MR. PULLMAN'S ELEGANT PALACE CAR

Books by Lucius Beebe:

Boston and The Boston Legend
The Stork Club Bar Book
High Iron, A Book of Trains
Highliners, A Railroad Album
Trains in Transition
Highball, A Railroad Pageant
Snoot If You Must
Comstock Commotion, The Story of *The Territorial Enterprise*
Mansions on Rails, The Folklore of the Private Railway Car
Mr. Pullman's Elegant Palace Car

Books in Collaboration with Charles Clegg:

Mixed Train Daily, A Book of Short Line Railroads
Virginia & Truckee
Legends of the Comstock Lode
U.S. West, The Saga of Wells Fargo
Cable Car Carnival
The American West
Hear the Train Blow
Steamcars to The Comstock
The Age of Steam
Narrow Gauge in The Rockies
Dreadful California
San Francisco's Golden Era

*the railway carriage
that established
a new dimension of luxury
and entered the national lexicon
as a symbol of splendor*

MR. PULLMAN'S
ELEGANT
PALACE CAR

LUCIUS BEEBE

Doubleday & Company, Inc., Garden City, New York 1961

The endpapers, by the distinguished railroad artist E. S. Hammack, depict the old *Golden Gate Special* on the Overland run between Chicago and California on the Central Pacific trackage between Ogden and San Francisco. The train has paused at a depot in deepest Nevada and the passengers from the Pullman Palace library–observation car *Sybaris* are taking the air against a background of the Humboldt Desert.

Green aisles of Pullman cars
Soothe me like trees
Woven in old tapestries. . . .
William Rose Benét

ACKNOWLEDGMENTS

This book has been made possible by the good offices and generous co-operation of many people, in whose debt the author stands for pictures, information and assistance, without which its eventual dimension would not have been possible. These include Richard Kindig of the Rocky Mountain Railroad Club, Gerald M. Best of the Railway & Locomotive Historical Society and Charles E. Fisher of the same dedicated group, Roy Graves, William Barham, Henry R. Griffiths, Jr., Ivan Dmitri, Fred Jukes, Andrew Merrilees, Howard T. Moulton, Dr. Philip R. Hastings, Edwin P. Alexander, H. W. Pontin, Douglas Craig Wornom, David Morgan of *Trains* magazine, Stan Repp and Howard Fogg. The author also owes a debt of special gratitue to E. Preston Calvert, Nora Wilson and Melvin Horn of Pullman Standard, from whose files a great majority of the photographs in this book derive, and to Everett L. De Golyer of Dallas, a collector of impressive proportions. And most urgently of all he must acknowledge the unfailing bounty and openhanded liberality of Arthur D. Dubin of Chicago, the leading repository of both the lore of the railroad car and its pictorial record. Mr. Dubin, an officer and director of the Railway & Locomotive Historical Society, placed at the author's disposal not only his rich store of iconography of the palace car, but also his definitive knowledge of the subject. The credit for this book belongs to these several people whose abundant helpfulness has made it possible.

PULLMAN STANDARD

CONTENTS

GENESTA   499

FOREWORD

THE name of George Mortimer Pullman does not, in the national lexicon of personalities, suggest a hotelier as explicitly as do those, say, of George Boldt of the old Waldorf-Astoria or Caesar Ritz, in whose name the several Ritz-Carltons were conceived, or Potter Palmer whose magnificent Chicago inn set a standard of ostentatious elegance that dazzled an entire generation of American magnificoes and foreign royalties.

Nor does one think of Pullman as a restaurateur in the same breath that one evokes the name of George Rector, Peter Delmonico or Oscar of the Waldorf Tchirky. He created no sauce that bears his name and wrote no memoirs replete with splendid doings amongst the game courses and vintage Madeiras.

Yet Pullman and, to a somewhat lesser degree, a small group of contemporaries in the field of railroad transport were in proper fact hoteliers and restaurateurs on a scale of operations and over a geographic spread to make even the largest operators of today, Conrad Hilton and Ernest Henderson, look like country innkeepers out of Dickens or roadhouse proprietors of obscure destinies and dimensions.

No hotel owner of the present time, let alone of Pullman's generation, could boast that his guests occupied 260,000 beds every night in the year or that the total registrations in his guest book came to 26,000,000 every twelve months. Or that he maintained clerks at 2,950 registration desks for the sole purpose of assigning guests to room and dormitory space.

Yet these are the figures for the operations of the Pullman establishment at the height of its effectiveness, while the amount of food and drink purveyed by Pullman services, though not available to statistical tally, were in astronomical quantities over the years. If further figures are required, it may be mentioned that in 1916 the Pullman Company maintained a linen closet that contained 1,858,178 sheets and 1,403,354 pillow slips valued at a total of something like $2,000,000 and during the year washed and ironed 108,492,359 pieces of bed linen, exclusive of hand towels, napkins, antimacassars and other incidentals to running a hotel.

Over and above the basic necessities of food and shelter, Pullman provided most of the luxuries available in de luxe hotels: barbershops, baths, both tub and shower, valets, manicurists and ladies' maids, cut flowers, periodicals and libraries of fiction, bars, cigar stands, telegraphic communications, news bulletins and stock ticker reports. On occasion, Pullman also carried the dead to rest and, in special Pullman cars devised for the purpose, the horses and carriages of travelers, thus maintaining a livery service of sorts in addition to more conventional conveniences.

And yet, despite all these aspects of hotelier and restaurateur, Pullman's basic service was one of transportation and the conveying of people from one place to another. He was primarily a railroad man and when, as occasionally happened, people complained that the charges for his hotel and restaurant services were out of line with those elsewhere, he blandly replied that no other hotel transported its occupants from 300 to 800 miles overnight and in safety and comfort altogether comparable to what might be expected in the most static hostel on Fifth Avenue or Nob Hill. None provided the fine views and constant change of scenery visible from the cars.

In the long light of history Pullman will be remembered as the man who put the American people on wheels, and also as the greatest single agency in the spread and appreciation of luxury on an almost universal scale.

There were, to be sure, others in the same field of carbuilding who contributed liberally to the national appreciation of clean linen, soft beds, well-prepared food, obsequious service and opulent surroundings, and Webster Wagner and the hilarious Colonel William D'Alton Mann will be given due credit in this book.

But the evidence is overwhelming that George M. Pullman was foremost among the prophets of the good life and loomed largest in the general imagination. It lies in the circumstance that his name became generic in the English language and, without capitalization, to go pullman is to this day to go first-class. Only Caesar Ritz is similarly honored by posterity as a purveyor of things de luxe whose name became part of the universal lexicon of luxury.

The impact of George Pullman's scheme of things on the general awareness will be more fully explored in the pages that follow, but before his first palace cars few enough Americans had any least conception of what constituted true luxury; three decades of first-hand contact with the manifestations of opulence available aboard the cars created a universal demand for rich living which had a profound effect on the American economy and national way of life that has not yet disappeared. For millions, their first contact with Turkey carpets, plate-glass mirrors and velvet portières was on the palace cars, and, to a degree that might make profitable its exploration by a more sapient commentator than the author of this book, Pullman left its impress on the entire national culture.

The concern of this book, however, is not alone with George M. Pullman, although his name provides a focus for its theme—overland travel in the *belle époque* of American railroading, the years from the close of the Civil War and the emergence of luxury conveyances until the decline of steam motive power and the disappearance of any appreciable character in rail transport.

It may or may not be coincidence that this period also embraces the years and decades of America's happiest destinies, whose various aspects today engage the attentions of a wide variety of historians concerned with what are loosely but affectionately known as The Good Old Days. It is only needed to scan the contents of any bookstall or repository of gramophone records to know that Americans of the sixties look with inextinguishable longing and envy at the years that came to an end with Sarajevo. Yesterday has become invested with all that is desirable, secure, homely and possessed of distinguishing virtue.

Americans never had it so good as in the decades directly after Appomattox, when the national economy was one of limitless abundance, a continental dimension beckoned and there was gold in the hills and buffalo on the prairie. A restless people rode to aureate destinies, and most of them rode the palace cars that were the showcases for the railroads of a land that could never have too many railroads. Amidst fringes, ferns and tassels, on plush and shrouded in velour, it beheld its own image in a thousand bevel-edged French mirrors set on mahogany bulkheads and between the wide picture windows of Pullmans and Wagners beyond counting. It drank champagne on the diners for breakfast and had supper off eight varieties of game on the dollar dinner and felt that it didn't need to tip its hat in the direction of either J. P. Morgan or the Medici. It was the most sumptuously upholstered landfaring in the history of human movement.

The years in which the ornate sleepers, diners and riotously uninhibited private palace cars of the nabobs rolled to glory were good years in the national riding and the Pullmans were a tangible expression of a determination to do it in style. Because it didn't occur to anybody that there could be virtue in conformity and sameness, the carbuilders gave free rein to the same rococo impulses that inspired Dundreary whiskers, octagon houses, deerstalker hats, the hansom kerridge, Gothic novels and dramas by Dion Boucicault. Nobody was asked to look, act, think or conduct himself like his neighbor, least of all the builders of railway equipment, and the results were as wonderful as the masculine attire at a Victorian shooting party. In an age innocent of the standards evolved by the Association of American Railroads and the industrial assembly line, no two Pullman sleepers were exactly alike in their interior decor or outer devising. Each was a little different from the next and possessed character of its own. Whoever rode them partook in some measure of an individuality that was unique and the good cheer that derives from an assured personality.

It may be a footnote to history that the decline of the railroads as an important factor in the American scheme of things corresponded precisely with the advent of unrelieved austerity of furnishings on the cars and that the decor that is known as *moderne* was almost overnight moribund as well.

Largely this book is intended as a chronicle of cheerful things in an age of hope and plenty, when a ride on the steamcars was a glorious adventure in a fairyland where there were cherubs painted on the ceilings and both terrapin and Porterhouse on the dollar dinner. In the mind's eye, it is still possible to revisit those golden yesterdays and share in good times as remote from the experience of today's generation as the pleasures of Augustan Rome. And there is no better way to achieve them than amidst the contented company that once peopled the lovely interiors of Mr. Pullman's Elegant Palace Car.

Lucius Beebe

MR. PULLMAN'S ELEGANT PALACE CAR

STEAMCARS IN THE MEADOWS

I N the mid-thirties of the twentieth century the Pullman Standard Carbuilding Company, then the world's foremost manufacturer of railway equipment, announced that it had built its last and final open-section Pullman sleeping car, the vehicular arrangement on which its fame and early fortunes had been founded and which had, over the years, made the word Pullman generic in the language.

Continental travel in the United States, Pullman explained, had reached a degree of sophistication where the open sleeping section had been rendered obsolete. All-private-room sleeping cars and, indeed, entire trains of all-room cars such as the *Twentieth Century Limited* and the *Broadway Limited,* constituted the new standard of first-class travel; henceforth the green aisles of Pullman section sleepers would be more and more relegated to secondary runs and less opulent sleeper assignments than those on the name trains that were the wonder and glory of the railroad world.

Americans pondered Pullman's decision and editorial writers perceived in it, with justice, a milestone in the national epic. The open sleeping berth, for bet-

ter or for worse, had become an integral part of the American consciousness and folklore. It was a property of vaudeville comedians and the anecdotes that passed as currency in its own smoking compartments. The potentialities for error or mischance to travelers inherent in a dim-lit, lurching corridor of green baize appealed inevitably to the national sense of humor. The open sleeping berth, sixty years previous, had come into being as a subject for controversy among moralists and profound commentators on *res publica*. It approached its terminal in almost the same status. In the intervening decades it had become institutional, one in the Yankee lexicon with baseball, Saturday night baths and the moral superiority of country folk over city dwellers.

In their concern for its impact upon national folk legend, the newspaper and magazine commentators on the Pullman milestone more or less overlooked the far greater impact upon American mores implicit in the name of clever George Mortimer Pullman. The convenience of the folding berth and the potentialities for the preposterous in their occupancy were of secondary magnitude compared to the over-all intimations of splendor which from the beginning associated themselves with the name of the carbuilder. The significance of Pullman has diminished since it first emerged as a synonym for luxury and convenience. Other and more modish influences followed and ensmalled its dimensions. Pullman style and decor inevitably became objects for the contempt of later stylists and molders of public taste, just as many other contemporary aspects of the Victorian age suffered a fashionable eclipse.

But when it was new the Pullman Palace car, and to a lesser degree the equivalent creations and artifacts of coeval carbuilders, was the greatest single agency of urbanity and sophistication available to the American consciousness. In the palace cars for the first time Brussels carpets, bevel-edged French mirrors, superbly inlaid woodwork and fine linen for bed and table could be experienced outside the private homes of the well-to-do and a very few exclusive resort hotels patronized by the same society. For the cost of an extra fare of extremely modest proportions Americans who had never before encountered anything but the essential elements of shelter and the most primitive decor found themselves part of a midst of velvet portières, splendid crystal chandeliers, hot and cold running water and at least some of the manners and comportment these amenities imposed or implied.

The presence of rich Turkey carpeting underfoot eventually inhibited the almost universal American habit of spitting tobacco juice, and where it was unable to stem the tide, it at least improved the national aim by providing tasteful spittoons located at strategic intervals. The wearing of boots to bed by gentlemen became impracticable in the face of clean sheets. A measure of sanitation was implied by the suggestion that passengers would please refrain from flushing toilets in the depot. In time a growing sophistication of travel convinced passengers that pulling the emergency air cord wasn't the way to summon the porter or conductor. Smoking was for smoking cars and, as in the better conducted saloons of the West, the open carriage and discharge of firearms wasn't in keeping with the general atmosphere of the palace cars.

The impact on public table manners of the dining car is a special field which will presently come up for consideration, but it may be remarked briefly that in it the influence of a single arbiter in the person of Fred Harvey was at least as conspicuous as that of an earlier Beau Nash on the habitués of Bath.

As with many another agency of civilization and even progress, the Pullman Palace car was not the product alone of a single specialized and dedicated genius, but of the right man and the right time. If George M. Pullman hadn't evolved the sleeping car, somebody else would have. There were, indeed, contemporaries who claimed to have done just that and took out various patents to prove it, but in the end Pullman engulfed or eliminated all of them so that even their names, Mann, Flower, Wagner, Marble and the rest, are known only to specialists and historians. Grandeur and durability from the beginning associated themselves both with Pullman's cars and his own progress and both rolled serenely into immortality long after their first protagonist was dead.

A later generation, and it may be remarked parenthetically, one that knows little that is as honestly good, may smile tolerantly at the plush and ormolu that ravished the senses of their grandparents. It cannot patronize the materials and the workmanship that went into the Pullman product for these were superlatively superb. No craftsmanship survives in the world today—unless it be that of a handful of private carriage makers still designing bodies for English automobiles—that is comparable in its pride and expertness to the so-called "Marquetry Room" where Pullman's cabinet work was done. In the annals of American manufacture its peer can be found only in the product of Abbot Downing & Co., of Concord, New Hampshire, builders of the horse-drawn stagecoaches that, like Pullmans themselves, have become an American legend.

In time the superiority of American carbuilding, one of the few fields of generally admitted superiority over English practice and manufacture, brought cars of Pullman build or of manufacture under Pullman license to England where they survive to this day, rolling grandly, among other assignments, between London and Southampton in the consist of Cunard boat trains. Shorn of its proper capitalization, Pullman became, variously, a type of apartment dwelling and an outsize portmanteau. It became, with capitals, the name of several American communities of varying degrees of importance.

In the field of railroad travel, where it most properly resides, Pullman came eventually to signify all first-class accommodations aboard the steamcars and that is the sense in which it is used in this essay.

Although in the eventual terms of history the company for the construction of railroad equipment founded by George M. Pullman became the dominant firm of carbuilders in the United States and the name of Pullman was permanently established in the national lexicon, the father of the sleeping car and future rich millionaire in the company of American capitalists was for many years only one of a number of other carbuilders practicing their calling, some of them with considerable success. He was, however, by long odds the most determined, acquisitive and tenacious of these, and in the end Pullman overwhelmed and outlived all of them but one of any consequence.

The yellowing pages of catalogues compiled by master carbuilders in the golden noontide of their craft and of the periodicals representing the railroad industry as a whole reveal a considerable multiplicity of firms engaged in the manufacture of rolling stock: T. T. Woodruff, the Mann Boudoir Car Company of the fascinating Colonel William D'Alton Mann, Jerome Marble's Worcester Hunting Car Company in Massachusetts, Flower, Billmeyer & Smalls, Kuhlman, Jackson & Sharp, Harlan & Hollingsworth, Brill, the Pressed Steel Car Company, Barney & Smith, and Webster Wagner, to name but a few. The firm of Jackson & Sharp in association with various minor builders and patentees eventually emerged as American Car & Foundry, which alone survived into the latter decades of the twentieth century in direct and unequivocal competition with Pullman. In addition to these concerns, many individual railroads, both early in the annals of the carriers and until now, built rolling stock of all sorts in their own shops. Notable were the Chicago & North Western, the Illinois Central, Central Pacific, Union Pacific and Central of Georgia, all of which specialized in the erection of fine passenger equipment in several categories and specially that of the private cars which represented the last word in carbuilding luxury and the *expertise* of their craftsmen.

If a seemingly disproportionate amount of space in this volume is devoted to private cars it may be cited in extenuation that their construction entailed the finest workmanship of all, that the romance associated with them is compelling above the average and that as a social property and status symbol they were significant for many years and to a degree far in excess of their actual number or ownership.

The railroading scene onto which the former cabinetmaker from Albion, New York, found himself projected at the close of the Civil War was comparable as an industrial bonanza to the bonanzas in precious metals which almost simultaneously were attracting the gaze of the world to the rich discoveries of precious metals in the Mother Lode of California and in the Comstock in Nevada and the wealthy multiplicity of strikes in the Colorado Rockies. Railroading in the United States was the greatest single symbol of Manifest Destiny and of the continental dimension that was then the theme of the nation's thinking. It was the preoccupation of pioneers and industrial moguls everywhere and enormous fortunes were coming into being as its traffic increased in density and dimension. The Vanderbilt dynasty was already an accomplished fact. The fortunes of Jim Hill, Edward H. Harriman and the overlords of Central Pacific, Leland Stanford, Collis Huntington and Charles Crocker were shaping up. On the fringes and outskirts of the excitement, men of disaster such as Jay Gould, Jim Fisk and Daniel Drew were wrecking railroad properties almost as fast as they could be built to recover salvage from the debris.

The collateral beneficiaries of railroad building, the ironmasters and steelmakers of Pittsburgh, land companies in the Middle West, locomotive and equipment builders like the canny Ames brothers of Boston, timber barons selling ties and bridge timbers to the carriers, the fuel barons of West Virginia and Pennsylvania, all were getting in on a good thing that got better with every mile of track that was laid. And thousands of miles of track, much of it between nowhere and nowhere, to be sure, but nonetheless expensive, were being spiked every year.

As yet nobody had made a fortune in passenger cars. Nobody had really given the matter of passenger accommodations much thought. George Mortimer Pullman, a pioneer with an eye to the main chance, was going to change all that.

Until the time of the Civil War a number of circumstances and conditions had discouraged even the most altruistic railroad managements, which were not conspicuously numerous, from investing too much money or attention on passenger equipment. For one thing the concept of a railroad as a through carrier for any distance had not yet been evolved. Railroads were largely short lines connecting with seaports or, in a casual manner, with other short lines. Often it was necessary to go across town from one depot to take the cars at another. Sometimes miles of countryside intervened. Union depots, connecting train schedules of arrival and departure between different roads and the through ticket were in the future. All of these were discouraged by hotelkeepers, saloonkeepers, stage proprietors and other tradesmen who profited from passengers obliged to stop over between trains.

The idea of through cars interchanging between different connecting railroads was discouraged by the carriers themselves, which laid their rails to a variety of gauges and made passage of the cars of other carriers over their tracks impossible. Saloonkeepers and restaurant proprietors in terminal towns were loud in viewing the idea of a universal gauge as a blasphemy against God. The longest trip anybody could take in one railroad car wasn't more than four or five hours. Often the passengers felt this was more than enough.

An example of what passed as a "connection" in the early days was the fairly important railroad city of Albany where the westbound trains of Commodore Cornelius Vanderbilt's New York & Hudson Railroad exchanged passengers with the recently consolidated New York Central running from Albany to Buffalo. The trains of both carriers used the same depot, and the wait between connections was seldom more than three or four hours, at least in the clement months of the year, although a day or two was not unknown in winter. The Commodore was covetous of the New York Central as part of a visionary scheme for through service all the way to Chicago over a single unified system, but he was of no mind to pay the going price for its shares. So one winter morning when the mercury was around zero and snow was falling, the up train from New York came to a halt at East Albany, a good two miles through the snowdrifts from the New York Central terminal at the west end of town.

There was a law, the Commodore said, preventing trains under his franchise from crossing the Hudson River, as they must do to make the Central connection. He was sorry he had been breaking it so long. Passenger traffic on the New York Central understandably began to decline. So did the value of its stock. When the moment was propitious, the Commodore bought up the New York Central at fire-sale prices and through connections were established next day.

In the end this maneuver contributed to the formation of the great New York Central & Hudson River Railroad over which such name trains as the *Twentieth Century Limited* and an almost equally fine flyer named for the Commodore himself were to roll between Manhattan and Chicago at eighty-five miles an hour, but at the time it was rough on the customers.

Things being ordered on these lines until the closing years of the Civil War, there was no great call for sleeping cars, diners, club cars or any of the long-occupancy rolling stock that was shortly to be in universal demand. No single railroad was long enough to warrant its maintenance.

The universal car for the accommodation of the passenger trade on American railroads was what came in time to be known as the day coach. This had started out on the primeval carriers of the 1830s as an adaptation of the highway stagecoach that had been hauling passengers and the mail in countries with roads for the past hundred years or so. The first railroad cars were simply stagecoaches removed from the thorough braces or other springing devices that supported them between the wheels, and mounted, insecurely as it often appeared, on flatcars, at first singly, then with three or four individual coaches to a unit. The general scheme of compartmentation survives in England and on the Continent until this day, but fairly early in the game it was modified in the United States to a single boxlike structure with access at each end instead of through individual doors giving to carriages of different classes.

The American-type pasenger car was widely heralded as an achievement of democracy, wherein all classes sat together in republican equality as a matter of choice. Actually the arrangement was necessitated by the great increase in traffic, which made the stages mounted on flatcars wasteful of space as well as dangerous. Then, too, passengers who rode on the roof, which had been the preferred position in good weather on the highways, found that cinders from the engine were burning grievous holes in their garments and drunks were falling, often with results fatal to themselves and the train brigade, under the wheels.

The center-aisle daycoach was the answer to these several problems and remained the only available accommodation on American railroads until the late 1860s. A sole concession to feminine sensibilities was the segregation of special coaches equipped with spittoons and non-flammable seat covering as smoking cars for men only. And in the Deep South, of course, there were designated accommodations aboard the cars and in depots for colored passengers.

There were microscopic exceptions to these generalities. As early as 1834 a group of snobs who commuted daily between Dedham and Boston had the management of the Boston & Providence Railroad set aside a special car morning and evening for their exclusive occupancy, and the first club car came into being. In 1841 when President-elect William H. Harrison was en route to Washington for his inaugural, an official of the Baltimore & Ohio asked his superiors if he should set aside "a select car" for the great man and his party, and the first private car emerged upon the page of history. During the same decade the Iron

Mountain Railroad, serving various Ozark spas noted for the curative properties of their waters, provided baggage cars in which cots had been installed for the accommodation of bedridden health-seekers, but only the most optimistic scholar would see in this arrangement the certified forerunner of the Pullman sleeper.

In May 1869, however, something happened to put an end to these parochial operations forever. At Promontory Point, Utah, the rails of the Union Pacific and Central Pacific railroads were joined to form a continuous and uninterrupted route over the better part of the continent, from Omaha to San Francisco Bay. Through trains were being inaugurated between New York and Chicago over two highly competitive systems, the New York Central and the Pennsylvania, both of which had set their caps for the then profitable passenger trade and for the prestige of being the world's finest railroad. Passengers were remaining aboard the same train without change of ticket for forty-eight hours and sometimes three days at a time.

The stage was obviously set for the entrance of the sleeper, the hotel car, the restaurant carriage and the eventual apotheosis of all these in the Pullman Palace car devised by the clever, bearded little man who was to become the ranking prophet of continental travel in terms of unimaginable luxury.

George Mortimer Pullman made his entry on cue.

PULLMAN STANDARD

Generally accepted as the first practicable sleeping car, Pioneer was designed by George M. Pullman for service on the Chicago & Alton Railroad in 1865.

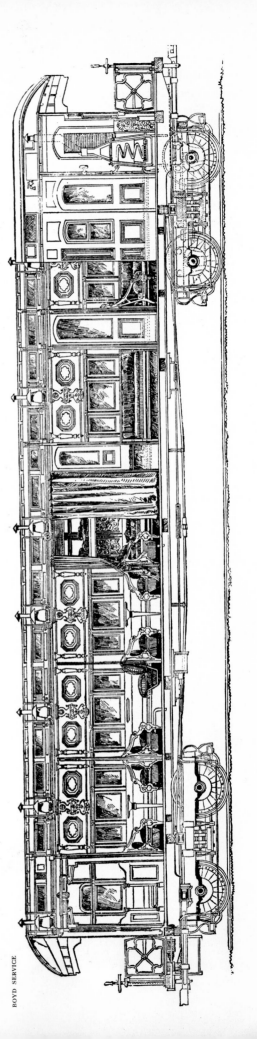

BOYD SERVICE

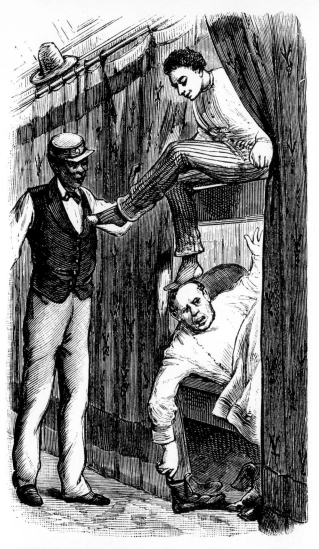

By 1859 Webster Wagner had placed in service a series of experimental triple-tiered open section sleepers on the New York Central Lines between Albany and Buffalo as reported in the drawing below in Frank Leslie's Illustrated Weekly. In the same periodical a few years later appeared the sketch at the left captioned "Must Step Somewhere," an indication that already Pullmans and sleeping car travel had entered the national vocabulary of humor and become part of the pattern of American folkways.

SLEEPING CARS NOW IN USE ON THE NEW YORK CENTRAL RAILROAD —

With its rails situated strategically through the
heartland of the continent, the Rock Island publicized a dollar dinner aboard its diners such as
this that included Lake Erie whitefish, filet mignon and prairie chicken.

ROCK ISLAND LINES

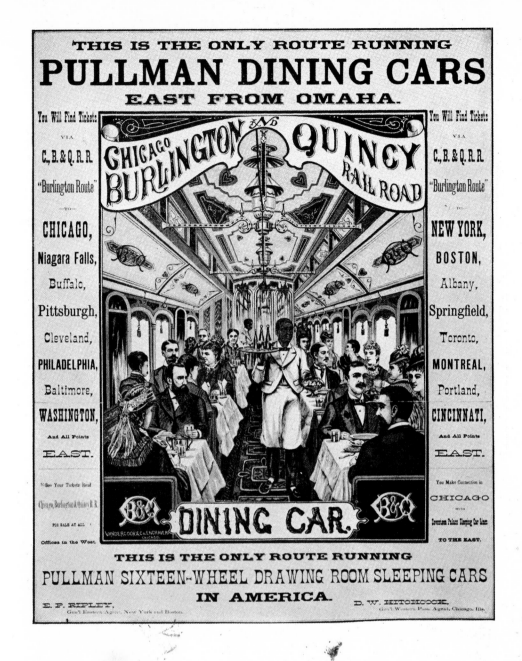

Realizing that its dining cars were the showcase of a railroad's wares, the Burlington advertised the food and service on its trains far and wide in the seventies. Missing no bets, it flattered communities along its main line by naming its luxury cars for them.

PULLMAN STANDARD

To ride the cars as one accustomed, grandma had to learn about the conductor's signal.

Coach travel on American railroads had changed between 1861, when a staff artist drew the above sketch on a Baltimore & Ohio train for the Illustrated London News, *and 1891, when Pullman built the truly splendid day coaches shown opposite for the same B. & O. and the Louisville & Nashville Railroad. Vestibules, six-wheel trucks and wide picture windows had come into being and passengers rode on plush and cut-velvet seats. The English sketch shows an interior with silk top hats and rustic chin whiskers dominated by a conductor, then known as the train captain, also in top hat and frock coat that were the professional attire of his important calling.*

Before the coming of the vestibule cars, such open platform parlor cars as this one built for the Ohio River Railroad by Pullman in 1895 were the last word in daytime travel comfort and gentility for people of quality.

In 1886 the Detroit, Grand Haven & Milwaukee Railroad added this de luxe parlor car to its Steamboat Express for the benefit of passengers who required privacy of more opulent accommodations than were available on the company's day coaches. The Steamboat Express ran between Detroit and Grand Haven, where it connected with "the elegant Steamer, City of Milwaukee," which sailed every midnight for the metropolis of its name. Privacy came at moderate cost on the Grand Haven's parlor car: twenty-five cents a seat over and above the regular fare. The sketch at the left depicts the somewhat more sophisticated interior of an "opera box" parlor car on the Pennsylvania a decade later.

BOYD SERVICE

Day coach travel on American steam railroads in the belle époque of carbuilding could be very de luxe indeed, especially in regions where competing lines flourished, and was often almost as ornate as its Pullman counterpart, as may be suggested by the interior of the Pullman coach exhibited at the Chicago Exposition of 1893 and shown on the opposite page. The Burlington coach shown below represented the other extreme of utilitarian lack of distinction. All classes of travel—coach, emigrant and luxury—appealed enormously to the pictorial artists of the golden age of railroading. Mostly, in keeping with the national spirit of the times, the people were happy, riding in whatever style to happy destinations. Passengers and types aboard the Erie Limited in the seventies provided pictorial material for a contemporary sketch artist on this page. That car windows, then as later, were balky and the artist observant, is suggested by the young man's pocket knife, used to hold up the venetian blind.

Interior View of Passenger Cars for
EASTERN RAIL ROAD COMPANY OF BOSTON.
May, 1872

This day coach with all the identifying properties of the era, venetian blinds, oilcloth ceiling, unprotected stove and narrow seats upholstered in plush, was built the year after the Revere disaster for the Eastern Railroad between Boston & Portland, possibly as a replacement for some of the equipment lost in that epic holocaust.

32

TWO PHOTOS: ARTHUR D. DUBIN COLLECTION

The superb period piece on this page is a combination sleeping car–parlor car built in 1895 by American Car & Foundry for service on the Georgia & Alabama Railroad on trains No. 20 and 21, which ran overnight over the 340 miles between Atlanta and Montgomery. A rare type of equipment, it was adapted to runs that couldn't support complete parlor and sleeping car facilities in separate cars. Beauty and utility were combined in this old coach that once rolled through moonlit plantations in the Georgia night upon the occasions of a now forgotten carrier.

The fine Wagner diner Ferdinand was part of the company's exhibit at the Chicago Fair of 1893, while the general service diner, shown below, with the wavy gold finelining that was a hallmark of Wagner manufacture was assigned to the New York Central's Lake Shore Limited between New York and Cleveland. It was handsome Wagners such as these rolling over the Vanderbilt roads that nearly drove George M. Pullman out of his mind.

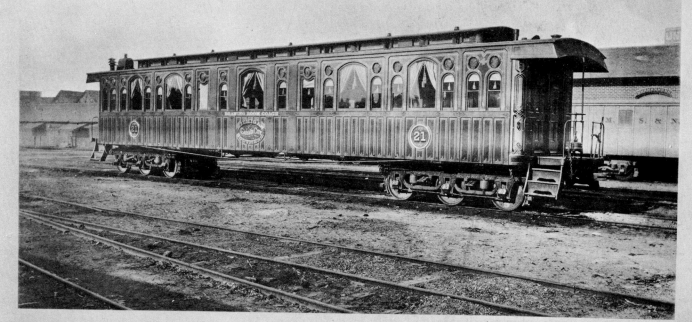

The resemblance in external appearance of Pullman and Wagner cars is illustrated by Pullman's Saranac and Wagner's Oakland, *the latter built in the mid-
seventies for service on the Lake Shore & Michigan Southern.*

The colonnade of little onyx pillars supporting the ceiling arch over the doorway of the Wagner sleeper *Inkerman* was the ultimate panache of Wagner elegance and the identifying hallmark of its manufacture. The twelve-section and drawing room car was one of the 480 sleepers that Pullman acquired when it absorbed the Wagner firm in 1899.

*The theme of
the sleeping car
Topeka was
Byzantine with
arches from
a Moorish mosque,
a decor widely
favored in
the nineties for
the den or smoking
room without
which no gentleman's
home was complete.
Only the camera
in the mirror
seems an intrusion
from the mechanical
Occident. Topeka
was assigned to
service on the Union
Pacific out of Omaha.*

The Pullman sleeping cars Anelo *and* Chicosa *on the page opposite are among the choicest examples of the carbuilder's artistry in the pre-vestibule palace car era, circa 1887–88, and* Chicosa *is known to have been assigned to the Denver & Rio Grande Western's Denver–Salt Lake run through the Rockies as soon as it was broad-gauged in 1892. The beautiful exteriors of these cars sustained the illusion of romance and far places implicit in plate-glass mirrors, velvet portières and snug berths in their interiors, the universal hallmarks of Pullman supremacy.*

THREE PHOTOS: PULLMAN STANDARD

39

40

TWO PHOTOS: ARTHUR D. DUBIN COLLECTION

Nearly four decades elapsed between the day in the seventies when Harlan & Hollingsworth built the Great Western day coach shown opposite and the date of American Car & Foundry's Missouri Pacific coach No. 6041, but the elegant touch had by no means disappeared from the hand of the carbuilder, as the beautiful etched and frosted window transoms attest in the long graceful arch that was an identifying hallmark of A.C.F. construction and design. On this page is evidence that life aboard the steamcars and death as well were an important part of the pattern of American society in the nineteenth century and occupied a prominent place in the contemporary public prints. Above, a car cleaner, presumably bored by his job, hangs himself on a day coach of the central of New Jersey, while, less melancholy, the wife and "the other woman" battle for the affections of a Baltimore businessman on the cars of the Baltimore & Ohio. What went on aboard the cars was very much news of the day.

The Grand Rapids & Indiana's stylish day coach Omena, *shown on the page opposite, was built in 1897 and boasted not only a name, but also enclosed vestibules. The Portland & Rochester's No. 23, six years its senior, was still fitted with wooden venetian window blinds of a type that had been in service on American railroads since before 1850. The Illinois Central's No. 616 was specially assigned, according to the lettering on its nameboards to the* Chicago & New Orleans Limited *predecessor of the crack streamliner* Panama Limited. *The well-known* Leslie's *artist Harry Ogden, shortly after the Civil War, sketched the interior (below) of a second-class coach on the South Georgia Railroad filled with colored members of the state legislature en route to Columbia, South Carolina. The Pullman coach at the left with neat venetian shutters is from the early eighties.*

The railed-in observation platform in its beginnings was on the side of the car instead of its rear end. The one next the engine at the right was posed on the Portland & Ogdensburg Railroad's Frankenstein Trestle at Crawford Notch, New Hampshire, in 1875. The trestle, incidentally, was of the Howe truss type that caused the Ashtabula catastrophe and many other fatal accidents of the time. The car below was in service the same year on the New Haven. It was probably Ymir, built by Monarch for the Connecticut River run. It was sixty-six feet long, with a buffet and three salons in the car's enclosed section. Outside it was painted brown and silver to suggest the White Mountains and had an icicle pattern under the eaves.

The classic rear profile depicted on this page had
no hesitation about proclaiming its private character and aloof social standing. Like the cars on
the page opposite, it was a New England property in service during the seventies on the Boston
& Lowell Railroad, subsequently part of the Boston & Maine.

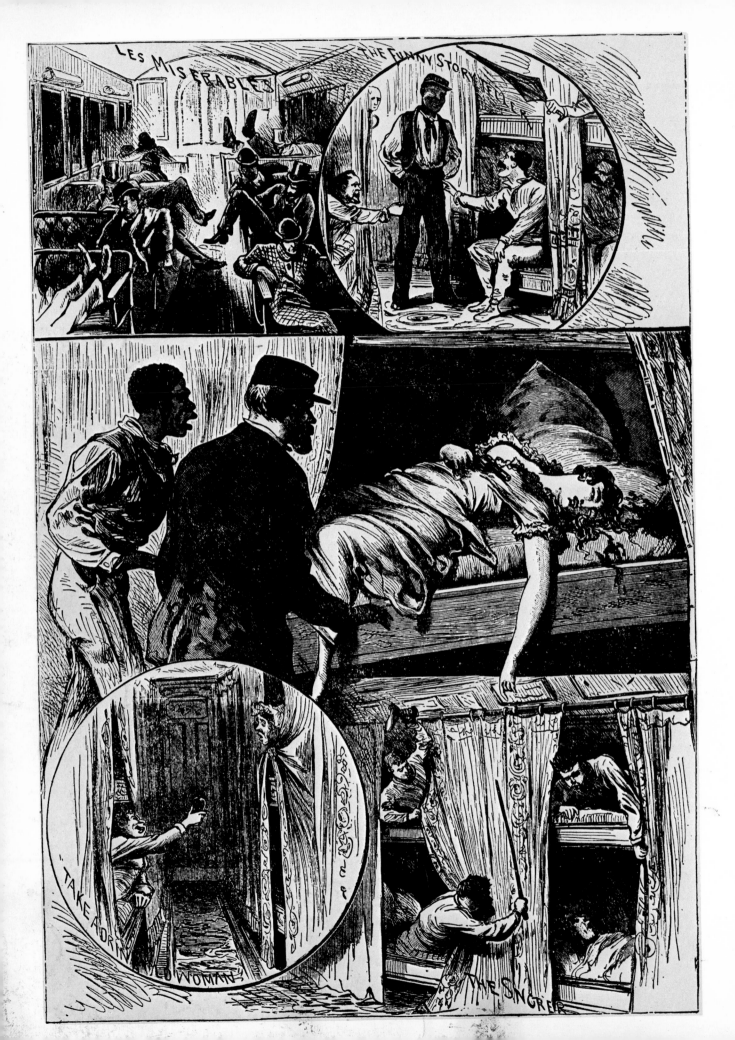

From the very beginning, the American imagination was captivated by the romance of the sleeping cars bound for the far places of the land and the adventure, comedy and tragic destinies that rode behind their green curtains. On the page opposite, a magazine artist of the eighties immortalizes the annoyances from drunks and other unquiet parties and "the fair unfortunate who started her last long journey by rail." Suicides on the cars were infrequent, but death from normal causes less so. On this page the interior of one of Pullman's open section sleepers of the period suggests the degree of luxury and ornate comfort expected by travelers and realized wherever the night cars ran.

The fine sleeping car shown is Australia, *companion to* New Zealand *and* China. *It was outshopped by Pullman at Detroit in 1889 and cost just $20,463.50.*

PULLMAN STANDARD

Beginning in the eighties, the White Mountains of New Hampshire enjoyed a supremacy in the esteem of many substantial vacationists, especially Bostonians, transcending anything Newport or even Buzzards Bay could offer. In summer months the Portland & Ogdensburg Railroad ran observation cars on all daylight trains and in 1880 Chisholm's White Mountain Guide remarked: "On your train there will be an observation car with open and windowless shades over which rain-shedding awnings are triced up, while revolving arm chairs occupy the floor. It is a ride of twenty-seven miles or not far from an hour and a half, up to the Crawford House; and the Duchess of Brookline and Lady Murray Hill settle themselves in becoming attitudes, while the American sovereigns of the male line unfold fresh newspapers and take out their cigar cases. Wiser travellers take seats on the right hand side of the cars, and bide their time." On the opposite page, at the top, three separate trains with an engine and car apiece on the Mount Washington cog railway await the Portland & Ogdensburg train with a baggage car and open observation car, while below a P. & O. train with no special equipment poses on Willey's Brook Trestle. On this page a P. & O. through train with observation car, as advertised, pauses in classic stance on Frankenstein Trestle at Crawford Notch in the heart of the White Mountains.

49

The palace car Baltimore and its sister car Saratoga were built in 1870 by Harlan & Hollingsworth to specifications by George M. Pullman and assigned on completion to the Pennsylvania Railroad. Their economy included ten sections and a drawing room finished in fumed walnut with Baker heaters, Hicks & Smith oil lamps, Janney link and pin couplers and a great deal of gold finelining on their exterior.

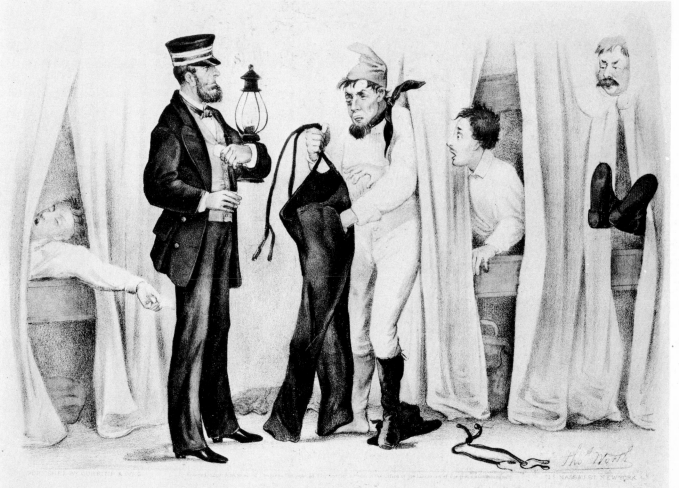

WAKING UP THE WRONG PASSENGER.
"I say old man! keep your hooks out of my trousers."

This innocuous cartoon was printed in lithograph by Currier & Ives in 1875 and found favor wherever men forgathered in pool halls, barbershops and saloons. It was a forerunner of many, as folklore gathered around the potentialities for mischance implicit in the lower berth.

Not notably a humorous man himself, George M. Pullman ironically sired an entire and well-defined body of risible absurdities and new vistas of fun opened up for stage comedians and raconteurs in the smoking compartments of the cars themselves. In time, however, the rustic conductor with down-East chin whiskers and his lantern balanced in the crook of his arm was replaced by the comparatively austere Pullman conductor (left), a highly trained and responsible company servant with great devotion to duty.

51

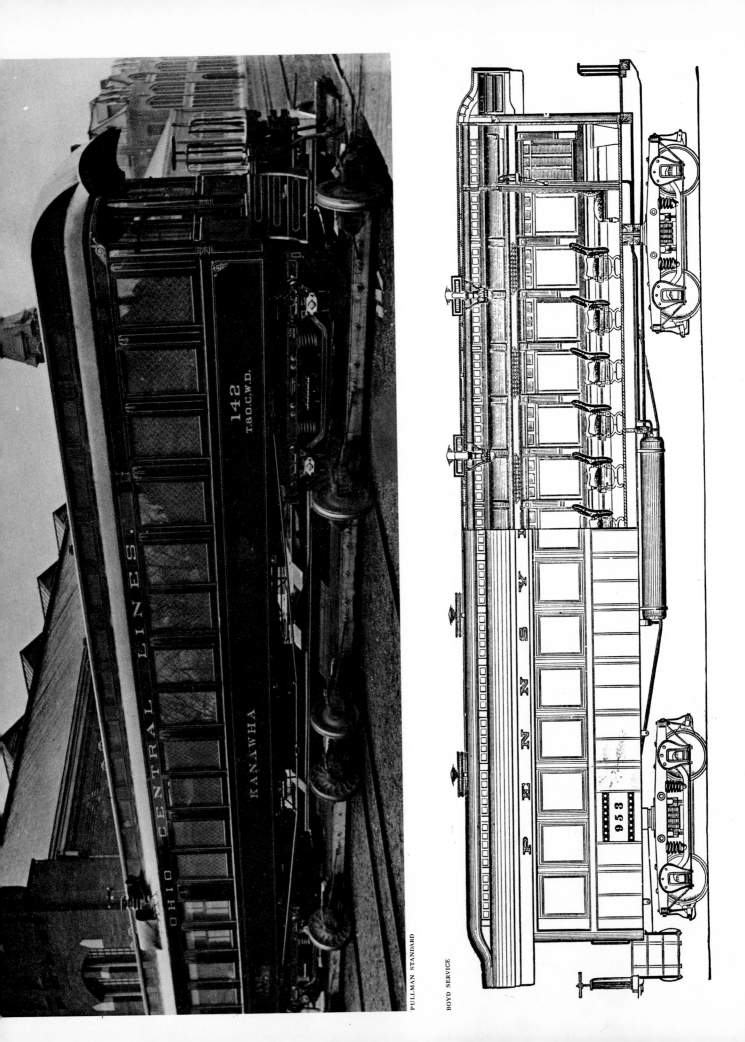

PULLMAN STANDARD

BOYD SERVICE

No matter what railroad a traveler might select, all were agreed that day coach travel in the nineteenth century abounded in tobacco juice, drafts of hot or cold air as the season might dictate and seats in which it was impossible to adjust the human body in attitudes of sleep. The line drawing of night life aboard a New York Central coach shown below was sketched by an artist for Harper's and is something of a classic of American folk scenes for the year 1868.

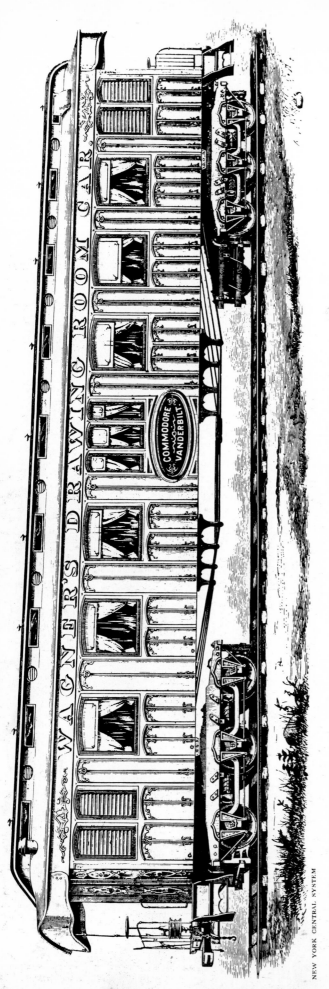

The earliest parlor cars, such as Commodore Vanderbilt's own car named for himself and the Woodruff-built Wawaka, were designed for day occupancy only and ran to central drawing rooms or salons with picture windows in the middle of the car.

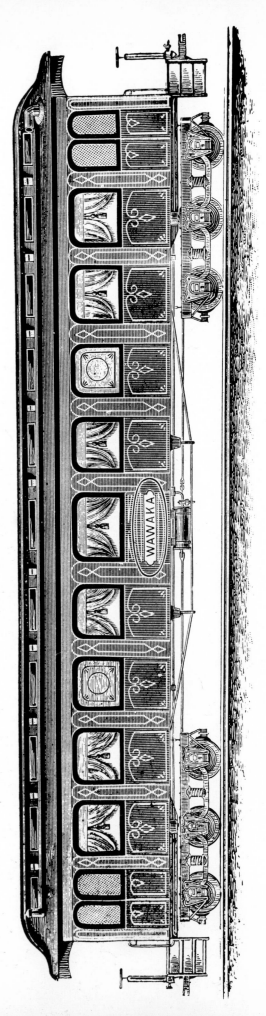

Vestigial traces of the centrally located main salon of times primeval survived into the eighties, when Pullman in such special equipment as the hunting car Davy Crockett *adapted the principal apartment as a room of common assembly and dining with berths as a measure of space economy. In this rare old-time interior the ubiquitous camera of Pullman's official photographer catches the bottle scars on the table and itself in the mirror, but even on a conveyance as utilitarian as a hunting car the meticulous Pullman craftsmanship is visible in the plain but superb upper berths now retracted for daytime convenience.*

PULLMAN STANDARD

Classic among American railway disasters, and one that spread destruction impartially between coach occupants and those of palace cars, was the wreck at Ashtabula, Ohio, on the Lake Shore & Michigan Southern in which eighty-five passengers perished. Its eventual victims included the well-born and highly placed as well as the conventional poor and lowly. Late one December night in 1876 during a tremendous blizzard the Vanderbilt road's crack Pacific Express, double-headed by two fine locomotives crashed through a Howe truss bridge, and its ten baggage cars, coaches and Wagner sleepers burned horribly on the ice of a creek 150 feet beneath. The fact that the Michigan Southern was no dubiously financed and managed streak of rust, but a proudly main-tained Vanderbilt affiliate, along with the gruesome details of the wreck, in which few bodies were ever identified, attracted national headlines. The day after the wreck the railroad's chief engineer, Charles Collins, who was a brother-in-law of the bridge designer William Howe, shot himself. A few days later Commodore Vanderbilt died, the end possibly hastened by shock. Five years afterward Amasa Stone, the Michigan Southern's once haughty president, took his own life. The Howe truss bridge was never again permitted in railroad construction and the lifework as an engineer of its inventor was reviled and repudiated. The little Ohio town of Ashtabula was permanently emplaced in the national lexicon of disaster.

During the seventies and eighties, when fast runs were making their first appearance on American railroads and wrecks reached a high-water mark, travelers acquired a prejudice against coach accommodations because, in many of the most sensational accidents, casualties in the day coaches ran far ahead of those in parlor and sleeping cars. Coaches were carried at the head of the train and suffered accordingly in head-end collisions, derailments and the collapse of trestles under the weight of locomotives. The palace cars at the far end of the train were less likely to be damaged, but they were more susceptible to rear-end collisions, which were frequent. Often enough, as in the Ashtabula wreck, the entire train, baggage and mail cars, coaches and sleepers were a total loss, a victim of flames ignited by the unprotected stoves with which all cars were heated in inclement weather. In the Wappinger Creek holocaust on the Hudson River Railroad, when a westbound express sideswiped an eastboard train of oil cars near Poughkeepsie, the coaches were engulfed in flames, while the three Wagner sleepers at the rear were uncoupled and pushed to safety by the train crew and passengers, a clue to the weight of equipment at the time. As long as wooden construction was universal, risk rode the cars and, until far into the age of steel safety in the twentieth century, seasoned veterans of earlier railroad travel could be identified by their insistence on sleeping space as near the middle of the center car of the train as possible. The potential of disaster involved in riding the cars in 1886 is suggested by the wreck, shown here, of the Fitchburg Railroad's night train near Greenfield, Massachusetts, in which six cars fell from a ledge more than 150 feet into the Deerfield River, with fatal results to twenty passengers. The event was important enough to be sketched for Harper's by the distinguished artist Charles Graham.

The luggage of travelers bound for California the Golden in the nineties rode grandly in such combination baggage and passenger cars as those built by Pullman for the Overland Limited and the Golden State Limited.

With the great surge of travel after the Civil War the baggage-master entered the demonology of the American people. The trunk destined for Boston and discovered in Kalamazoo became a part of folklore. Too much luggage when traveling became a national vice, and travel guides and handbooks took to publishing pictured warnings, such as that at the left entitled "The Green Traveler."

THE GREEN TRAVELER.

The baggage room of any depot was regarded by most travelers as a sneak preview of Hell. There chaos and old night reigned supreme.

The railroad accidents and steamboat wrecks of the eighties aroused widespread indignation against the carriers, nowhere more than in the pages of Harper's Weekly, whose celebrated cartoonist Thomas Nast drew the grim sketch at the right with the title "Our Constant Traveling Companion." Another Harper's indictment of the railroads, shown below and entitled "The Modern Altar of Sacrifice," was enormously influential in abolishing the unprotected car stove and replacing it with steam heat from the engine.

OUR CONSTANT TRAVELING COMPANION.

Ironically Pullman's great rival in the carbuilding field, Webster Wagner, was killed in a wreck at Spuyten Duyvil on the Hudson in 1882 while riding on the New York Central, which had been his best customer and with which he was closely associated. Commenting on the disaster, Harper's remarked bitterly: "Within a few feet of water, there were no buckets on the train . . . no axes at hand to cut open the burning cars. . . . But for the wretched and criminal parsimony of the company in heating the cars with stoves, the train would not have taken fire." That the carbuilder should meet a Wagnerian end on cars of his own manufacture was a topic for several sermons the following Sunday.

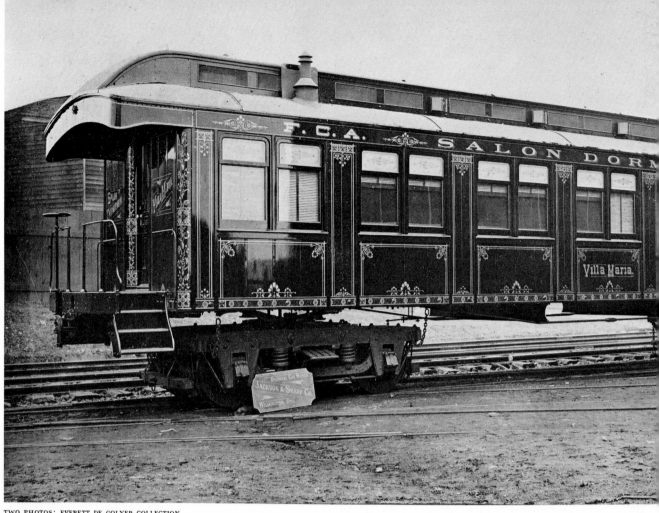

TWO PHOTOS: EVERETT DE GOLYER COLLECTION

In the year 1870 the New Jersey Railroad &
Transportation Company, now the Pennsylvania,
posed its fine New York to Philadelphia express
at Academy Street Junction in Jersey City for
a rendezvous with immortality (see below).
Then as later, the New Jersey countryside offered
pastoral vistas from the car windows, as is suggested above. At the left is the builder's photograph of Jackson & Sharp's "Salon Dormitorio"
the Villa Mario for Argentine export. The year
is 1875.

No more comely equipment was ever built for any American carrier than the narrow-gauge Colorado & Southern's business car No. 911, a Pullman product of such antiquity that when this photograph was taken in the thirties two different types of journal boxes adorned its trucks in the coach yard at Denver.

The seats of passengers were staggered, two on one side, one on the other, for even distribution of weight aboard such narrow-gauge coaches as Denver, built by Jackson & Sharp in 1871 for the Denver & Rio Grande Western Railroad in the Colorado Rockies.

By the mid-seventies passengers traveling between New York and Chicago over the Fort Wayne & Pennsylvania connections might expect to encounter the same comforts aboard Pullman's Hotel Cars as in the then-building hotels which were to make America the standard of innkeeping in the nineteenth century world. A rara avis is the Pullman sleeper Viceroy *on the Great Western Railway, shown below, with eight-wheel trucks. A series of Burlington diners were also built with this wheel arrangement, but for the most part luxury cars were designed with six-wheel trucks until the end of Pullman Standard operations.*

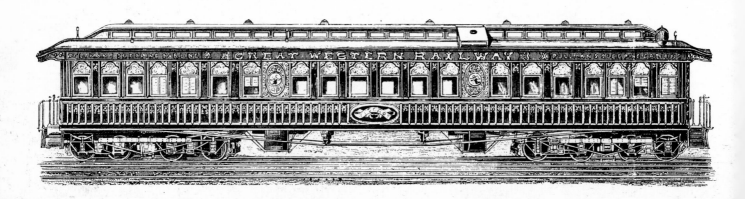

When, after viewing the Centennial Exposition at Philadelphia in 1876, Emperor Dom Pedro of Brazil, only regnant royalty to have visited the United States until then, went to San Francisco as the guest of Leland Stanford at the Palace Hotel, he went aboard the Pullman Palace Hotel Car *Metropolitan*. The Emperor is shown aboard the car in two drawings at the right, the *Metropolitan itself below*.

What its cathedrals were to Europe of the Middle Ages, its depots were to nineteenth-century America, a focus for the excitements of a nation on the move. Dearborn Street Station in Chicago has seen the coming and going of many cars since 1885, when this picture appeared in Harper's—the Santa Fe, Monon, Wabash and Grand Trunk among them. Opposite, a generation of New Yorkers jam Grand Central to board the New York Central and New Haven for the Fourth of July week end, then as now. The year is 1878.

SHADOW OF THINGS TO COME

WHILE the completion of the Pacific Railroad may be taken as the event that gave luxury carbuilding its greatest single impetus in the record, there had been premonitions of comfort and luxury on Eastern railroads before this time and, prophetically, George M. Pullman had briefly been associated with them. In view of this, it may be profitable briefly to recapitulate the first primeval beginnings of the amenities of comfort aboard the steam-cars.

As early as 1843 the Erie—then a carrier of consequence building its line westward from New York with an eventual destination on the shores of the lake for which it was named—introduced two "Diamond Cars," so called from the shape of their windows, whose black horsehair seats could be converted into a form of reclining couch. As the Erie's then longest run was only three hours, sleeping facilities were not an important consideration.

More essential to the well-being of passengers was the still earlier provision made by the management of the Philadelphia, Germantown & Norristown Railroad of a men's bar at one end of each of its two cars named *President* and *Victoria*. The presence of drink-ing facilities may be noted with reassuring regularity throughout the entire history of railroad travel. It was evidently a first consideration on the part of managements with an eye to passenger traffic, and even in the Deep South in the years immediately following the Civil War, when the railroads were in deplorable condition and their rolling stock of almost unbelievable antiquity and obsolescence, the presence of a bar somewhere in the train was noted by commentators on travel. Often it was a crude arrangement in the baggage car, but no man need go thirsty. It was an age when neither regulation nor custom inhibited train crews from drinking on duty, and it may well be that conductors, or train captains as they were then known, saw to it that refreshments were available on their assigned runs.

Generally speaking, railroad managements in the years before the Civil War inclined to view a considerable degree of decoration as a substitute for comfort and privacy. The coaches of the period, while they were characterized by an almost complete absence of springing and often the merest apology for covering or upholstery on their hard wooden seats, ran to an opulence of visual decor that gladdened the hearts of travelers, although their bones might be in anguish. Bright colors predominated everywhere. Trains were often painted in cream and gold, and crimson and green trim and fine lining abounded. Early cars were splendid with painted landscapes on their exteriors. Some of these depicted natural wonders or beauties that might be encountered along the right of way. Others showed the lively imagination of the artist with beasts of the jungle or scenes from classic mythology. When Samuel Hopkins Adams's grandfather took passage on the Rensselaer & Saratoga Railroad in the York State forties, he was offered a choice of coaches emblazoned with a winter scene from the Swiss Alps or a lifelike Bengal tiger snarling at the bars of a painted cage. "Grandfather was advised that the tiger coach was the safer."

Travelers, especially the more impressionable among them, seemed to concur with the management in the theory that lavish ornamentation was an adequate substitute for practical comfort. Sophisticated travelers who were literate enough to set down their impressions of train travel might view with disapprobation the primitive toilet facilities and republican accomodations generally, but a large majority of railroad patrons seem to have been conned into comparative quiescence and tranquillity by the suggestion of luxury rather than its factual accomplishment.

This understandable yearning for magnificence on the part of people whose domestic existence was homely in the extreme was to be reflected in the interiors to be provided by far more sophisticated carbuilders only a few years hence. Neither Wagner nor Woodruff, nor least of all George Pullman, underestimated the appeal of luxury, either real or implied, and their success was in large measure to be determined by the degree in which they gratified a growing public taste for opulence.

During the 1850s there first began to appear on the better established railroads intimations of the privacy through compartmentation that was to be the identifying hallmark of luxury travel in years to come. In 1853 there was designed for the Hudson River Railroad an experimental car of advanced design whose long shadow was to fall over carbuilding practice for decades to come. Built by the firm of Eaton & Gilbert of Troy, it may well have been the first all-compartment car in the record and contained five staterooms for private occupancy within its over-all length of forty-five feet. "Each room is calculated for a party or family," said the admiring *Scientific American* of this prototypal vehicle, "and is furnished with a sofa, four chairs, a looking glass and a small center table. The panels are painted in landscapes, the ceiling hung with silk, and the floor richly carpeted. The rooms are entered from a side passage and each is well ventilated and lighted. There is a washroom in the front of the car. It is the first experiment of its kind in the United States."

A contemporary gesture in the direction of luxury was indulged by the up and coming Erie whose management, while not yet thinking in terms of staterooms, was agreeable to giving the passengers aboard its day coaches the red carpet treatment, even though the phrase was a century in the future. Its new cars built at the company's Piedmont shops boasted "twenty windows on each side of the car with a single plate of double thick French plate glass. . . . The seats throughout are C. P. Bailey's patented reclining day or night seats. They . . . are splendidly upholstered, the covering being a rich velvet plush costing five dollars a yard. Over 100 yards of plush were used."

The rich carpets and fine cabinetwork in rare woods that delighted early travelers on the cars were to last until well into the twentieth century. But the skill of scenic artists whose landscapes and lions had appeared on the panels of the first ornate coaches was in little demand after the fifties. The foremost practitioners of this pleasant calling like John Burgum and his son Edwin drifted to Concord, New Hampshire, where they found employment in the coachworks of Lewis Downing and Leon Abbot, ornamenting the doors and side panels of their magnificent product with the heraldry of the United States Mails and the natural wonders of the countryside. After the last Concord coach had been sent west for the service of Wells Fargo & Co., they were reduced to depicting the Lakes of Killarney on safe doors and enlivening the interiors of saloons. But once their craft had been a noble one, dedicated to portraying Commodore Vanderbilt on the headlights of locomotives and the national eagle on the sides of the cars that were making history in the land.

Premonitions of the full hotel facilities that were

ultimately to be devised by Pullman and his contemporaries and competitors in the boom days after Appomattox already existed in the minds of forward-looking editors and commentators on the travel scene. As early as 1842 when the internal-expansion steam locomotive had barely supplanted the horse in general railroad practice, the *American Railway Journal* forecast great things to come.

"On the whole it would be difficult to imagine any improvement that could be desired," it said in commenting on some particularly commodious cars outshopped that year at Cambridge, Massachusetts, "though we dare say these Down Easters will rig up some new notion ere long that will furnish board and lodging as well as mere passage on the railroad."

The first lounge car had already made its appearance in what may be described as the Early Ordovician period of train travel. It was placed in service on the Philadelphia, Germantown & Norristown Railroad in 1836, the fruit of genius in a Richard Imlay who forthwith patented it together with several less essential aspects of innovation. The body of *Victory* was dropped between the trucks, a design which was to be incorporated with spectacular results some years later in the celebrated Gothic director's car of the Chicago & North Western, while at the two ends of the car, over the trucks, were located a water closet and standup bar, respectively. The car was a resounding success with the patrons of the road who were enchanted with the progressive aspects of drinking and answering the demands of nature while in motion.

As early as 1850 the Baltimore & Ohio, for many years the standard of operational railroading of the entire world, had been experimenting with sleeping cars. It built several with three berths one on top of the other, and thus early in the game the risible aspects of sleeper folklore were established as a staple of American humor.

"As the Baltimore & Ohio was always noted for its sharp curves, many amusing accidents occurred during the journey from Baltimore to Wheeling," wrote a contemporary, "when the traveller, in a state of dishabille, frequently dropped from the third tier in the dead of night, awakening his neighbors with a groan when he reached the floor of the car."

The groans of sleeper patrons, together with their mating cries and the nocturnal tribal rites of Pullman patrons were to resound from vaudeville stages and be reflected in the popular press for decades to come.

Beginning as early as 1836 when the Cumberland Valley Railroad placed in service its primordial bunking conveyance named *Chambersburg* between Harrisburg and Chambersburg, the mention of sleeping cars, both projected and factually accomplished, flits through the annals of railroading, an elusive will-o'-the-wisp compounded partly of patents and blueprints and occasionally of an experimental model in revenue service.

In their thinking then and later, carbuilders and railroad managements had natural recourse to the already established techniques of naval architecture and the design of ships' interiors. No land vehicle had ever before been planned for prolonged occupancy or with an eye to more than the most cursory possibilities of eating and sleeping. Men had, however, been living comfortably at sea for uncounted generations, and it was no random parallel, a few years later, when an observer compared the elaborate private car built by Colonel William D'Alton Mann for the actress Lily Langtry to Cleopatra's barge.

Popular legend, unsupported by any positive evidence, has long held that George M. Pullman was inspired to the invention of the folding upper berth by the practice of building tiered bunks he encountered in the mining camps of Colorado. Pullman himself never gave support to this suggestion. No record exists of any folding upper bunks in the miners' cabins of Georgetown or Central City; rather, those that existed were fixed and permanent parts of the domestic architecture, and tiered berths had already been experimented with both on the New York Central and the Baltimore & Ohio before Pullman turned his hand to sleeping cars. The preponderance of evidence would seem to be against the mining-camp theory.

Long before the firing of the first shot at Sumter, the Patent Office at Washington had recorded fully twenty cars or their components designed to afford sleeping accommodations while moving. Some of these remained in the drawing-board stage, while a few saw actual nocturnal service on the weird and wonderful network of vaguely interlocking railroads that were coming into being everywhere that stages and canal

CHICAGO, Burlington AND QUINCY RAILROAD.

IS THE ONLY ROUTE RUNNING

PULLMAN 16-WHEEL

DRAWING ROOM SLEEPING CARS

IN AMERICA.

PULLMAN SIXTEEN WHEEL SLEEPING CAR.

BURLINGTON

THE ONLY ROUTE RUNNING

PULLMAN DINING CARS

FROM CHICAGO TO OMAHA!

The Press and Traveling Public pronounce it the Favorite Route for all points in

Nebraska, Wyoming, Colorado, Utah, Idaho, Montana, Nevada, Oregon, Arizona

AND CALIFORNIA.

You will find Tickets at General Office, 59 Clark St., Central Depot, Indiana Ave. and Canal St. Depots.

W. B. STRONG, Gen'l Sup't, Chicago, Ill. JAMES WALLACE, City Pass. Agent, Chicago. D. W. HITCHCOCK, Gen'l West'n Pass. Agt., Chicago, Ill.

CHICAGO EVENING JOURNAL PRINT.

boats previously had trafficked. In 1854 H. B. Myers filed patent application on a primitive arrangement of folding coach chairs which, with the aid of a qualified mechanic, could be transformed into a sort of double-decker berth, without curtains or any suggestion of privacy, to be sure, but at least space on which a man might stretch out if he were not too tall. His patent later became one of the properties of the Central Transportation Company, one of the earliest builders of sleeping cars.

Myers was followed by Theodore Tuttle Woodruff, sometimes spoken of as the father of sleeping cars, with an arrangement so complicated and ponderous in its mechanism that it might have served as a prototype for one of the devisings of Rube Goldberg. Woodruff's patents, too, entered the stream of railroad history and appear recurrently as financed and then rejected by an adventurous young capitalist named Andrew Carnegie. Plymon Green, an Illinois photographer, devised a car seat which, along with many other claimants, he subsequently declared had been misappropriated by George M. Pullman to his, Green's, fiscal detriment and professional disadvantage. An upper berth invented by Edward C. Knight was slung on ropes with counterweights and had to be secured firmly in its lowered position to prevent its returning to the car ceiling with results injurious possibly to the person of its occupant and certainly to his dignity.

A down-East Yankee named Asa Hapgood actually had sleeping cars of his own manufacture in 1861 on the Boston–New York run via Springfield. Nathaniel Thompson patented a sleeper whose daytime seats were arranged back to back down the center of the car, a device subsequently pirated by William Flower with bad feeling and legal see-here-nows on both sides.

These are only a cross sampling of the invocations of Morpheus that appeared before the Civil War. By the seventies, when such eccentric geniuses as Colonel Mann, Christian E. Lucas, J. A. Schmitz and R. J. Montgomery were in full cry across the landscape, it was hard to gain admission to the anterooms of general managers of the more important railroads because of the press of wild-eyed inventors in dented hats and with rolls of blueprints spilling from their coattails. Sleepers were by now an accomplished fact and profit-

able beyond all previous dreaming, and everybody was anxious to get in on the act.

Railroad travel, at least up to the time of the Civil War, was regarded, of course, as adventurous, which it was, and a form of pioneer endeavor which it also was. But only a handful of uncommonly farsighted venture capitalists foresaw its possibilities or imagined that it might be the major preoccupation of the entire American nation, as it was to become in the fullness of time and for three whole decades.

There is in existence an enormous body of literature on the primeval aspects of rail travel, far more for example than is available in the later bibliographies of flying or the automobile. Everyone who ventured aboard the cars felt obligated to set down his impressions with the implicit suggestion that a good deal of heroism was involved in merely taking passage, or booking a seat as the custom at first was, following the practice of the staging lines. When in turn the airplane arrived upon the scene a large segment of the traveling public merely accommodated its luggage to the weight requirements and set off into the wide blue yonder with a yawn. The American who was going places simply transferred his patronage complete with the manners and customs of mass travel to the planes in much the same manner that he had, without fuss or wonderment, changed from the horse-drawn hack to the auto taxi.

Things were different when the first steam engines and their train brigades commenced operations following the river roads of New England or upper York State. A ride on the cars became the subject for a starred chapter in the memoirs of every literate person, and as a result we have a very complete and fascinating report on every aspect of train travel: the cars themselves, their personnel and conduct, the wonderful locomotive engines that drew them, the eating, drinking, smoking and spitting habits of the customers, the architecture of the principal depots (almost invariably questionable), the food at luncheon stops (something to establish continuity with the Borgias) and the sensation of riding up to a mile a minute, which was accomplished in 1848 and which one and all concurred was perfectly splendid.

Except among an unreconstructed fringe of churls and curmudgeons, everybody fell under the spell of steam locomotion. There were country squires who objected to the invasion of their estates and privacy. There were in the South, feudal overlords who foresaw, correctly, social trouble as one of the cargoes the cars would bring in. There were canal-boat proprietors who viewed it as against God, and housewives who objected to the sooting up of their laundry. But by and large the railroad was viewed with almost uninhibited delight by those who rode it and those who viewed it from a prudent distance.

There were, to be sure, many contretemps and disappointments. The first proud owners of locomotive engines imported from England, where for a few years the best of these were built, refused to allow them out in wet weather, and if it rained, the train didn't go. There were occasional mishaps. Commodore Cornelius Van Der Bilt, as he then spelled his name, was involved in one of these in New Jersey. It smashed him up considerably, and the Commodore swore he'd never have anything to do with the thrice-damned cars again. There were cruel accidents involving bystanders and animals and when a fast train in 1840 on a Maryland carrier collided with a horse carriage

carrying two ladies, killing one of the occupants and doing grievous smash to all and went on without stopping, public resentment suggested a quick lynching for the conductor.

But it was wonderful how soon things got straightened out. Rights of way became fenced, and crossings were guarded by village ancients. The cars met the steamers at Stonington or Fall River with an exactitude that was marvelous to behold, and the engines, which were shortly being made in this country, went out in all weather and with a reliability that was little short of sensational. On the Western Railroad of Massachusetts, a road built by the father of James McNeill Whistler, the motive power was an Eddy engine so precise and reliable in its work that it became known as an "Eddy Clock." People began riding up and down the line not only upon occasions of business, but for the sheer pleasure of it, and very early in the game the excursion ticket became recognized by managements as a potent source of passenger revenue. Militia regiments, chambers of commerce, fraternal groups and chowder and marching societies all took to the cars, sometimes with saluting cannon

mounted on a flat, often with a baggage car filled with hampers of champagne, and always with oratory and civic enthusiasm that caused the eagle to scream in concert with the whistle on the engine up ahead.

Perhaps the most dramatic social impact of the coming of the railroad was upon the estate of the men connected with it. The age of railroad presidents whose frock coats, silk top hats and gold-headed canes were the hallmark of authority was yet in the future, but the operating personnel, trainmen, superintendents and general managers assumed a prestige status in their communities comparable to that of shipmasters in sailing ports such as Nantucket or Newburyport. In a time before hundred-mile-long operating divisions, a conductor or engineer was apt to live at home and be home to supper, and in his community he was a dignitary, if not on a parity with squire or the banker, at least with deacons of the church and other solid men.

Engineers were Mister. Conductors enjoyed the title of Captain, and master mechanics in the local roundhouse and shops for some now forgotten reason were identifiable by a top hat long after other operating employees had switched to more practical headgear. In group photographs of the shop personnel as late as the nineties, the master mechanic is still distinguishable among the cloth caps and dungarees by his top hat and Prince Albert coat.

In all this clamor of events and changing times, only one thing seems to have remained almost completely static while all else was change and mutation, and that was the accommodations provided for railway passengers. From the middle thirties, when the stagecoach body was being discarded in favor of the center-aisle common passenger coach—built like a box on wheeled trucks until the years immediately after the Civil War—no basic change and few changes in the details of construction of railroad cars were effected. Inventors tinkered with patent ventilators and improved water closets. Crackpots dreamed of a time when cars should be built of iron, steel not being then even thinkable, and precarious devices were perfected so that doors at both ends of the car couldn't be open at the same time with the resultant draft that threatened to blow passengers and all out the rear door. The immutable window latch was brought to the fullest flower of perfection, as it remained for nearly a century, and the emergency bell cord for signaling the engineer was strung overhead, where for decades old ladies thought it was for hanging parasols. But the essential basic economy of the passenger coach remained the same. Everybody said there was room for improvement, but like Mark Twain's weather, nobody did anything about it.

Then came the war and priorities for the armies took precedence over convenience for travelers. For four long years the cars grew grimier, grimmer, more confining and more inflammable. Many of them were destroyed in actual hostilities; others simply fell apart when threading was pulled off bolts and nails rotted in the frames.

Toward the very end there were intimations of things to be on the railroads of the future. Appropriately the two most significant of these had their origins with the two heads of state engaged in implacable warfare. The United States Army Railroad administration built a private car for the use and occupancy of President Lincoln. And when the fall of Richmond was obviously at hand, President Jefferson Davis sent his wife south out of the beleaguered capital on a special chartered for the occasion on the Petersburg Railroad. Mrs. Davis and her suite occupied a private car and, just to be one up on Mr. Lincoln, her carriage together with a complement of horses and grooms went with it on a flatcar.

The age of luxury travel by railroad was at hand.

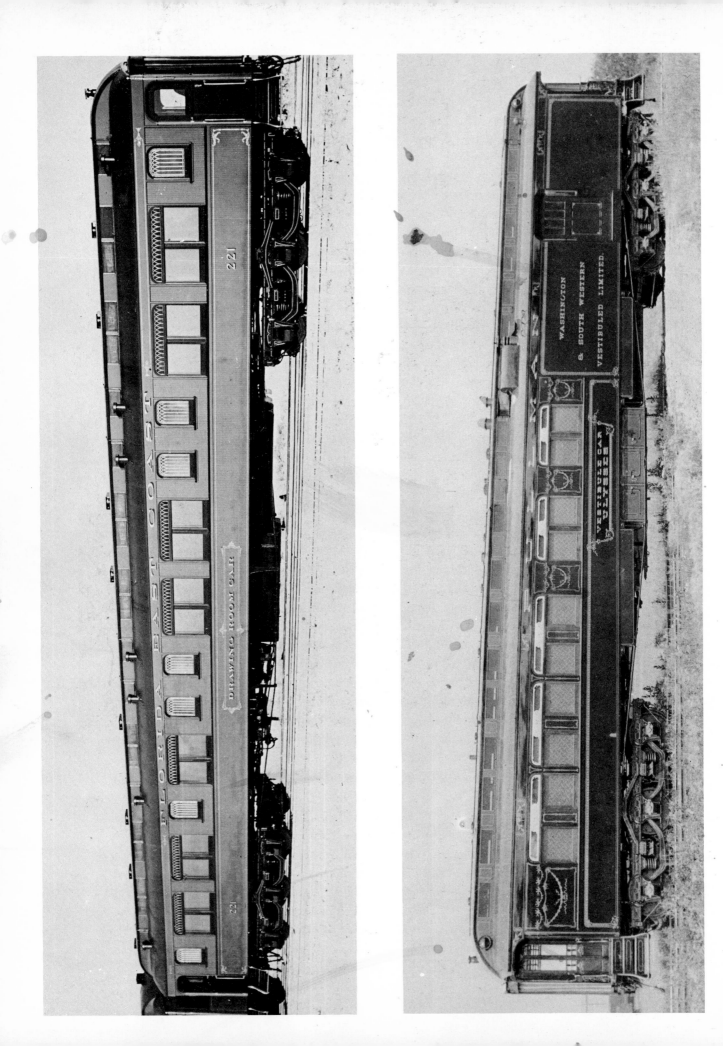

The lush age of Pullman design knew no more voluptuous concept of general service transport than the cars represented here. The Florida East Coast was still dominated in 1906—when it ordered the stunning all-room sleeper on the opposite page—by Henry M. Flagler, a man of great determination in the matter of divorcing unwanted wives and making Florida the winter playground of the nation. Palm Beach was coming into its own, and such notables in its annals as Edward T. Stotesbury and Colonel Edward

R. Bradley, when not riding the private cars of other nabobs, demanded the best of everything. The superb all-room sleepers on the F.E.C. were the answer. The buffet–smoking car combine Ulysses on the page opposite and the sleeper Chile shown here were built for the Richmond & Danville's Washington & South Western Vestibuled Limited, an all-Pullman, extra-fare run between Washington and New Orleans. It too catered to the luxury trade and spared no expense in comfort, or detail of ornamentation.

Superb examples of American Car & Foundry craftsmanship are these two palace cars from the collection of Arthur D. Dubin. The Père Marquette's parlor–cafe No. 25 was built at A.C.F.'s Jeffersonville shops in 1903 and assigned to the Northern Michigan vacation service on trains No. 1 and 5, and Nos. 9 and 10, the Resort Special. Of this train the public timetable for 1905 of the Great Central route of which the Père Marquette was a component, says, "Trains No. 1 and 5 will stop at Little Manistee River (Fishing Camp) on signal," an index of casual operation in good old summer days. The car was characterized by a curved rear bulkhead with plate-glass windows to match, giving onto an observation platform of uncommon depth. The Georgia & Alabama Railroad, represented by buffet No. 90, was successor to the Savannah, Americus & Montgomery and ran between Montgomery and Savannah, a distance of 340 miles over its own tracks and those of the Central of Georgia. It ran buffets in its daily train each way and A.C.F. combination parlor–sleepers on its overnight.

TWO PHOTOS: ARTHUR D. DUBIN COLLECTION

Dinner aboard the cars in the years of the Georgia & Alabama's flowering was a matter of unhurried ease in an uncomplicated world.

The melancholy celebrity of the wreck on the Toledo, Peoria & Western Railroad near Chatsworth, Ohio, in August 1887 derives largely from a mawkish and inaccurate music-hall ballad circulated immediately after the accident. But the wreck was a classic in railroading annals because of the great destruction and loss of life resulting from the collapse of a minor trestle not more than fifteen feet long and ten deep. The train, an excursion to Niagara Falls, carried more than 600 passengers in five coaches, two parlor cars and six sleepers, to which were coupled at either end a baggage car and the business car of the road's general manager, all drawn in an im-

pressive doubleheader by two fine engines. The trestle, weakened by a brush fire, failed under the combined weight of the locomotives, and the cars telescoped one on top of the other in the shallow ditch, the six Pullmans and the business car at the rear of the train remaining safely on the track. Fire, which broke out immediately, was extinguished, but there were seventy-odd fatalities and nearly 300 injured. Depicted on this page is the interior of one of the coaches at the moment of impact; on the page opposite: the debris, including the crushed truck of one of the forward cars.

THREE DRAWINGS: AUTHOR'S COLLECTION

On the night of February 6, 1871, the west-bound Pacific Express, *crack New York Central flyer on the New York–Chicago run, sideswiped a train of tank cars filled with oil while passing over a drawbridge across Wappinger Creek, near New Hamburg on the Hudson River, to provide one of the sensational wrecks of the age. The head-end equipment was deluged with petroleum which immediately took fire as survivors fled across the ice of the creek. A footnote* to the car construction of the period is that three Wagner sleepers at the rear of the train were uncoupled and pushed out of range of the flames by manpower. On the page opposite, the Pacific Express *poses on Harlem Trestle between 100th and 116th Streets, New York City, with Wagner cars on the head end instead of the rear. Above, a Michigan Central parlor car of the same period with wicker furniture in place of the more conventional plush.*

One of the less commonly encountered and more exotic types of Pullman, the observation sleeper somehow possessed a cachet of romance unknown to the vestibule-enclosed cars in the middle of the train. To take the air before breakfast from the open platform of one's sleeper gave almost the dimension of riding a private car. Norseman, built in 1908 for general service, was an open section car of wooden transom construction with all-steel underframe. Neponset had conventional open sections with a stateroom and drawing room.

TWO PHOTOS: PULLMAN STANDARD

In an age when gentlemen wore stiff collars and boiled shirts with business attire, the men's washroom at the end of the sleeper was the pre-breakfast trysting place for masculine passengers, largely, be it said, in crosspatch mood. Here emerged the straight-edged razor of Toledo steel, here in a setting of misplaced collar buttons and overset shaving kits, was knotted the improbable Ascot cravat, here adjusted the Fireman's Friend galluses. Last night's club car whisky and good fellowship were miles behind; unsteady hands had trouble with button-top boots, and toothpaste became unmanageable. Both the spacious dimension of the apartment and the suggestion of Chesterfieldian manners in this propaganda painting from a Burlington travel folder of 1910 are strictly spurious.

87

THE

CHICAGO AND NORTH-WESTERN R'Y

RUNS

SOLID VESTIBULED TRAINS

AND FURNISHES

PERFECT DINING CAR SERVICE

BETWEEN **CHICAGO** AND

PRINCIPAL POINTS

WEST AND NORTHWEST.

THE PACIFIC LIMITED.

LEAVING CHICAGO 11.00 P. M. DAILY. ALL MEALS SERVED IN DINING CARS BETWEEN CHICAGO AND PORTLAND, OREGON, AND TRUCKEE, CAL.

THE DENVER LIMITED.

LEAVING CHICAGO 6.00 P. M. DAILY. ALL MEALS SERVED IN DINING CARS BETWEEN CHICAGO AND DENVER.

THE ST. PAUL LIMITED.

LEAVING CHICAGO 6.00 P. M. DAILY. ALL MEALS SERVED IN DINING CARS BETWEEN CHICAGO AND ST. PAUL AND MINNEAPOLIS. BREAKFAST SERVED IN BUFFET SLEEPER TO PASSENGERS FOR DULUTH.

THE OVERLAND FLYER.

LEAVING SAN FRANCISCO 7.00 P. M., PORTLAND 9.00 P. M. DAILY. ALL MEALS SERVED IN DINING CARS THROUGH TO CHICAGO.

THE CHICAGO LIMITED.

LEAVING DENVER 9.15 P. M. DAILY. ALL MEALS SERVED IN DINING CARS BETWEEN DENVER AND CHICAGO.

THE VESTIBULED LIMITED.

LEAVING ST. PAUL 6.50 P. M., MINNEAPOLIS 7.30 P. M. DAILY. ALL MEALS SERVED IN DINING CARS THROUGH TO CHICAGO. SUPPER SERVED IN BUFFET SLEEPING CAR TO PASSENGERS FROM DULUTH.

THROUGH PALACE SLEEPING CARS

CARRYING PASSENGERS IN **FAST TIME** BETWEEN CHICAGO AND

San Francisco, Portland, Denver, Omaha, St. Paul, Minneapolis, Duluth, Sioux City.

W. H. NEWMAN,
3rd Vice Pres't.

J. M. WHITMAN,
Gen'l Manager.

W. A. THRALL,
Gen'l Pas. & Ticket Agt.

Christmas Dinner—1890.

—•—

BLUE POINTS.

GREEN TURTLE. OX TAIL.

BOILED CALIFORNIA SALMON, WITH FRENCH PEAS.
BAKED RED SNAPPER—PIQUANTE SAUCE.

MUTTON—CAPER SAUCE. CAPON—EGG SAUCE.

BEEF.
TURKEY—STUFFED WITH CHESTNUTS.

DUCK—CURRANT JELLY.
GOOSE—APPLE SAUCE. ROAST QUAIL—STUFFED. WILD TURKEY—GRAPE JELLY.
GROUSE MACEDONIA STYLE.

SWEETBREADS—POTTED—SMOTHERED WITH MUSHROOMS.
BAKED RABBIT PIE—AMERICAN STYLE.
CROQUETTES OF OYSTERS.
ORANGE FRITTERS. CHICORY AND LOBSTER SALAD.

CELERY. LETTUCE. CHOW CHOW. QUEEN OLIVES.

BOILED SWEET POTATOES.
MASHED POTATOES. STEWED TOMATOES.
ASPARAGUS. GREEN CORN.
GREEN PEAS.

ENGLISH PLUM PUDDING—BRANDY SAUCE. COCOANUT PUDDING—WINE SAUCE.
MINCE AND PUMPKIN PIE.
CHARLOTTE RUSSE.

NEW YORK ICE CREAM. LEMON ICE, CAKE
EDAM AND ROQUEFORT CHEESE. BENT'S CRACKERS.
COFFEE.

MALAGA AND CATAWBA GRAPES. APPLES.
BANANAS.
ORANGES. RAISINS.
ASSORTED NUTS.

Times have changed on railroads everywhere since Christmas 1890 when the diners of the Chicago & North Western Railway listed—among other items—green turtle soup, roast quail, wild turkey, grouse, baked rabbit pie and oyster croquets, while the absence of any mention of tariff suggests that the meal may have been on the house, although this is purely speculative. That the good things of life still survive aboard the cars is suggested by this enticing buffet displayed for the benefit of a photographer aboard the Santa Fe's crack flyer, the Chief, only a few years back. Fred Harvey himself would have admired it.

In 1905, when Pullman built for it this fine cafe–chair car, the Wisconsin Central was attempting to compete with the Burlington, Chicago & North Western, Milwaukee and Illinois Central on the Chicago–Twin Cities run. Failing to make the grade, it merged with the Soo four years later, but connoisseurs remember with pleasure its Tuscan red trains with bright gold trim. Wisconsin Central interiors matched the outside with many mirrors, old-gold plush upholstery and Wilton carpets.

TWO PHOTOS: PULLMAN STANDARD

The handsome cafe–parlor car Schenley was built for the Baltimore & Ohio by Pullman in 1901 and was still in service at the end of the First World War.

The buffet car shown at the left was built by Pullman for the Grand Trunk in 1899 and reflected the taste of the time with coal-oil lamps, fringed portières and recessed and mirrored alcoves for flowers. The Illinois Central lunch counter car (below) was more utilitarian and was built with a wide corridor so that passers-through need not jostle patrons of its highly polished steam tables and coffee urns.

PULLMAN STANDARD

ILLINOIS CENTRAL RAILROAD

The transition in a period of a little more than ten years—from the open platforms and mahogany finish of the sleeper Olesa to the cream striping and art glass transoms of London—in the special livery of the Pennsylvania only served to intensify the implications of the word "varnish" as a synonym for fine passenger equipment.

The open sections of *Lapland,* albeit somewhat less ornate than some of its contemporaries, bespeak the genius of T. T. Woodruff rather than of Pullman, into
whose custody the car finally passed. It was a ten-section, drawing room sleeper–
buffet car with open platforms, solid cabinetwork, Pintsch lamps and uncommonly attractive star-spangled upholstery.

THREE PHOTOS: PULLMAN STANDARD

93

No single calling or occupation more faithfully patronized the steamcars in the days when 260,-000 Pullman berths were occupied every day and night in the year than did the confraternity of drummers—travelers in every sort and brand of merchandise, from lowly hawkers of dollar watches and electric belts to exalted promoters of heavy industrial merchandise, such as Diamond Jim Brady who wrote hundreds of millions of dollars worth of business every year. Every night they rode in thousands, in lowers and uppers, staterooms and compartments as their means and status dictated, forgathered in washrooms to smoke cigars and exchange anecdotes of questionable propriety and market tips and descended from the sleepers at inconvenient hours of the morning to register blearily at a hundred Commercial Hotels and Windsors from Bangor to Los Angeles. Nights spent in the mysterious jungle life that prowled the green aisles of Pullmans and days spent in sample rooms in Memphis, Seattle and Fort Worth left an indelible stamp of worldliness on the drummer of classic times, who is shown here, in a contemporary drawing by Harper's *staff artist T. de Thulstrup, doing business in a Western hotel, while in the barroom in the background, even bigger deals are being shaped.*

Accidents such as the one depicted above were frequent
aboard moving trains with open
car platforms like those at the
right. Colonel Mann's boudoir
cars showed the way to the first
platforms enclosed in narrow
vestibules (below), which were
soon adopted by all major builders of palace cars.

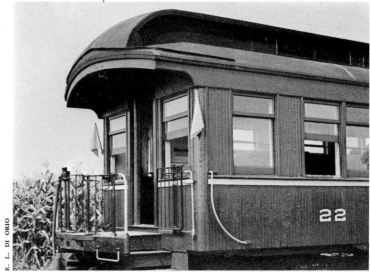

E. L. DI ORIO

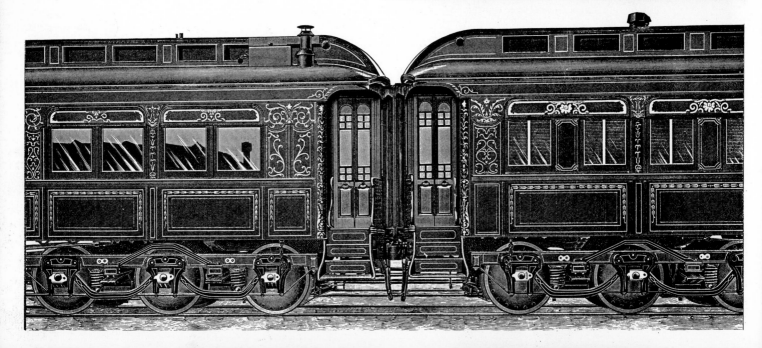

The ultimate objective of Pullman's design and construction of palace cars was easy and continuous access between the elements of a moving train and safe continuity between their various resources of sleeping, dining, lounging, private apartments and special services such as barber and library. The illusion of living under the roof of a luxury hotel was heightened, as is suggested by these two photographs, by tight-locking draft gear, close-fitting vestibule diaphragms and interlocking footplates. The wide vestibules such as those shown here were the logical outgrowth of the first narrow passageways, and passengers were encouraged to move from car to car, where every facility for living and recreation was at hand for a minimum of effort and inconvenience.

TWO PHOTOS: PULLMAN STANDARD

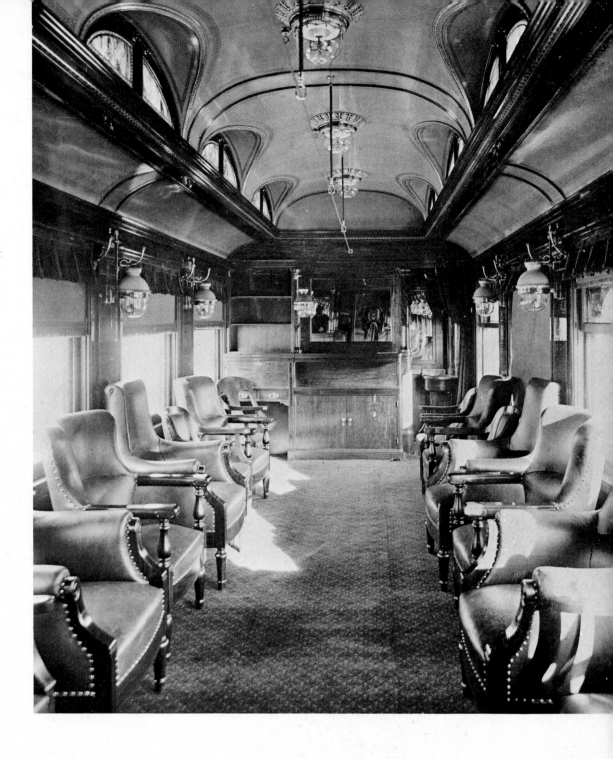

Jay Gould had two more years to live in control of the Missouri Pacific when the vintage buffet car on the page opposite was built by Pullman in 1890. The Burlington's uncommonly handsome cafe–parlor car Wisconsin was placed in service in 1902 with a gravity water system, wooden undersills and both Pintsch and electric illumination. Wisconsin was one of two cars classed by the railroad as DO-I; it lasted until 1929, when it was dismantled and the body sold at Aurora. On this page is a rare Chicago & North Western buffet of 1911 vintage, unusual by reason of the individual illumination furnished by bracket lamps activated by Pintsch gas along the walls in addition to the conventional ceiling fixtures.

Because the honored position at the end of the train occupied of necessity by observation cars has usually been assigned to more august conveyances, day coaches with observation platforms are comparatively rare on the rosters of steam carriers. Exceptions that prove the rule that the rear car be an observation sleeper, parlor car or cafe car, are the observation coach *Tymochtee* on the once active Hocking Valley, shown on the opposite page, and the Gulf, Mobile & Ohio's No. 390, which ran between Bloomington, Illinois, and Kansas City, a trackage acquired by the G.M. & O. from its consolidation with the Chicago & Alton. On this page, in the fearful and wonderful feminine attire of the year 1908 is shown Olga Nethersole, a contemporary pet of the lobster palaces, as she and her party prepared to depart from Colorado Springs for a tour of the Cripple Creek diggings on the platform of an observation day coach of the Colorado Springs & Cripple Creek District Railroad. This was the run up the escarpment of the Rockies which, a few years earlier, had moved Theodore Roosevelt to the sentiment that it bankrupted the English language to describe its scenic wonderments. The coach shown in the photograph survived for many decades and saw service on the final run of the Midland Terminal, last of the Cripple Creek complex of carriers, in the mid-fifties.

DENVER PUBLIC LIBRARY: WESTERN COLLECTION

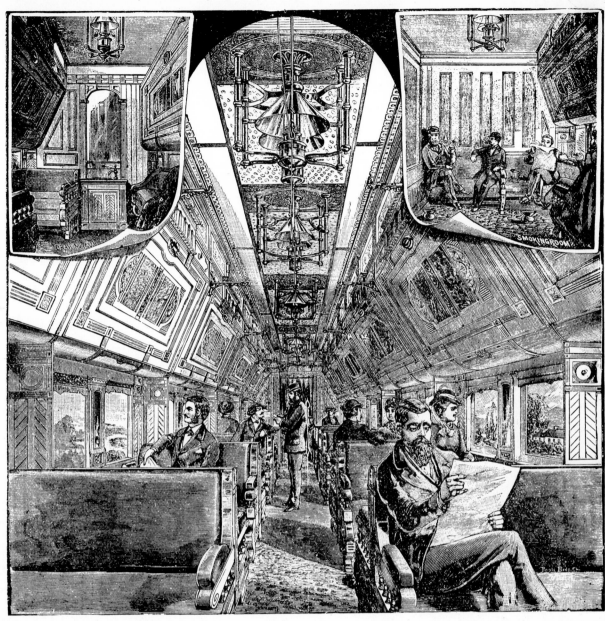

The winter of 1884 was one of great floods on the inland waterways of the United States. From the Great Lakes to the Gulf scores of railroads were flooded for varying lengths of time and at Cincinnati the important Ohio & Mississippi suspended operations for six full weeks. Four feet of water stood in the main street of Richmond, and throughout the Deep South emergencies were declared. Near Orlando, Florida, the trains of the Tavares, Orlando & Atlantic Railroad maintained service by sending track walkers ahead of each train with torches. Passengers were thrilled as water rose to the level of car platforms and made jokes about the lucky occupants of upper berths. When the cars eventually reached Jacksonville the passengers were glad to tell their exciting experiences to Charles Graham, the celebrated staff artist for Harper's, who drew the sketch opposite "from a passenger's notes." The Tavares Railroad patronized Monarch, but Pullmans such as the one shown above experienced similar excitements on the inundated rails of the nearby Louisville & Nashville.

Champagne doings aboard the cars became a cliché of magazine illustrations as a symbol of high life in the seventies and eighties.

The fine mahogany dining car shown here was built in 1915 by American Car & Foundry for the Nashville, Chattanooga & St. Louis Railroad as a rolling exemplar of Southern hospitality in the grand manner.

WINE LIST.

CLARETS, ETC.

Imported by Cavaroc & Co., New Orleans.

	QT.	PT.
St. Julien, "very fine."	$1.00	$ .60
Haut Sauterne,	1.25	.75

CHAMPAGNES, ETC.

	QT.	PT.
Goldlack (extra fine),	$3.00	$1.75
Mumm's Extra Dry,	3.00	1.75

Sherry (extra dry),	20c.
Bass Ale, bottle,	30c.
London Porter, bottle,	30c.
Frankfürter Lager Beer, bottle,	25c
Budweiser " " (very fine)	30c.
Whiskey, Old Bourbon,	20c.
Cognac (very old),	30c.
Gin (old Holland),	20c.
Apollinaris Water,	25c.
Congress Water,	25c.

CIGARS AND CIGARETTES.

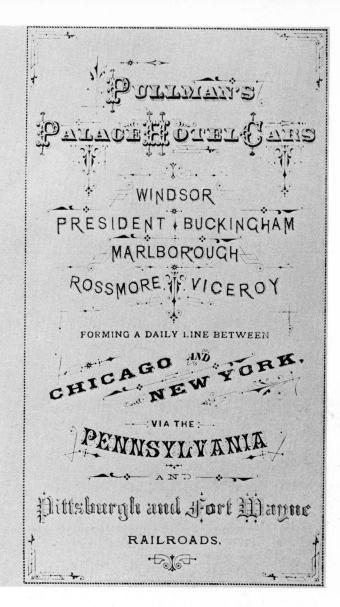

PULLMAN'S PALACE HOTEL CARS

WINDSOR
PRESIDENT ⊹ BUCKINGHAM
MARLBOROUGH
ROSSMORE ⊹ VICEROY

FORMING A DAILY LINE BETWEEN

CHICAGO AND NEW YORK,

⊹ VIA THE ⊹

PENNSYLVANIA

AND

Pittsburgh and Fort Wayne

RAILROADS.

Menus on Pullman's hotel cars such as this could not, of course, attempt to compete with the multiplicity of fish, game and meat courses, entrees, joints and desserts on regular dining car bills of fare because of lack of space. The reverse of this handsome specimen of type faces listed whole prairie chicken, 90c; quail, 60c; golden plover, 90c; Porterhouse steak for two, with mushrooms, $1; half cold lobster, 60c, and other conventional supper dishes at commensurate prices. There was no hardship involved in going Pullman.

TWO PICTURES: ARTHUR D. DUBIN COLLECTION

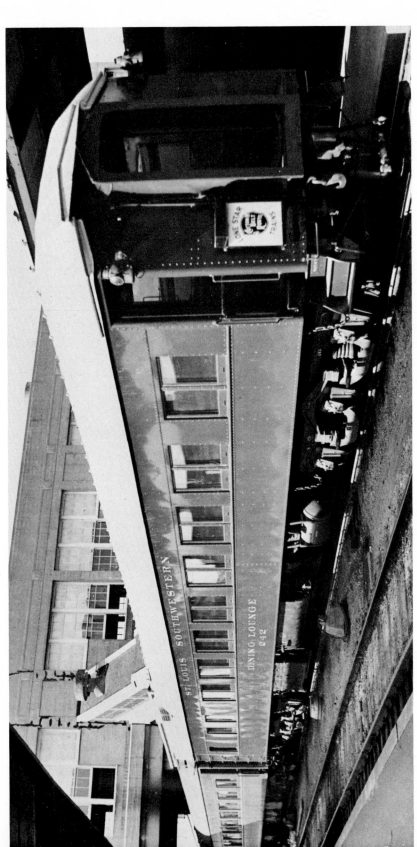

The St. Louis–Southwestern's cafe–lounge car at the right was unique in having been rebuilt from a private car of forgotten ancestry and may well have been the last diner in service with wicker armchairs in its lounge section and an open observation platform. No. 242 was rebuilt at the Cotton Belt's Pine Bluff shops from an eight-section Pullman sleeper. When the road needed additional restaurant cars during the Second World War it purchased two more from the Delaware & Hudson.

TWO PHOTOS: EVERETT DE GOLYER

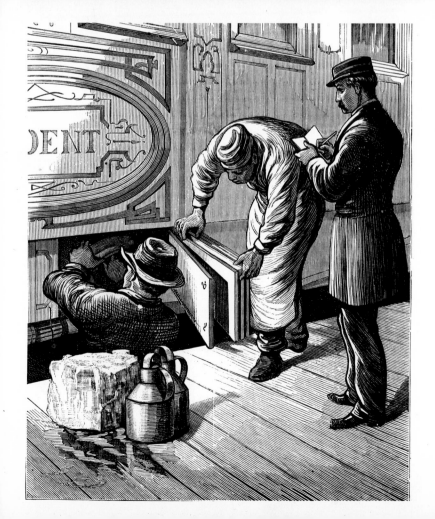

Differing only in detail is the process of provisioning the Chief *and that of stocking Pullman's palace hotel car* President *seventy-five years earlier, as shown in Leslie's for 1875. The skullcaps favored by crewmen off duty remained the same over the years.*

107

In that now dim and distant age when a trip down East was a real adventure and the Maritime Provinces a sleeper haul, both the Boston & Maine and Maine Central maintained superb diner and cafe car services and menus well-provided with Yankee table fare: broiled lobster, baked beans, scrodded codfish and, in season, Penobscot salmon and Cotuit oysters. Groceries came, of course, from S. S. Pierce or Cobb, Bates & Yerxa.

The handsome, if relatively austere, parlor car *Evangeline* was originally built by American Car & Foundry for the Union Palace Car Company and passed to Pullman ownership in the merger of 1889, to be placed in service on the Boston & Maine. Aboard it the proper Bostonians of a more gracious era embarked in Boston's venerable North Station for Casco Bay or the distant resorts of the Belgrade Lakes. Reading matter acceptable to its patrons was the Boston Evening Transcript *or the venerated* Atlantic Monthly *or possibly a novel by Mary Roberts Rinehart, generally esteemed to be at least part New Englander, since she summered at Bar Harbor. Evangeline's era was one in which the cloth traveling cap for gentlemen replaced the more formal top hat or derby aboard the cars and fastidious masculine travelers and practically all women wore gloves. The black silk skullcap which many men had favored in transit a generation earlier was definitely out of fashion.*

On Sunday morning July 29, 1923, the special bearing President Warren G. Harding and his official family arrived at the Southern Pacific's Third Street depot from Portland. Shown on this page are Mrs. Harding waving to friends (right) and (below) chatting on the observation platform of the Presidential car with Herbert Hoover, a distinguished native son and Secretary of Commerce at that time.

Six days later the President was dead in the Palace Hotel and the Southern Pacific was scheduling a funeral train and pilot train to convey his body to Ogden via Tracy and the Dumbarton Cutoff. Shown above with General John J. Pershing at attention, the military guard of honor is lifting the coffin through the window of an Espee business car. Below, his widow, in deepest mourning, is being helped aboard for the President's last journey east.

Thos Hogan Del.

Beginning the day after the Golden Spike ceremonies at Promontory Point, Utah, in May 1869, the West became accessible aboard the steamcars, and the two dominant American preoccupations of the time, railroading and the Western continent, were fused in a single availability. As Westport Landing and St. Joseph, Missouri, had been the entrepôts of Western commerce in the days of covered wagons and the first pioneers, so Omaha took rank to itself as the eastern terminal of the Union Pacific. Although within a few years Omaha was to be achieved by

THE
OVERLAND
TRAVELLER

both the Rock Island and the Burlington, travel from Chicago was mainly over the English-financed rails and left-hand operations of the Chicago & North Western, one of whose westbound trains is shown here, leaving the North Western depot, Chicago, in the early seventies, in a classic drawing from the pages of Harper's Weekly *of the time. Here and on the following pages are depicted the steamcars and the life that rode aboard them, following the Overland Route westward through the decades of steam toward California the Golden.*

The Central Pacific's Silver Palace cars shown in various aspects here may not seem luxurious by contemporary standards, but in their early years almost as much revenue was taken in aboard the sleepers from the frankly curious as from legitimate through passengers. All across Nevada, according to Oscar Lewis, ranchers, miners, Indians and assorted frontier characters gladly paid the extra fare, if only for a few miles' ride, to experience the red plush cushions, plate-glass mirrors and rare inlaid woods that were part of the facade of de luxe travel. In the stereo view above and at the right, the photographer, working from the stateroom at the end of the car, has let his derby hat show. Below and right, many of the Silver Palace cars were equipped with a patent brake that wound up on a spring and when released, snapped the cars to a halt with such violence that flattened wheels and the complaints of passengers soon brought about its discard.

FIVE PHOTOS: SOUTHERN PACIFIC CO.

The first luxury cars, sleepers, diners and buffet cars, used by the Central Pacific between Promontory, Utah, and later Ogden and San Francisco were the Silver Palace cars built by Jackson & Sharp at Wilmington, Delaware, and the service continued until July 1, 1883, when Pullman Palace cars replaced them. Luxury travel exerted a powerful hold on the general imagination throughout the last three decades of the century, and thousands viewed such cars with pleasure in the Currier & Ives lithograph below, depicting "The Lightning Express."

EVERETT DE GOLYER COLLECTION

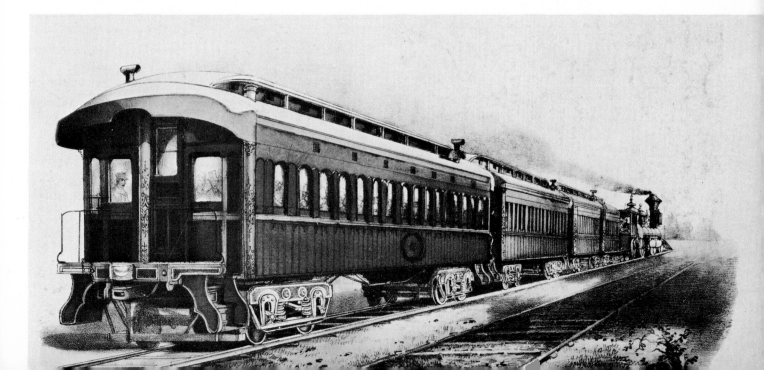

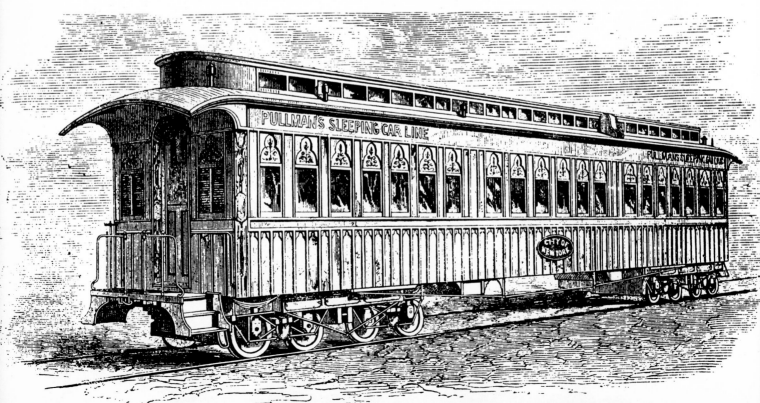

By the fall of 1869 transcontinental sleeper service of regular and imposing dimensions was available between Omaha and California over the joined rails of the Union and Central Pacific Railroads. For the first few months the joint terminal and interchange point of these two carriers was maintained at Promontory Point, scene in May of the Golden Spike ceremonies, and passengers changed cars there from the Pullman sleepers of the U.P. to the Silver Palace hotel cars of the Central Pacific. The entire world was fascinated by the operation of through trains across two thirds of a continent and in its issue of October 2, 1869, the Illustrated London News ran the three fine sketches shown on these pages from the pen and scratchboard of their staff artist Frederick Whymper, who depicted the Pullmans on what the News chose to call "The Pacific Union Railway." Note the eight-wheel trucks of the City of New York, which was then rolling in splendor over the Great American Desert to a rendezvous with destiny and the Central Pacific on a windy upland in the Utah hills.

THREE DRAWINGS: ILLUSTRATED LONDON NEWS

A generation that never ceased to wonder at the comforts and conveniences afforded aboard the steamcars was vastly impressed by the presence on the Wagner-built palace cars of the Central Pacific of organs and pianos for use in communal singing, and they were a favored theme with artists recording the details of transcontinental travel. This particular version appeared in a popular German language periodical of the seventies with a Teutonic music professor at the console.

NEW YORK CENTRAL SYSTEM

By 1890 when Palmyra was again photographed (below) it had been downgraded to the estate of tourist sleeper and its once proud parlor organ supplanted by the utilitarian linen closet of the Pullman porter.

The factual existence of parlor organs on the transcontinental Pullmans of the Union Pacific is photographically attested by the interior of the sleeper Palmyra, shown above, in 1872. Palmyra was already a celebrity in its own right, having been in the Boston Board of Trade special in 1870. Twelve years later a traveling Englishman described a pleasant musical evening spent around Palmyra's organ while passing over the Great Plains, indicating a fair longevity in strenuous service.

At Battle Mountain in the Humboldt Desert of Nevada the Central Pacific cars paused and passengers sought diversion for half an hour by weighing themselves on the baggagemaster's scales or buying prairie dogs from small boys. A few miles farther, they craned from the cars to view "The Maiden's Grave," a regional landmark to the memory of a California pioneer who had fallen by the way in gold-rush times.

Although the comforts of such Pullman palace cars as Rover, *shown here, were an obvious improvement over the covered wagons of only a decade previous, the long trip from Omaha to Oakland could not be altogether free from boredom, and passengers eagerly followed their own progress in one of the many guides such as Crowfoot's and Williams', then popular accessories of the overland traveler. One of the sights on the U.P. run was the high trestle at Dale Creek (below) near Sherman Summit, between Cheyenne and Laramie. When such excitements failed, Williams' Guide advised passengers* "to sit and read, play games and indulge in social conversation and glee." *The last of these diversions was not further identified.*

PULLMAN STANDARD

The interior of one of Union Pacific's Pullman-built hotel cars of approximately the same time as Waud's sketch on the page opposite is shown in this rare photograph with the tables invitingly set up for a meal. Although air conditioning was in the still unforeseen future and smoke and dust a commonplace of travel, most commentators were unanimous in admiring the crisp linen, fresh flowers and general neatness of the hotel car appointments.

An innovation at which travelers never ceased to marvel aboard the Overland Express as it traversed the Great Plains was the appearance each morning at breakfast of the newspaper The Great Pacific Lines Gazette, which was gotten up in the smoking car from telegraphic dispatches picked up during the night.

Chicago, Rock Island & Pacific Railroad
·GREAT·
HIGHWAY of NATIONS between OCCIDENT and ORIENT.

All MEALS from Full BILL of FARE 75 cents.

All Lunches can be obtained in Restaurant at Reasonable Rates.

The Only Line of Dining and Restaurant Cars
IN THE UNITED STATES ARE OWNED AND RUN BY THIS COMPANY
BETWEEN CHICAGO and OMAHA.
WE OWN OUR SLEEPING CARS,
and the Charges between OMAHA and CHICAGO are $1 less per Section than any other line.

ALL MEALS ARE SERVED IN THESE CARS, AND TRAINS DO NOT STOP AT DINING STATIONS.
A. KIMBALL, General Superintendent.   E. ST. JOHN, Gen'l Ticket and Pass. Agent.

The St. Paul and Minneapolis Line—The Milwaukee Route.

As far as Omaha one dined on the cars of the Rock Island. West of Omaha one traveled in the Union Pacific's hotel cars, as sketched in 1869 for Harper's by the distinguished artist A. R. Waud.

This rare old-time photograph from a faded
print in the possession of the Society of California
Pioneers is identified in an inscription on its mar-
gin as "a restaurant on the San Francisco–New
York railroad" and hence may have been taken
aboard one of the Union Pacific Pullman diners
of the early seventies or one of the Jackson &
Sharp cars built for the Central Pacific. It is
not a Silver Palace hotel car as is suggested by
the absence of upper berths, but table wine was
available in abundance, as were the cuspidors,
inevitable in even the most genteel surroundings
of the times. In the Chicago & North Western
advertising on the page opposite, it is apparent
from the lifted glasses that most gentlemen took
advantage of the liberal cellars with which all
hotel and dining cars of the time were stocked.

Despite the handsome and occasionally gaily ornamented exteriors such as that of a Chicago & North Western coach on the page opposite and its less ornate counterpart on the Central Pacific, day coach travel for any extended period in the seventies could be wearisome in the extreme, as is suggested by the contemporary drawing reproduced on this page. The drawing was made by one of the staff artists who comprised Frank Leslie's celebrated expedition of 1876 to report to his readers on the newly opened Far West and may have been made either aboard a Union Pacific transcontinental train or aboard its Central Pacific counterpart west of Ogden, Utah.

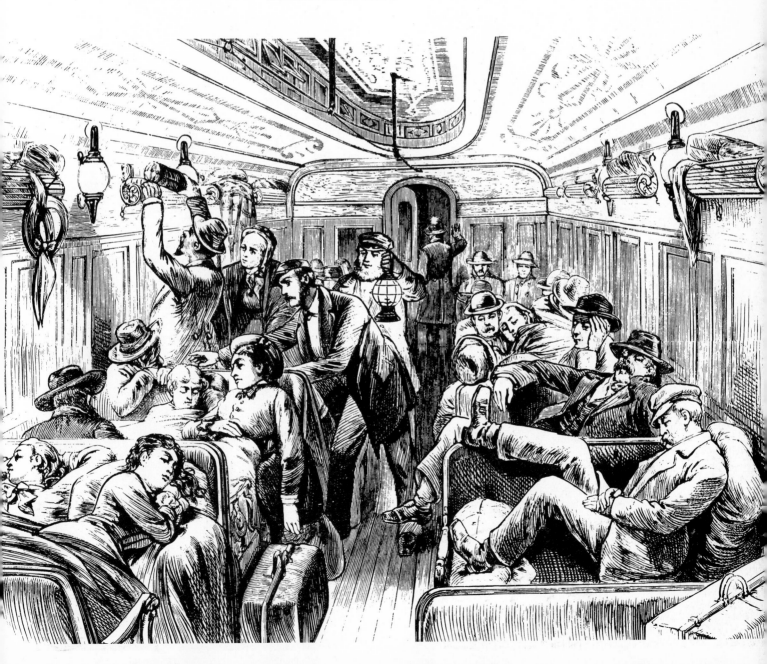

ROBERT HALE

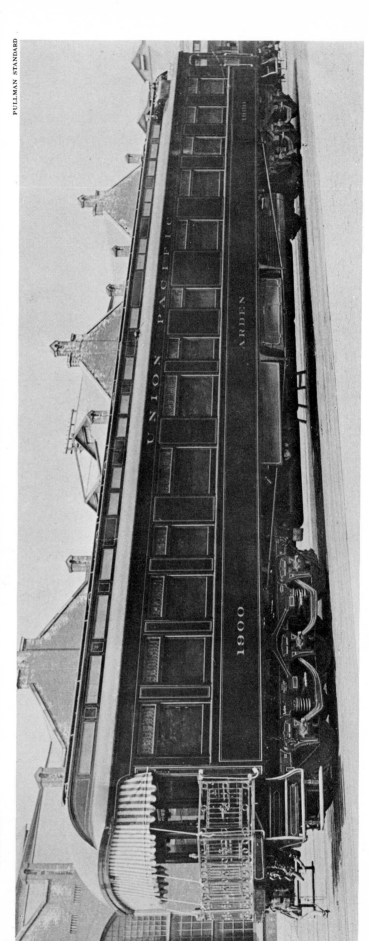

PULLMAN STANDARD

Successive generations of Union Pacific residents have prowled the Overland Trail in style aboard their business cars, ranging in decor from E. H. Harriman's celebrated Arden, *dating from the turn of the century and depicted above and on the page opposite, to A. E. Stoddard's stream-lined No. 100 shown in the Cajon Pass in a photograph by Robert Hale. Between these in its period is No. 100 of Pullman standard construction (below), dating from 1917, used in an effective and spectacular term of office by William Jeffers, a man who got things done in a big way.*

The overleaf photograph is Fred Juke's magnificent action shot of the Overland Limited *eastbound on the Southern Pacific at Elko, Nevada, in 1916. Some of its equipment is depicted on these two pages.*

On the opposite page the cachet of the Overland Cigar, a proprietary brand merchandised
by S. S. Pierce & Company, the princely firm of
Boston grocers, is testimony in pure Havana to
the celebrity of one of the greatest of all American name trains. Below is the interior of one of
the Overland's club cars, its smoking compartment separated from the through corridor by a
partition with elaborate art glass windows. On
this page is the interior of the combination
smoker and baggage that rode the head end of
this splendid flyer between Chicago and San
Francisco in the age of steam.

UNION PACIFIC RAILROAD   PULLMAN STANDARD

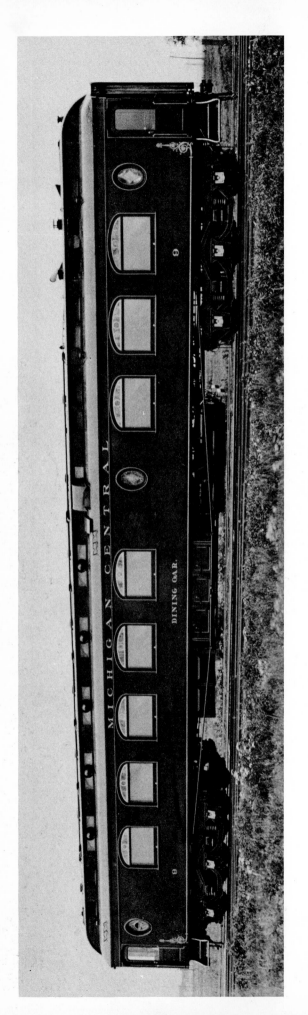

There is a well-established school of Pullman aficionados and students of car-building, of whom Arthur Dubin of Chicago is a leading exponent, that feels that the classic apotheosis of car design was in the decade from 1900 to 1910, rather than in the ornate splendors of the satinwood nineties. The elegant simplicity of 1907 diners on the Vanderbilt lines goes a long way toward justifying this opinion.

Diners aboard the New York Central's crack Lake Shore Limited *that had been flagship of the Vanderbilt fleet until the coming of the* Twentieth Century Limited *still did themselves well at table in the year 1907. Air conditioning was still in the unforeseen future, but the dollar dinner was in its glorious noontide aboard the dining cars of the land and the New York Central was already identified with the watermelon pickle, which was to be a hallmark of its service for decades to come. Outside the picture windows the lordly Hudson furnished an incomparable backdrop for the operations of a railroad of imperial dimensions.*

NEW YORK CENTRAL SYSTEM

MAKE DOWN LOWER SIX

GEORGE MORTIMER PULLMAN came to the business of carbuilding with complete appropriateness through being a cabinet-maker. Born in Brocton, New York, on March 3, 1831, he followed the classic pattern of Yankee apprenticeship to greatness by clerking in a country store during his boyhood at Westfield, New York, and shortly packed up and removed to the equally country town of Albion, where an older brother, A. B. Pullman, had founded a small firm of joiners and woodworkers. For a full decade Pullman followed the cabinetmaker's trade that was to be the basis of the operations of the vast carbuilding firm that was to bear his name, acquiring an understanding of woods, tools and the refinements of an occupation that was to be the keystone of the fortunes of the Pullman Palace Car Company.

So celebrated were the artisans that he was to recruit from the Black Forest regions of Germany to serve as personnel in his Marquetry Room at Pullman that people with no interest in carbuilding were to seek their services on private occasions, and when he had made his fortune and was building in Denver the finest residence money could afford, Fred Bonfils, one of the founding partners in *The Denver Post,* personally journeyed to Chicago to borrow experts from the Pullman Company to install his library and dining room.

Skill in woodworking was the basis of everything Pullman.

During Pullman's ten years in Albion he achieved a local reputation for moving buildings as a sideline to cabinetmaking when times were dull. The Erie Canal, the Work of the Age, passed through Albion and the Pullman brothers supplemented their earnings as joiners by contracting to move buildings out of its path so that when, answering the Westward call of destiny, George M. moved to Chicago in 1855 he was already expert in an operation in great request on the shores of Lake Michigan.

In the beginning everything had been jerry-built in Chicago—sprawling factories, tenements, residences and business blocks which sprouted on marshes and swamplands along the lakefront and south of the Chicago River. Now the town was busy pulling itself out of the mud, both literally and figuratively, and George Pullman attracted widespread and favorable attention raising entire business blocks to more secure foundations and even relocating them intact at more advantageous sites. In the course of his business activities he naturally encountered some of the first citizens of the booming community, among them Cyrus H. McCormick, the reaper man, Marshall Field and Levi Z. Leiter who had advanced ideas of merchandising, and Joseph Medill, a newspaper publisher, who, for a time anyway, didn't think trains were practical enough for the transport of the mails. The letters, he said, would blow out the car doors and their recovery would present a problem.

The muse of history made no note of the exact date or the source from which Pullman received the inspiration for building the first Pullman railroad car, but in 1858 he was hard at it. He had propositioned a minor executive of the Chicago & Alton Railroad—one of the then numerous carriers building out of Chicago to all points of the compass—to allow him to experiment with a sleeping car to be placed in service between Chicago and Bloomington, Illinois. Pullman was given a couple of downgraded day coaches, each forty feet long with flat roofs and single sash windows a foot square, and the railroad then stood clear to watch the result.

The potential loss involved was slight and you never could tell what might come of it. The Pullman boy looked and sounded rational and he had a record of achievement behind him as a contractor of sorts.

Pullman hired an assistant, Leonard Seibert, and went to work to produce the first two sleeping cars to go into actual revenue service on an established carrier. The results, while not spectacular, were gratifying. The cars each had ten sleeping "sections," as Pullman was pleased to designate a combined lower berth and folding bunk above it, a washroom at either end and a linen locker. The cars cost perhaps $2,000 each and were financed by the designer; they were finished neatly in plush and cherry wood with oil lamps and heated by box stoves.

There was nothing about the cars that might not have been devised by any contemporary car master commissioned to build a car for night occupancy, with one exception: the folding upper berth. Nobody to date had come up with the idea of a six-foot-long box swung on stout brass hinges which folded up against the ceiling and was secured there by a patent

lock and which, when not in service, was still commodious enough to hold the mattresses and bed linen not only for itself but for the bunk beneath it. The lower berth was composed of two reversible seats with demountable elements which combined to make a secure platform or bedframe and were not appreciably different from half a dozen inventions then current or in process of being patented. The secret was the folding upper.

The sleeping coaches were put into service by the Alton and were successful enough to justify the construction of a third on the same lines, but patronage shortly dwindled and the company eliminated the expense of a special sleeping-car conductor by handing over the making up and assigning of sleeping accommodations to the regular train conductor, in addition to his other duties. Most of the patrons were men. Few of them removed their boots before going to bed.

Significantly the name of Pullman was not attached to these primeval slumber vans. George Mortimer was reserving that association for something far more pretentious.

This was to be the first sleeping car built from the ground up and specifically designed as a sleeping car and nothing else. Its floor plans, construction, fittings, furnishings and entire aspect were unequivocally the components of something absolutely new, a sleeping car by night and a comfortable chair car by day. It wasn't a conversion: it was a revolution. It was the first car, among other things, to be known by the name of its designer and builder. It was all Pullman.

The *Pioneer*, as it was christened, rode on cast-iron trucks with coil springs reinforced by blocks of solid rubber. It was a foot wider and two and a half higher than any railroad car that had yet been outshopped. In beauty and richness of furnishings it left beholders gasping. Costly brocaded fabrics covered the seats and seat backs; beautifully matched woods of exotic grain were worked into doorframes, windows and panels at the ends of the car itself. Coal-oil lamps were trimmed in silver and there was a profusion of mirrors which reflected their light in dimensions that seemed actually palatial. On the floor a red Turkey carpet discouraged spitting and the bed linen was the finest that Pullman could buy from his friends Marshall Field and Levi Leiter.

Pioneer had cost an unbelievable $20,000, the entire sum of Pullman's savings, and three or four times what had been spent on any single railroad car until that time. The Chicago & Alton Railroad, despite the somewhat negative circumstances that the car's dimensions wouldn't clear its station platforms and bridges, was so captivated by this wonderful vehicle that it acquired it on sight. As an afterthought it started enlarging clearances all along its right of way so that it could carry the car in its trains.

An authentic predecessor in sleeping car service to that supplied the Alton by Pullman may be mentioned in the so-called Gothic cars commissioned in 1855 by the Illinois Central and placed in regular service on July 1, 1856, in the carrier's *Lightning Express* between Chicago and St. Louis. The cars, six of which were contracted with Daniel J. Townsend of the Buffalo Car Company, Buffalo, New York, were each fifty feet long and ten feet wide and fitted with sleeping berths and stateroom under the direction of Colonel Roswell B. Mason, the I. C.'s superintendent of operations.

On July 8, 1856, and under the heading "Luxurious Railroad Car," the *Memphis Appeal* carried a news story about them, lifting its account, as was the almost universal custom of the time, from another paper, the *Detroit Advertiser:*

The *Detroit Advertiser* says the cars of the Illinois Central Railroad for comfort and convenience excel those of any other road in the West. One of them contains six staterooms, each room having two seats with cushioned backs long enough for a person to lie upon. The backs of the seats are hung with hinges at the upper edge, so that they may be turned at pleasure, forming two single berths, one over the other, where persons may sleep with all imaginable comfort. In one end of the car is a small washroom with marble wash bowls, looking glasses, etc. The other five cars each have two or three similar staterooms.

The designation of these primeval sleepers as Gothic cars is completely in period. It was an age when Gothic architecture for residences and public structures, Gothic decor generally and, above all, the Gothic novel in English literature were at their zeniths. Unhappily no likeness of the I. C.'s Gothic sleepers survives, but a decade later the Chicago & North Western, whose master carbuilder may very well have been exposed to them, built at the company shops at Fond du Lac, Wisconsin, a sensationally Gothic director's car with tall pointed windows straight out of a ruined chapel or moated grange in any of the popular English novels of the period.

Notable, too, was the designation of the Illinois Central's Chicago–St. Louis night run as the *Lightning Express,* which must place it well in the front rank of name trains in point of time as well as in the distinction of carrying special luxury equipment.

Recouped by the Alton for his outlay with presumably something to show in the way of profit, Pullman promptly set about getting the cars that were now universally associated with his name accepted by other carriers. The year was now 1865 and all sorts of improvisations masquerading as sleepers were in service on overnight runs and journeys long enough to justify them. Mostly they were built in the car shops of individual railroads from blueprints in the heads of carmasters and at a minimum of outlay. Despite the $20,000 invested in *Pioneer,* most railroads felt that $4,000 was plenty for a car and wondered if patronage would justify even that much expense. This whole night-travel business might prove to be just a fad and in a year or two everyone might go back to sitting up in the coaches. Also, there was a war on.

A road that was now running a number of improvised sleepers on overnight hauls was the Michigan Central, and Pullman talked the management into putting his and its divergent theories to the test. He built four cars, largely on credit, that went *Pioneer* one better and cost $24,000 each and advertised them for service between Chicago and Detroit with a surcharge of $2 for their use. In the same trains the Michigan Central made available space on their old cars at the established rate of $1.50.

The public decision was overwhelmingly in favor of Pullman. As a contemporary put it: "In a short time the only travelers who rode in the old cars were those unable to secure space in the new." The Michigan Central began to get most of the trade in its territory, and its competitors, unable for a time to procure cars with the magic name of Pullman, began withdrawing their overnight runs altogether. It was a clear-cut victory for the quality product.

Pullman now had rolling showcases for his product in scheduled service on two well-established and expertly conducted railroads and was beginning to experience the satisfactions deriving from a favorable press. Excepting only the Pullman strike and industrial unrest of the nineties, Pullman always enjoyed a good press, and in the early years it was rhapsodic.

"Pullman is a benefactor to his kind," effused one editor. "The dreaded journey from Chicago to New York becomes a mere holiday excursion in his delightful coaches, and by the way, there will soon be through service over this route, in which a man need never leave his place from one city to the other." This prophetic reference is presumably to the New York Central Lines and their connecting Lake Shore & Michigan Southern, a combination that, far from proving an asset to Pullman, was soon to be the chiefest thorn in his side. But Webster Wagner's alliance with Commodore Vanderbilt was still in the unforeseen future.

In 1866 Pullman sleepers *Atlantic, Pacific, Aurora, City of Chicago* and *Omaha* went into service on the Chicago, Burlington & Quincy Railroad and George M. was making a bold bid for recognition on the far side of the Mississippi as well as in the industrial Middle West. In spare moments the Alton ran excursion trains to publicize its sleepers, and the press was gentled aboard them with those restoratives which have never failed to arouse friendly sentiments in the breast of the American newspaper reporter. The press waxed lyrical in its praise of Pullman's "French plate mirrors suspended from the walls," "the rich window curtains looped in heavy folds" and chandeliers "with exquisitely ground shades hanging from the ceiling," "painted with chaste and elaborate designs upon a delicately tinted azure ground." Patrons, assured of the chaste intent of the decor, were also exhorted to admire the "handsomely scrolled black walnut woodwork and the richest of Brussels carpeting."

From the very beginning, George M. Pullman played upon the inborn American yearning for luxury and the native longing for rich fabrics. You could ride in safety and expedition on the cars and you could sleep as man in motion had never slept before, but you could also feast the senses on beautiful things such as few Americans at that time had ever experienced. By the close of 1867 he had forty-eight sleeping cars in operation, each of them a radiant advertisement for the standard of luxury the word Pullman was coming to suggest.

The evolution of Pullman's original firm into the Pullman Palace Car Company, which made him one of America's wealthiest capitalists and achieved a near monopoly in the carbuilding field, was at the suggestion of Pullman's associate in a number of business ventures, Andrew Carnegie.

Some years earlier Carnegie had profitably invested in the future of another carbuilding genius who may well have been the true father of the sleeping car, T. T. Woodruff. Carnegie encountered Woodruff, a rustic inventor type, aboard a Pennsylvania Railroad smoking car where Woodruff showed him a working model of a folding berth adapted to installation in a car otherwise designed for daytime occupancy. Carnegie, who was already on good terms with the railroads, induced the great Tom Scott of the Pennsylvania, to place two of the Woodruff cars in service on his road, where they were an unqualified success. Carnegie had even loaned Woodruff $200 to tide him over a period of financial embarrassment, and the sleeper receipts constituted the first considerable sum he had made from venture capital. Carnegie looked with favor on carbuilders.

More recently Carnegie and Tom Scott had invested heavily in the Woodruff Sleeping Car Company which had changed its name and was doing business in a big way with the Pennsylvania, among others, as the Central Transportation Company. The firm held contracts for sleepers for most of the important carriers east of the Mississippi, while Pullman was already established in the good graces of the then wildly expanding lines west of Chicago. The Union Pacific had come into the market for sleepers for its transcontinental run and the rival companies were underbidding each other ruinously in the hope of securing its patronage.

Pullman and Carnegie personally attended a meeting of Union Pacific officials in New York, where the two titans of finance met face to face for the first time. They were stopping at the same hotel, the St. Nicholas, which was handy to the U.P.'s New York offices. After dinner one evening as the negotiations were under way, Carnegie seemingly by chance encountered Pullman in the lobby of the hostelry and boldly buttonholed him.

"Mr. Pullman," he said without preliminaries, "are we not making a pair of pretty fools of ourselves in this deal?"

"What do you mean?" asked Pullman, who had no time for impertinences.

"Tell you what I mean," said Andy brightly, "we're cutting off our noses to spite each other. The Union Pacific will beat us down to where there's no profit for whoever gets the contract. You and I ought to organize as one big company and take the cream of the business for ourselves."

Pullman instantly saw the light.

"Come up to my room and have a cigar," he invited. "Now what would be the name of this company you suggest?"

Andy, who knew another egoist when he saw one, had the answer on the tip of his tongue.

"The Pullman Palace Car Company!" Before the evening was over Carnegie had invested substantially in Pullman and the way was paved for the carbuilder to become one of the rich millionaires of his time. Soon afterward Carnegie got Pullman an exclusive contract with the Pennsylvania and became the largest single shareholder outside of Pullman himself. The Woodruff Company withered on the vine. Carnegie's change of allegiance had scuttled it. Neither Pullman nor Carnegie gave it a second thought.

The assets of the Woodruff Sleeping & Parlor Coach Company emerged briefly upon the business scene a few years later when, in 1889, they were combined by Job H. Jackson of Jackson & Sharp with those of the Mann Boudoir Car Company to form the Union Palace Car Company. The merged companies claimed to operate a total of thirty-four palace cars on carriers routing them over about 5,000 miles of track, mostly in the Deep South and Middle West. Within sixty days of its incorporation, Union Palace was bought up by Pullman for an announced price of $2,500,000 and Woodruff and Mann made their exit together from the scene, at least as carbuilders.

Colonel Mann, of course, was just warming up for his spectacular careers as publisher of *Town Topics*, the ranking blackmailer of American society and a New York character of epic dimensions. Although his cars were soon retired from railroads in the United States, so that even their photographic likenesses are today a curiosity, their various patented components continued in service on European railways for many years. The loose patent protection of the times prevented the Colonel from realizing any substantial income from this source and he was forced to turn his hand, with radiant success it may be remarked, to shaking down erring members of New York's then flourishing four hundred.

Despite the gaudy overtones of Colonel Mann's bravura performance on the New York scene, his instincts as a carbuilder were strangely prescient. Almost alone in his time he advocated staterooms, which he preferred to designate as boudoirs, for single occupancy, and built cars entirely composed of private sleeping apartments. The concept was half a century in advance of its general practice. The single private stateroom was already at the time a conventional feature of Pullman general service sleepers and available to double occupancy, or even three if the uncomfortable sofa was pressed into use, but the compartmented corridor car was not to emerge on a large scale for years to come.

The year 1867 which saw the emergence of George Pullman as one of the rising industrialists of the ever-crescent business scene in America through his associations with Carnegie and the Pennsylvania Railroad also saw the evolution and emergence of a new type of car bearing the name and imprimatur of Pullman. The Great Western Railroad of Canada had recently approached Pullman with the idea of an improvement on the sleeping car which should not only provide passengers with nighttime accommodations but also with food while in motion. Complete hotel service was what it wanted, so that on trains featuring such cars it would no longer be necessary to pause at irregular intervals to find refreshment at dubious depot restaurants, an aspect of travel that railroading had inherited with little modification from coaching days.

Pullman promptly came up with something called a hotel car. *Western World*, in addition to its conventional berths for sleeping, contained complete restaurant facilities served from a diminutive kitchen at one end of the car. Meals were served by an attendant on tables set up in the sections from a fairly comprehensive menu that included oysters, an assortment of cold cuts, broiled beef, mutton and ham, eggs in all manners—among them, French omelettes with rum —Welsh rarebits and light snacks. *Western World* was almost immediately joined in the Great Western by two more hotel cars, *President* and *Kalamazoo*, which were hailed with rapture in the daily press. The newspapers, with some justification, saw ordinary passengers exalted by their surroundings to the estate of millionaire men.

The crowning glory of Mr. Pullman's invention [said the *Detroit Commercial Advertiser* on June 1, 1867] is evidenced in his success in supplying the cars with a cuisine department containing a range where every variety of meats, vegetables and pastry may be cooked on the cars, according to the best style of culinary art.

The hotel car is not to be confused with the dining cars which shortly followed it and whose predecessor in eating facilities in motion it was. Its vestigial traces may rather be discerned in the private car, which was yet to emerge upon the scene as the ultimate in affluent transport.

In addition to the sleepers already commissioned for the Burlington, Pullman was now authorized to build six full-service hotel cars for that expanding granger line and in September 1867 the *Daily Quincy Herald* announced that four of them, the *City of Aurora, Plymouth Rock, Western World* and *City of New York,* were already in service. *Western World,* apparently, after its initial bow on the Great Western, had been transferred.

The furniture [said the paper] is of solid black walnut, handsomely carved and ornamented and upholstered with royal purple velvet plush imported from England expressly for this purpose. The finest Axminster carpets cover the floor. The night curtains for the berths are of heaviest silk; splendid chandeliers are pendent overhead; elegant mirrors grace the walls. Luxurious beds invite repose by night and when made up for the day the cars betray no trace of the eating or sleeping uses to which they can be put. The total cost of each car is $30,000, a fact which speaks for itself of its unrivalled magnificence and commodiousness.

In Chicago, *Western World* attracted favorable at- tention and a great deal of newspaper space, especially from the collation served to the press and chosen guests: choice beefsteaks, fried oysters and liberal quantities of the best champagne "chilled to perfection." A later-day columnist, O. O. McIntyre, was fond of remarking that the only place he ever thought of ordering bottled water was aboard the cars, and there is reason to believe his feelings were reflected by an earlier generation of travelers in champagne, as wine salesmen soon came to recognize Pullmans and other luxury equipment as one of the best outlets for their product.

As a capstone to his widely acknowledged triumphs in the field of sleepers and hotel cars, Pullman now achieved fresh laurels as a benefactor of the traveling public with the dining car. The year 1868 saw the building in Chicago of the first of all restaurant cars, appropriately named *Delmonico* as a tribute to New York's most stylish restaurateur and inevitaby placed in service on the Chicago & Alton. In *Delmonico* the breach with the on-line station lunchroom was complete. The service of food and drink aboard hotel cars was limited to the patrons of these cars alone, and no facilities were extended for refreshment to passengers in the other cars of trains in which they ran. Even though hotel car patrons might have dined regally at forty miles an hour and would now be enjoying perfectos and vintage cognac as the scenery flew past, still the train must pause at Hornelsville or North Platte or wherever, while the coach passengers bolted their meal at a lunch counter in the conventional twenty minutes.

Delmonico obviated the eating stop altogether, and for all classes the diners which followed were to be available to everybody aboard. The car was, of course, a handsome advertisement for Pullman travel, with its richly upholstered seats, silver-nickle lamps suspended from the central transom and ball-and-fringe portières at doorways and windows. The kitchen was of far more ample dimensions than was possible in the limited space available on the hotel cars, and the menus expanded accordingly. If all tables were taken at the moment, there was waiting space at the end of the car handy to the steward's wine locker, and passengers could have a nourishing cocktail in the interval.

The dining car immediately became the novelty of

the moment that the sleeper had been before it, not to mention the hotel car, and newspaper editors assigned their best reporters and sketch artists to record the scene and sensation of dining in motion. Without exception, their findings indicated that the gastronomy of the cars reflected the material abundance of the age in which they came into being. The trays of waiters towered with comestibles in a variety and quantity suggestive of Henry VIII having a snack with Cardinal Wolsey. Breakfasts were of the massive order only encountered today aboard Cunard Liners, and hock, claret and champagne were suggested as appropriate breakfast wines. Dinners came in successive courses to satisfy Mrs. Astor, whose guests remained at table four full hours.

All this the newspaper reporters and magazine artists passed on in faithful detail to readers, whose greatest ambition immediately was to ride the diners and partake of Lucullan repasts in the cheerful company of folk who were always going somewhere else and doing it stylishly beyond compare.

Pullman, who always kept an eye on the main chance, easily foresaw the almost limitless possibilities for luxury equipment implicit in the opening of the Far West to railroad travel. He rightly guessed that Union Pacific and its connections would not be the only line to the Pacific but that until other transcontinentals could be built, Union Pacific was potentially the most important user of Pullman equipment. Simply it ran over the greatest distance.

To captivate the imagination of Dr. J. C. Durant, vice-president of the U.P. in charge of operations, Pullman sent *Western World* to New York and asked the doctor and his directors to come west aboard it on a trip of inspection of their property, then building across Nebraska into Wyoming. Durant and Pullman were men who saw eye to bird's eye maple in the matter of luxury and a contemporary described Durant's offices as probably the finest in New York, beautiful with paintings and statuary, and enlivened with the singing of birds.

The U.P. directors listened to Pullman's smooth sales talk and rolled comfortably across the prairies on *Western World* to the end of track where Jack Casement's Irish paddies were picking up the rails and laying them down in the right place, and Pullman

shortly went home to Chicago with Union Pacific contracts in his brief case for an assortment of rolling stock in keeping with the grandeur of the over-all project.

Pullman sleepers and drawing room cars were heading westward out of Omaha long before the rails met at Promontory and on that historic occasion itself Pullman was represented by the business car of Dr. Durant in the windy Utah uplands. Photographs show that in addition to the usual Pullman elegance of French mirrors and inlaid woodwork, this early varnish car carried a stand of arms racked above a doorway—handy to have around as long as Indians were off the reservation.

George Pullman's genius for publicity and his fetish of perfectionism combined in what may be termed the Early Ordovician age of continental travel to produce a railroad exploit of almost stupefying splendor. It took the form of a specially built all-Pullman train of eight cars chartered by the Boston Board of Trade in 1870 for a trip to California over the newly completed rails of the Pacific Railroad. Probably it was the first all-Pullman train ever to be marked up on a trainmaster's sheet.

Boston in 1870 was at the zenith of its fortunes, and its destinies loomed larger on the national horizon than they have since as New England yielded its preeminence in such varied fields as banking, commerce, learning and social character to other cities and regions. To involve the Boston Board of Trade in a promotional gesture was as splendid a coup as could be imagined and the prestige that accrued from the union of State Street, Beacon Hill and Pullman was a major triumph for the carbuilder.

The Board of Trade Special was composed of eight of the finest available specimens of railroad luxury rolling stock. A baggage car contained spacious iceboxes for the preservation of the wines and choice viands essential to any occasion of rejoicing, either static or mobile, of the times. There was also a battery of type cases and a small press on which was printed a daily newspaper, the *Trans-Continental,* that has since become a rare and much-wanted item of Western Americana.

There followed a smoking car which sheltered such various conveniences as the editorial rooms of the newspaper, a wine room or cocktail lounge and "a beautifully fitted hair dressing and shaving saloon." A bartender was on constant duty to serve the array of fizzes, cobblers, crustas and other restoratives of contemporary favor, and there is internal evidence in the files of the *Trans-Continental* to suggest that the train barber had access to the car's resources of wines and spirits. He kept missing the train's departure at various western stops and was continually having to catch up through the agency of a following train or special engine dispatched for the purpose.

Then came two hotel cars, *Arlington* and *Revere,* tactfully named for Boston suburbs, the two saloon cars *Palmyra* and *Marquette* and finally two commissary and restaurant cars the *St. Charles* and *St. Cloud* aboard which, if contemporary accounts are to be believed, the proper Bostonians did carnage among the antelope steaks and quail in aspic as the cars rolled westward at an electrifying twenty-two miles an hour.

The arrival of this glittering entourage was a signal for municipal rejoicing and civic hospitality at Chicago, then shaping up as the greatest of all railroad terminals, at Omaha and Ogden. Local first citizens stepped aboard to admire the "two well stocked libraries, replete with choice works of fiction, history, poetry, etc.," and marvel at the two parlor organs around which passengers gathered of an evening for secular music and on Sundays for divine service.

More than a decade later the *Palmyra* was still in service, although it seems to have been downgraded from the glittering estate it achieved on the Board of Trade Special. An Englishman, W. G. Marshall, rode aboard it on the Union Pacific and recollected its homely comforts in a book, *Through America.* "We have a little eight-stop organ in our sleeping car, the *Palmyra,*" he wrote, "and this evening we bring out its tone and our companions in the car contribute a few songs. The instrument has two manuals but will only sound in one, and the upper part is devoted to pillow cases and blankets. So for two hours we amuse ourselves with singing and playing, our conductor who was a bit of a musician in his way, coming and treating us to a few songs. I believe if we had only room enough we would have got up a dance."

Do the thin little tunes of *Palmyra*'s patent Burdett parlor organ still linger in the night air at North Platte, at Laramie, at Julesburg and Lodge Pole?

The strangle hold maintained for nearly a quarter of a century by Webster Wagner's palace car company on the patronage of the New York Central and its subsidiary Vanderbilt lines between New York and Chicago caused Pullman to search for another through carrier by which his cars could achieve the shores of Lake Michigan. This he found in Erie, which was then, in spite of the powerful Vanderbilt competition, making a serious bid for through traffic.

In November of 1875 Erie through trains to Chicago, comprising sleepers, hotel cars and drawing room cars all bearing the Pullman imprimatur, went into service. The hotel cars, predecessors of entire cars devoted to restaurant purposes, attracted special attention with such richly various menus, studded with game and seasonal delicacies, that the *New York Tribune* was moved to comment editorially: "Should the Erie have a monopoly of such comforts? Why does not Wagner imitate or improve on Pullman?"

That Wagner took the hint almost too closely to heart is suggested by the fact that six years later the Pullman Palace Car Company brought suit for $1,000,000 against Webster Wagner and his New York Central Sleeping Car Company, claiming infringement on Pullman basic patents in the manufacture of Wagner sleepers.

No matter. A contemporary newspaper account nicknamed the Erie cars "French Flats," a reference to the newly popular innovation of apartment houses with origins in Paris, and waxed lyrical over their delights and comforts:

All modern conveniences of a first class house are condensed into these hotels on wheels. The beds at night are put away to make room for spacious seats by day, between which a table is placed covered with damask cloths and napkins folded in quaint devices, at which four may sit with ease. The whole car—a Pullman—is luxuriously fitted up, and one end is partitioned into a store room and kitchen; there is a smoking room for lovers of the weed, and a separate toilet room for ladies. As the porter of the car blacks the boots and there is a telegraph office at each stopping place, the waggish question often is "Where is the barber shop?" But this may come, too, in time, as last summer an excursion of ladies and gentlemen took a hair dresser with them over the Erie to Niagara Falls and two of the three ladies actually *had their hair crimped* while traveling thirty or forty miles an hour! At this time, while game is plenty in the West, the Pullmans with their facilities and two fast trains each way per day, are able to make a bill of fare and serve it in a style which would cause Delmonico's to wring its hands in anguish. The service is on the European plan; that is you pay for what you order, and we quote the prices to show at what a reasonable rate one can take a superior meal of fifty or a hundred miles long. Prairie chicken, pheasant and woodcock, whole: $1.00; snipe, quail, plover and blue winged teal, each 75 cents; venison, 60 cents; chicken, whole, 75 cents; cold tongue, ham and corned beef, 30 cents; sardines, lobster and broiled ham or bacon, 40 cents; mutton and lamb chops, veal cutlets or half a chicken, 50 cents; sirloin steak, 50 cents, etc. Every traveller who has missed his dinner to catch a train will rejoice in knowing that a warm meal awaits him at the cars, and that he can wake up in the morning and choose his time for breakfast, instead of bolting it down at the twenty minutes convenience of the railroad company.

The *Erie Limited* and other crack trains of that harried yet triumphantly operative carrier on the New York–Chicago run remained for some years a showcase for Pullman improvements. In 1883 Pintsch illuminating gas was first introduced in Pullman equipment on the Erie. A brilliant illuminant, Pintsch gas had for some years been commonplace in Europe, but it remained for Pullman to give impetus to its use in the United States.

To Dr. Samuel Johnson, a nice ride aboard a stagecoach "was the sum of human felicity" and in the golden age of the steamcars millions of Americans felt the same way about a ride on the train. Another of Dr. Johnson's great delights, after a coachride through the countryside, was to sit down to a good dinner and this, too, the railroad was able to provide after the coming of the diners. It is no risk to assume that Dr. Johnson would entirely have approved of railroad travel once George M. Pullman had set about putting its details to rights.

146

GLORY TIMES AND LORDLY WAYS ON THE PENNSYLVANIA

Some idea of the rich variety of good things available to travel on the Pennsylvania in the early nineties is suggested by this stunning, if busy, interior of a Pullman-built buffet–sleeper under whose hospitable roof the cheerful traveler encountered at once shelter, refreshment, transport and repose. The champagne was Heidsieck Monopole, a popular wine of the time. In the background is a glass cabinet housing a nice display of china such as might be found in any well-to-do private house. Nothing worth mentioning was lacking from the car's self-contained resources of pleasure and utility. It is worth noting, as a footnote to vanished times, that the taste that ordained the finest chinaware and silver on the cars and the costliest linen, still decreed stunning brass cuspidors in all public apartments frequented by gentlemen.

Chin-whiskered and proudly posed in the uniform frock coat of his office, this Pennsylvania conductor of the seventies might be taken as the prototype of a calling that was invested with authority and respect beyond the average. His word in the conduct of his train was as absolute as that of the master of a vessel at sea, and from earliest times until comparatively recently his title was that of Train Captain. When this photograph was taken the conductor's silk top hat of the fifties had yielded to the more utilitarian uniform cap, just as, after the turn of the century, the skirted frock coat was to give place to the dark blue cutaway. Unchanging over the years, although not visible here, was the heavy gold Albert watch chain, glory and oriflamme of the calling from Bangor to the Golden Gate.

Pride and glory of Alexander Cassatt's far-flung Pennsylvania system in the nineties was the all-Pullman Pennsylvania Limited *(page opposite), predecessor of the* Pennsylvania Special *and the* Broadway Limited *on the New York to Chicago run. With the combination baggage–smoker* Premier *on the head end, it represented the last word in Pullman beauty and through–train lux-* *ury in the pre-vestibule era. On this page is the interior of an early and wonderfully ornate Pennsylvania parlor car* Flora. *The date of* Flora's *flowering is unknown, but the white top hat on the knee of the gentleman in the foreground is in the style of the early seventies. In all probability the car was a Woodruff product.*

TWO PHOTOS: EDWIN P. ALEXANDER COLLECTION

Occupying two pages on the overleaf is the ornate observation end of the Pennsylvania Limited, *posed on Horseshoe Curve in 1893 with a group of passengers en route to view the wonders of the Chicago Fair. From the collection of Arthur D. Dubin.*

Pennsylvania Railroad passengers in the years following the close of the Civil War were largely masculine, as is suggested here, and read James Gordon Bennett's New York Herald in relaxed attitudes. This group was sketched en route to Philadelphia to view the wonders of the Centennial Exhibition of 1876.

In the thirties it was always possible to identify one of the Pennsylvania's great name trains, *even if the name plate on the* Spirit of St. Louis *(below) was somewhat blurred.*

One of the features of the magnificent cars built by Pullman for the original Pennsylvania Limited *in the eighties were barbershops such as this one aboard the* combine Premier. *Below, a conductor of a later generation in the twenties of the* Broadway Limited, *successor as flagship of the Pennsylvania fleet, compares watches with his engineer at Harrisburg. On the opposite page is a rare picture of the* Pennsylvania Limited, *taken at speed in 1902, when it was inaugurated; it was renamed* Broadway *in 1912.*

EVERETT DE GOLYER COLLECTION

PULLMAN STANDARD

EDWIN P. ALEXANDER COLLECTION

Once the Pennsylvania Limited and other westbound through trains had cleared for the evening, the main line through Merion, Ardmore, Radnor and Paoli was clamorous with commuter trains. Here the homeward-bound of 1887 crowd the platform at dusk as snowflakes fall.

Passengers aboard the composite baggage and library–buffet car Cassius, *riding at the head end of the* Pennsylvania Limited *westbound, might have looked up from the pages of Munsey's Magazine to witness briefly such a platform tableau as that on the opposite page as their train flowed smoothly over the main line out of Philadelphia.* Cassius *was built specially for the Limited in 1898 and painted in the vermilion livery of the owning road.*

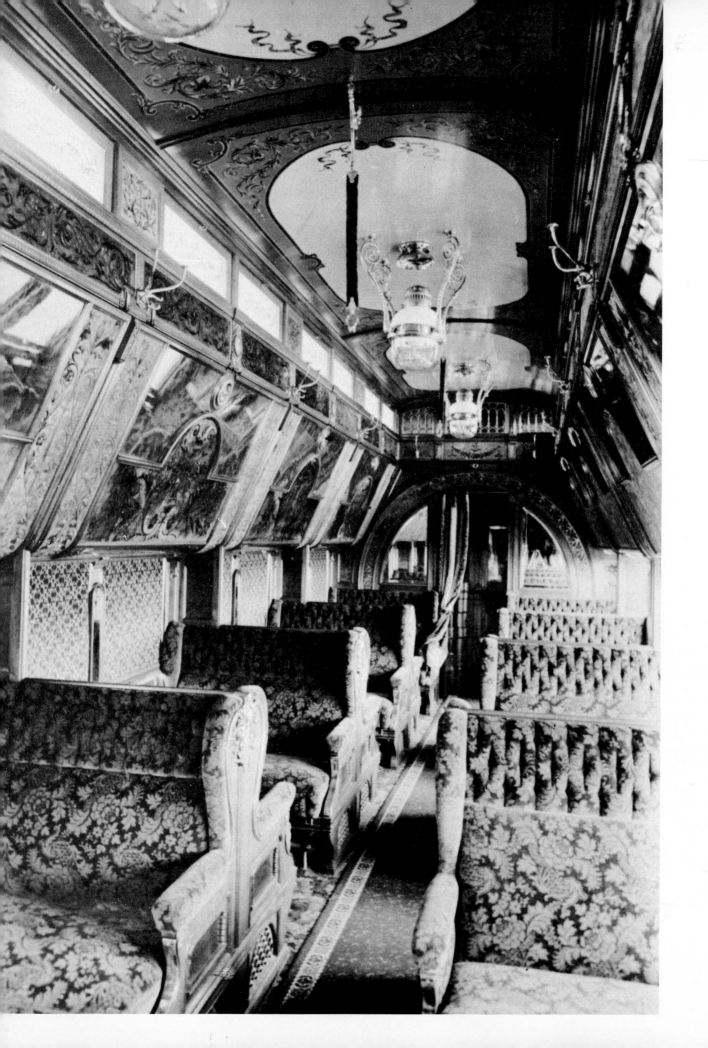

In 1891 the Pennsylvania Railroad opened what was to be a decade of uncompromising elegance everywhere by assigning the two cars shown on this and the opposite page to the crack *Pennsylvania Limited* on the New York–Chicago run as flagship of its fleet of limited trains, many of them all-Pullman extra-fare flyers. Satinwood berths, intricate marquetry work and beautifully frescoed ceilings characterized the sleeper *Fano* on the opposite page. Shown below is an example of the "opera box" decor in parlor car construction, which had a brief but ornate vogue on drafting boards of both Pullman and Wagner. Nooks, recesses, stalls and paddock-like enclosures nestled in thickets of potted plants for the sequestration of the ultra-diffident and erected an unobtrusive barrier around their occupants. Although Americans liked to boast of classless railroads, Pullmans in fact represented first-class travel and coaches the equivalent of second class in other countries. The opera box in parlor cars provided a sort of Diamond Horseshoe of mobile exclusiveness.

PULLMAN STANDARD   EVERETT DE GOLYER COLLECTION

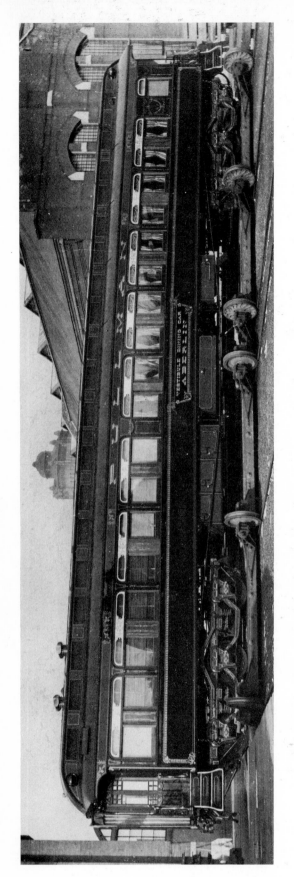

The diner Aberlin with narrow vestibules and the novelty of electric lights was built by Pullman in 1891 for the crack Pennsylvania Limited on the New York–Chicago run. Diner No. 7586 was built in 1901 for general service on the same carrier. The intervening decade saw the complete transition in car styling and construction from narrow vestibules to platforms enclosed flush with the car walls that were to be standard for the next sixty years.

Of a piece with such decorative and luxurious diners of the period as Parisian, La Rabida *and* Shohola, *Pullman's* Wellington, *assigned to general service, expressed the elaborate taste of the nineties in mirrored recesses for flowers, rich leather upholstery on the banquettes and a beautifully inlaid ceiling of baroque pattern, the whole illuminated with floriated Pintsch lamps reflected in French mirrors at the bulkheads.*

THREE PHOTOS: PULLMAN STANDARD

On the opposite page the Pennsylvania Limited, *glory and flagship of the Pennsylvania's fleet of name trains, poses in 1900 at Rockville Bridge, near Harrisburg, Pennsylvania. It was widely advertised as "the first de luxe passenger train with all-electric lights" and the steam exhaust from the roof of the combination baggage–smoker Utopia on the head end indicates a power plant in the baggage compartment activated by a steam line from the locomotive boiler. Above is Utopia, as it emerged from the Pullman works. Why it was first painted in solid color when specifically designated for the Limited where it is shown in the full-dress cream and chocolate livery of the railroad is a mystery.*

Shown below as it left the Pullman works in 1897 in the cream and chocolate livery of the Pennsylvania with the observation parlor car Esther on the rear end, the Congressional Limited was hailed as the most beautiful string of all-Pullman varnish ever built until then. Esther's interior (above) boasted the new electric light as well as Pintsch illumination.

The splendor that was the Pennsylvania in its glory days in the nineties is suggested by the observation–buffet–lounge car Jupiter that rode the end of the Pennsylvania Limited and the vestibule library–smoker Caesar that was assigned to the Washington–Boston run in the Colonial Express over the rails of the owning carrier and its affiliated New York, New Haven & Hartford via the Shore Line.

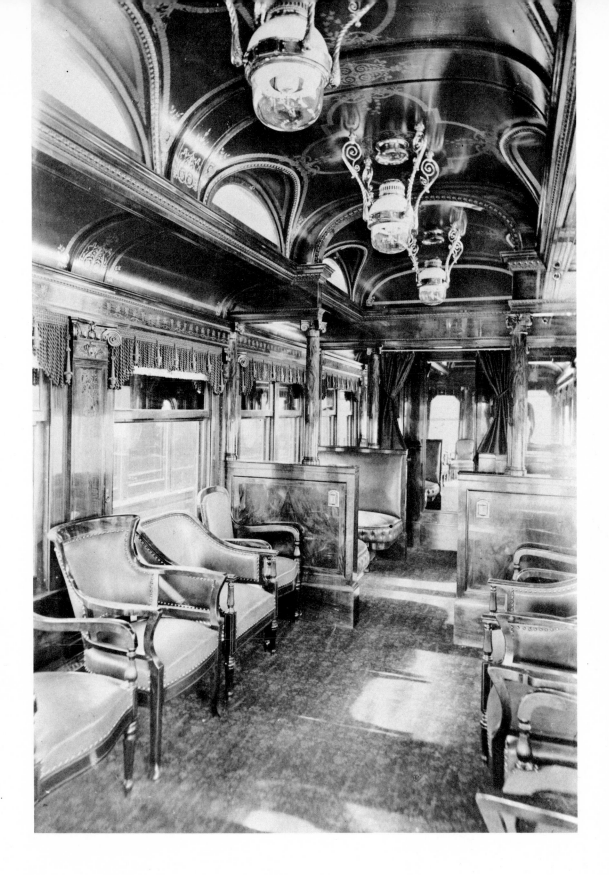

The name Jupiter *with its connotations of* Olympian aloofness and majesty appealed to *such aristrocratic railroads as the Pennsylvania* and its beautiful interior as shown here was ap*propriate to the godlike captains of finance and* industry who rode between Chicago and New York on the Pennsylvania flagship. Jupiter *was* built by Pullman in 1898 for the Pennsylvania Limited, *but twenty years previous Pullman had* outshopped one of the earliest parlor cars on record with the same name.

Stan Repp painted this rainy evening view of Englewood depot platform a few miles out of Chicago in the glory days of Pullman Standard when the Pennsylvania's keystone insigne blazed regally from the rear observation platform of the Broadway Limited. Passengers in its lounge read Collier's Weekly and were sluiced with Heublein's bottled cocktails by three bar attendants in white jackets. Elsewhere in the observation car was a master suite with its own shower bath. On the far track at Englewood, the opposition in form of the New York Central's Twentieth Century Limited is just moving out to pace the Broadway minute-for-minute if not quite mile-for-mile to overnight Manhattan. Opposite is the combination baggage–lounge car Ulysses, built by Pullman in 1898 for the Broadway's predecessor as flagship of the Pennsylvania's fleet; Pullman liked the name. Another Ulysses had been built a few years before for the Washington & Southwestern Vestibuled Limited, crack all-Pullman flyer of the Richmond & Danville Railroad between Washington, D.C., and New Orleans.

PULLMAN STANDARD

STAN REPP

The Gulf to Rockies route had three cafe cars in pool service on each of its component roads, the Fort Worth & Denver and the Colorado Southern, in 1900 running the full way between the Queen City in Colorado and the Texas cow capital in trains No. 1 and 2. They were Pintsch-lit and maintained à la carte service in connection with conventional Pullman sleepers. The rugged run along the escarpment of the Rockies and into the Texas Panhandle via Trinidad has always been an important artery of Colorado commerce. Today's successors to the picturesque operations over the mountains are the Texas Zephyrs, running with the fine original equipment of the Denver Zephyr. The galley range and hot water heater at the left was designed for private car use or in combination buffet cars.

The look of the Old West still clung to railroading out of Denver when this photograph was taken in 1900 of the Fort Worth & Denver's train No. 1 about to leave Union Station. The classic American type eight-wheeler No. 145 is of Union Pacific origin, and its diamond stack suggests how close railroading in the Plains States remained to pioneer times even after the turn of the century. Trains No. 1 and 2 carried through vestibuled, gaslit buffet sleepers, as shown at the rear of this consist between Denver and Fort Worth and on to Houston via the Houston & Texas Central from Fort Worth through Ennis.

R. H. KINDIG COLLECTION

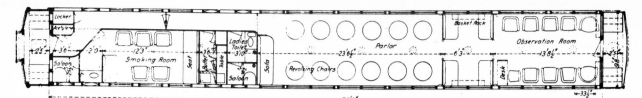

Fig. 225. Parlor Buffet Car. Pére Marquette. American Car & Foundry Co., Builders.

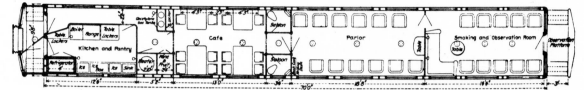

Fig. 226. Observation Café Car. Chicago Great Western. Pullman Co., Builders.

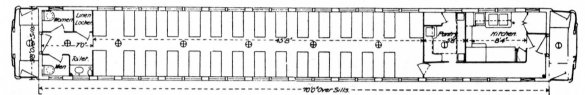

Fig. 227. Café Coach. New York Central. Barney & Smith Car Co., Builders.

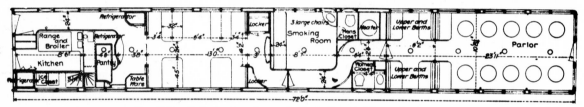

Fig. 228. Café Parlor Car. C., B. & Q. Pullman Co., Builders.

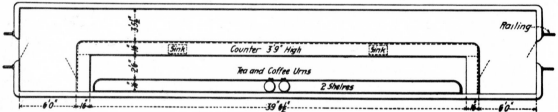

Fig. 229. Lunch Counter Car. Pére Marquette.

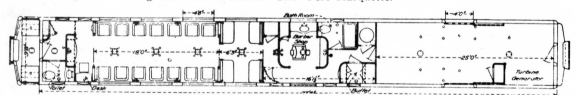

Fig. 230. Composite Car. Pennsylvania Railroad. Pullman Co., Builders.

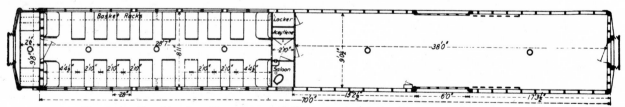

Fig. 231. Combination Passenger and Baggage Car. Chicago, Burlington & Quincy.
American Car & Foundry Co., Builders.

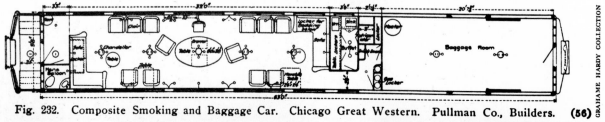

Fig. 232. Composite Smoking and Baggage Car. Chicago Great Western. Pullman Co., Builders. (56)

Some idea of the multiplicity and profusion of passenger cars being designed and built in the golden age of rail travel may be suggested by the floor plans on the page opposite, which are only a modest sampling of the many pages of such examples contained in the Car Builders Encyclopaedia for 1909. The interior of the Chicago Great Western composite smoking and baggage car shown at the bottom of the page is depicted here, evidence of the degree of luxury available even to coach passengers on a secondary granger railroad in the Middle West.

Shortly after the first Pullman parlor car was put into service in 1875 to give the polite lie to the belief that no class distinctions existed on American trains, the car Weimar *was placed in service, its seats equipped with adjustable backs and little footrests that could be extended on casters. Less exalted passengers also rode* Weimar, *as is attested by the mirrored image of another compartment equipped with conventional coach seats in the rear of the parlor accommodations.*

The Chicago & North Western's parlor car Elburn *was built by Pullman in 1891 as a handsome example of the already disappearing open platform car for luxury equipment.*

TWO PHOTOS: PULLMAN STANDARD

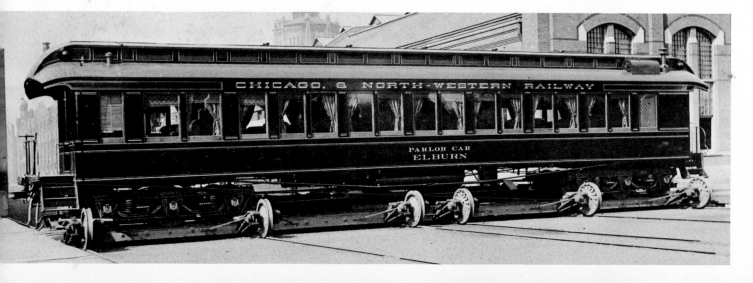

Although other types of luxury car were more exacting of construction, Pullman in the nineties lavished great and affectionate care on the decor of its parlor cars, various examples of which will be found in their appropriate places in this book. In the private drawing room of one of them, Mrs. Grover Cleveland, young and pretty wife of the President, took passage to visit friends in Memphis in 1893. She made so pleasant a picture among the flowers of well-wishers that an artist sketched the scene for Harper's *as the Southern landscape rolled past the wide picture windows.*

In 1892 a sketch artist for Harper's drew this picture with the caption "A Snow Blockade at Lamy, New Mexico; Passengers Removed From the Cars of The Santa Fe Railroad." Whether the main line was blocked or only the branch up to Santa Fe the artist didn't specify, but the suggestion is explicit that in the nineties the railroads of the Far West were still occasionally at the mercy of the elements, even the august Santa Fe with Boston backing and State Street antecedents. Ten years later Pullman outshopped Brazito for service in the California Limited (page opposite), and if passengers were snowbound aboard it, they had the satisfaction of knowing that they were inconvenienced aboard one of the finest all-compartment cars built till that time.

In the thirties the Santa Fe's Centennial
State *rolled bravely out of Denver in steam.*

LUCIUS BEEBE

Pullman Hunting Cars Rover & Pickwick

The vogue for hunting expeditions on the newly opened West which moved numerous well-to-do Easterners to organize safaris to Colorado, Wyoming and the Dakotas in the seventies and eighties inspired several carbuilders to design special hunting cars for more or less prolonged expeditions in the wilds. Pullman was agreeable to building such cars on order but came by its own fleet of per diem cars when it purchased the assets of the Union Palace Car Company in 1889. Among these were the private sleeping cars with full living accommodations, Rover, Pickwick, Mayflower and Davy Crockett. The exteriors of Rover and Pickwick are shown opposite, while the interior of Rover is depicted here. The cars were of Mann Boudoir and Woodruff ancestry and are of special interest to railroad historians because of their heterogeneous background and final ownership.

179

THREE PHOTOS: PULLMAN STANDARD

The exterior views on these two pages are of a Northern Pacific house car, especially designed for the occupancy of hunting parties on the plains, that was chartered one year by Jerome Marble and a friend, C. C. Houghton of Worcester, either when no Marble hunting car was available or when the safari had split up at its western terminal. The bearded huntsmen in the photographs are Marble and Houghton and the women are the Mmes. Houghton and Marble. The interior is that of the Pullman hunting car Izaak Walton, one of the several similar conveyances built for charter parties similar to those who patronized the Marble Company in Massachusetts.

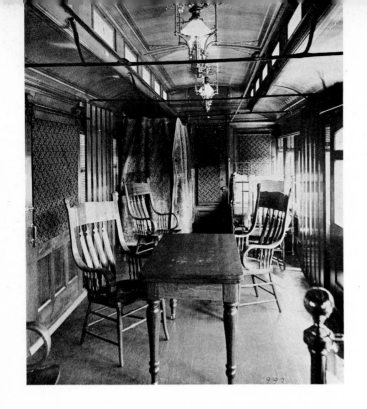

Pullman not only maintained a pool of per diem hunting cars, such as Izaak Walton and Nimrod, but built them to order for customers such as the San Antonio & Aransas Pass Railroad in Texas. Fern Ridge *(left and page opposite)* was maintained by the Lone Star carrier for the pleasure of directors and important shippers. Brass beds behind curtains occupied the four corners of its principal salon, and wide doors facilitated egress with arms and bulky fishing tackle.

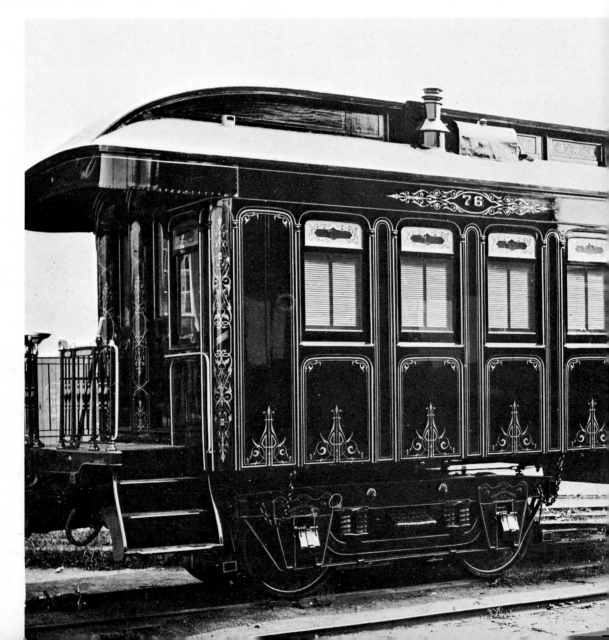

The City of Worcester, *shown below, was not only the flagship of Jerome Marble's fleet of hunting cars operating out of Worcester, but a superb example of the car-builder's craftsmanship that aroused universal admiration.*

Perhaps the most elaborate of the eight hunting cars which over the years accommodated the guests and patrons of Jerome Marble was the City of Worcester, *which was built to Marble's order by Jackson & Sharp at Wilmington, Delaware, in 1876. Marble took the* City of Worcester *and a select party of sportsmen west that year on his first hunt the far side of the Missouri River, where General George A. Custer marveled at its conveniences and fine fittings while he still had his hair. Local legend around Worcester to this day holds that the car of its name was the first private car to be built in the United States, a patent misconception, but it was one of the handsomest and provided a great deal of pleasure for its occupants.*

Here the celebrated artist team of Frenzeny & Tavernier depict a hunting scene for antelope on the great plains against a background of prairie fire. In an age of casual dispatching and no great density of traffic, trains with hunters aboard often stopped for their convenience. At the bottom opposite, the City of Worcester poses with its complement of hunters on the Dakota prairie, while above, Mrs. Jerome Marble and a friend, Mrs. C. C. Houghton, assume resolute attitudes and masculine attire during a Far West safari. Their expressions suggest something less than voluptuary enchantment with their surroundings.

TWO PHOTOS: HAYNES STUDIOS

A familiar sight in the railroad yards of the West at the time the scene on the page opposite was photographed was the private car of Buffalo Bill, somewhat redundantly named for its owner: Cody. Extensive research has failed to turn up the car's pedigree or antecedents, but the record shows that nothing even faintly resembling Rule G (against use of liquor) was ever observed by Pahaska (Cody's Indian name) when aboard it. The piano in its salon was strictly a prop, but the legendary great of the Old West gloried and drank deep on Cody in its times of splendor.

The stylish ten-wheeler standing in Denver's Union Station at six seventeen of a summer's evening in 1900 in forty-five minutes would head out across the Great Plains for Chicago with the Santa Fe's train No. 6 with Pullmans, mail and coaches for Chicago. Behind it with locomotive No. 708 on the head end is the Rio Grande's train No. 3, the Trans-Continental San Francisco Butte & Portland Express, *surely one of the longest names on record. The caption on the drawing to the left in a Santa Fe travel folder of the time read:* "The dining service, under management of Fred Harvey, is the best in the world."

ARTHUR D. DUBIN COLLECTION

Overnight service between New York and Boston via Worcester and the Shore Line was a long-established feature of the New York, New Haven & Hartford Railroad in 1900 when the combination baggage–stateroom car shown above was placed in service. Ten years later Pullman improved on this conveyance with two sleepers for the Second Midnight Express, each equipped with a brass bed, a table, chairs, electric fan, thermostatic controls and a private toilet in each of its seven bedrooms. One of these luxury cars is shown below. A contemporary commented: "This service is likely to remain unique for some time since it is doubtful if there is another place in the country that would sustain it."

The nocturnal excursions of the New York, New Haven & Hartford at the time when it was the elder J. P. Morgan's favorite investment, despite its reputation for wrecks which occasioned remark in Life With Father, were varied and useful over the years. The various Owls included a New York–Providence car and a New Haven–Boston sleeper, while their Boston–Philadelphia counterpart was set out from the through night train between Boston and Washington. All-compartment cars appeared on the Shore Line in the nineties, and in the thirties the Owl usually carried two or more all-stateroom cars with permanent beds named Night Cloud, Night Sky and the like. At times of communal academic rejoicing such as Harvard-Yale football games or boat races at New London, the New Haven's night runs became a sort of mobile uproar, but ordinarily their progress was tranquil and conducive to repose as the long green trains rolled smoothly through sleeping Bridgeport, Westerly and Madison.

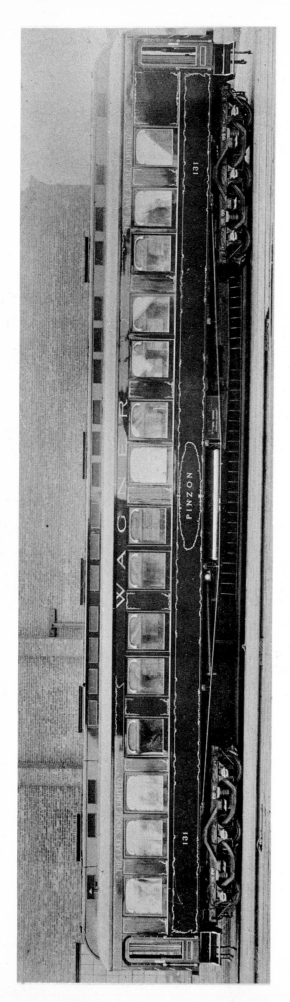

The Wagner Palace cars Malacca and Pinzon ran in the Lake Shore Limited of 1897 over the Michigan Southern, New York Central and Boston & Albany between Chicago and New York–Boston. Pinzon was a parlor car with twenty chairs. Its stateroom and buffet were finished in satinwood and gold, and its main salon was "Shakespearean in design with English oak trim and provided with two cases filled with select books."

The Wagner Palace car Malacca *ran in the* Lake Shore Limited *over the rails of the Michigan Southern, New York Central and Boston & Albany and was a sleeping car with ten open sections, two drawing rooms and a buffet. It was one of three identical cars, one each on the Chicago–New York run, one between Cleveland and New York, and one on the Boston & Albany section between Boston and Chicago. According to the* Railroad Age Gazette *for June 1898 the*

exteriors of these fine trains were painted pale olive with gold striping and lettering on their proud nameboards. At the same time these cars were in service on the Vanderbilt lines, the Burlington made a bid for the women's trade with the above view of the lady's retiring room on one of its sleepers with the suggestion that its female patronage derived solely from close relatives of the Ogilvie sisters.

THREE PICTURES: ARTHUR D. DUBIN COLLECTION

TWO PHOTOS: PULLMAN STANDARD

The end of the line for Pullman Standard all-steel construction and for the open sleeping section of Pullman legend was almost at hand when *Gothic Tower* was built in 1942. The roomette car and all-room train such as the Broadway and Century *were making obsolete a staple of folklore and an American institution, even as lightweight construction and roller bearings were supplanting Pullman Standard design. The transition is represented on the page opposite. No innovation, however, could retire the train captain, shown in his ancient pose of office in the Ivan Dmitri photograph at the left, and the Chicago & North Western's speedy 400 shown below was dustless, noiseless and vibrationless where once the palace cars had rolled on the Twin Cities run from Chicago.*

IVAN DMITRI   RAIL PHOTOS: W. G. FANCHER

In 1891 when Pullman built the parlor car Laurita for the Baltimore & Ohio's New York–Washington run, the vogue was for nooks, alcoves and opera boxes, where the diffident or the haughty, as the case might be, could avoid the general gaze. In Laurita, which later passed to the Pennsylvania, exchanging its royal-blue livery for Tuscan red, it took the form of a sort of padded box stall entered by a curved Dutch door and shielded by velvet portières under demilunes of elaborately carved woodwork. Creamy figured-velvet upholstery must have given the maintenance department long thoughts in an age still forty years removed from air conditioning. Opposite, the diner on the Illinois Central's Daylight on the Chicago–St. Louis run gives equally illuminating insight into the mode of women's hats in 1905.

196

Henry Villard,
first president of
the Northern Pacific,
was a brilliant pioneer
but poor executive
who soon lost his
property to crusty
and cantankerous
James Jerome Hill.

In a day when railroad locomotives and, to an only slightly less degree, the Pullmans that rode splendidly behind them were household names along the main lines of the continent, the fine Pullman sleeper Oriole *was a familiar property of the Northern Pacific on its crack* North Coast Limited *between Minneapolis and the Northwest. A magnificent example of the craftsmanship of Pullman's Marquetry Room,* Oriole *had art glass transom windows, berths decorated in a Chippendale pattern and a Byzantine arch separating the open sections from the stateroom at the end of the car. From its windows passengers looked down from the mountainside near Livingston, Montana, in the scene depicted on the opposite page by the artist Charles Graham for* Harper's *in 1886.*

In the late sixties the Old Colony Railroad, long an institutional New England carrier, inaugurated service on its Boston to Fall River run with the British-type compartmented coach shown in these drawings. "Its apartments are elegantly fitted up," said Leslie's in describing the innovation, "and the fare is only a small sum more than to ride in the democratic way. We are rapidly approaching that time in the luxuriance of travel when we shall step into our suite of rooms in New York and have no occasion to leave them until we arrive at St. Louis or New Orleans." Two of these coaches were built but were soon supplanted by the Pullman parlor cars Violet and Pansy.

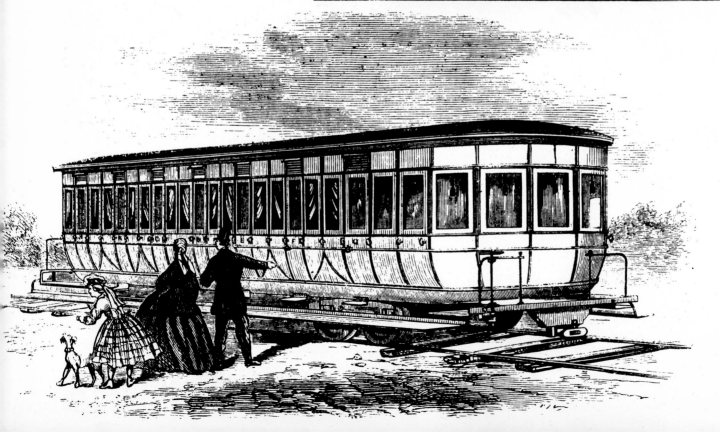

A generation before today's Grand Central Terminal Oyster Bar was dreamed of patronized the Gentleman's Buffet at an earlier Grand Cen-tral in lunch-hour crowds of almost equal dimen-sion. Then, as now, Grand Central was one of the world's great crossroads.

Although much abused by the envious inferiority that resents success, William H. Vanderbilt was one of the most sapient operators of the age that saw railroading dominate both the American economy and consciousness. Unlike his father, the Commodore who regarded business as a continuous and delightful Donnybrook, William H. regarded it in the light of solid achievement and preferred the orderly operation of a conservative property to the incessant alarms that had enchanted his father. Under his administration his family fortunes doubled and the Vanderbilt lines became the standard railroads of the world.

In the day when railroad presidents rode grandly as gentlemen in their own private cars and did business on a lordly scale with Pullman, Wagner and Mann, a railroad president looked the part and acted it. Witness the persons of Robert Garrett of the Baltimore & Ohio and George Gould of the Missouri Pacific on the page opposite, and on this page, from top to bottom, Thomas Oakes of the Northern Pacific, George Coppell of the Denver & Rio Grande and Collis P. Huntington of the Southern Pacific. Such magnates George Pullman met as peers and entertained magnificently at his homes in Chicago and Burlingame and at the Florence Hotel in Pullman itself, and their orders and those of several score, equally powerful general managers and chairmen of the board ran into millions annually. The side whiskers and grand manner of railroading have long since gone, but in their time they were worn by magnificoes second to none in the American social and economic scheme of things.

SWITCHED OFF.

IN THE EMIGRANT TRAIN.

FRENZENY & TAVERNIER

Until well after the turn of the century life aboard the cars was a major preoccupation of the American people and this was reflected in the newspaper and picture press of the period with great fidelity. Enormous fortunes were being achieved through the agency of railroading, lives were being lost in wrecks and derailments; the cars were freighted with drama and excitement for everyone. Not only was space accorded the steamcars and the people aboard them in the responsible picture press—Harper's, Leslie's and Scientific American—but its more sensational aspects were grist for the mill of the Police Gazette and its archrival the Police News whose sketch artists enjoyed vistas of impious potentiality impervious to their more staid contemporaries. Infidelity in the staterooms of the Erie, gamblers working their wiles in the smokers of the Missouri Pacific, millionaires and other fast company opening wine in the salons of private palace cars, all found a wide and appreciative audience in readers of the pink pages of the Gazette and the imitative art layouts of the News. The cars themselves, of course, with their rich furnishings provided a matchless setting for scenes of revelry and license into which it was possible for the public imagination to project itself without either effort or factual contamination. Few Americans penetrated the residences of Goulds and Vanderbilts or commanded wine at Delmonico's, but hundreds of thousands were at first hand familiar with the palace cars, already invested with beautiful furnishings and the romance of far places. On the opposite page are two of the more reputable school of railroad illustration, scenes of emigrant travel by the famous team of Frenzeny & Tavernier in Harper's. Here a stirring scene from the Police Gazette purports to show how "He Won With the Revolver; Col. Youmans, a Faro Bank Squealer of New Orleans, Loses His Winnings on the Queen & Crescent Line."

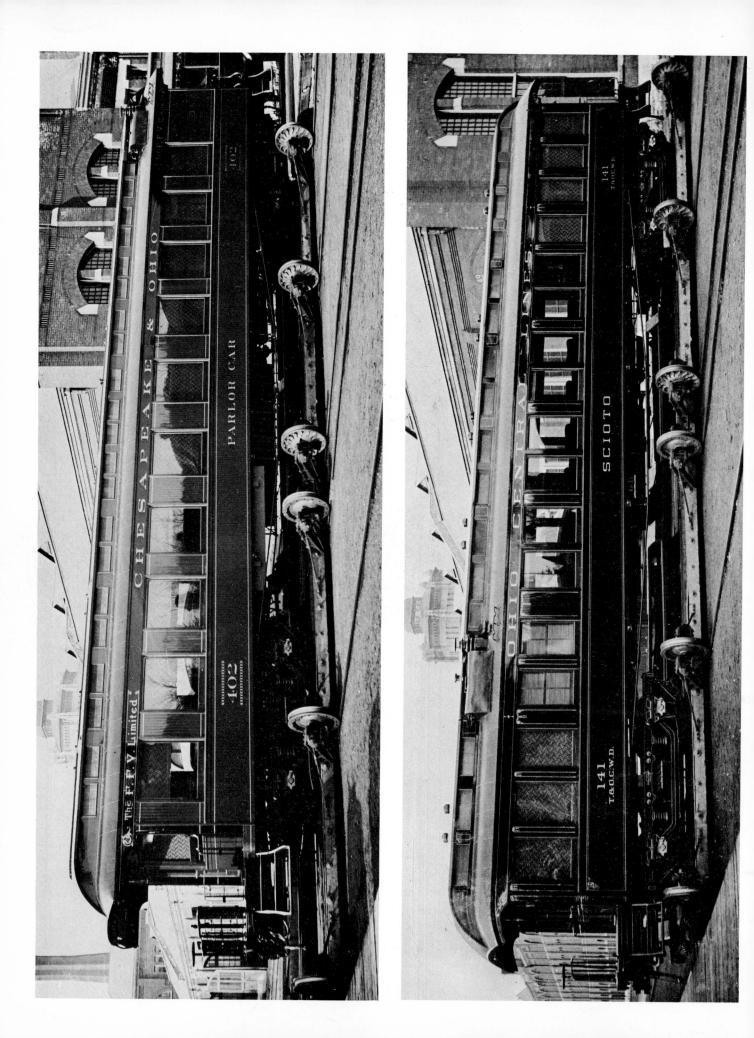

Pullman travel in terms of parlor cars was for many decades the hallmark of daytime respectability and genteel aloofness. The Chesapeake & Ohio's comely No. 402, shown opposite, rode for years in the crack varnish the Fast Flying Virginian, while the Ohio Central's Scioto reminds us that pleasant times once rode on railroads now largely forgotten. The interior shown on this page is of a parlor car built by Pullman in 1895 for the Boston & Albany, a Yankee road of irreproachable patronage and ancestry, having been built by the father of James McNeill Whistler.

209

PAVANE OF THE CARBUILDERS

I T WOULD BE a mistake of the first order to imagine that only George Mortimer Pullman designed, patented, manufactured, leased and operated the railroad carriages that soon after the Civil War came to be known as palace cars. In time the name became generic so that the word pullman without capitalization entered the language as a synonym for luxurious or hotel travel by rail. In time, too, palace cars became a proprietary or trade name and both Pullman and his arch-rival in the field of de luxe railway carriages, Webster Wagner of Palatine Bridge, New York, incorporated the words into their business style as the Pullman Palace Car-Building Company and the Wagner Palace Car-Building Company. So did several others.

Anything that Pullman did Wagner saw merit in, even when it came to incorporating, and if it is true that imitation is the most conspicuous form of flattery, Webster Wagner flattered George Pullman in tones of uncommon unctuousness.

But the two titans in the field of carbuilding were far from the only competition that made a bid for the ever-crescent railroad business of the nineteenth century. As in the later field of motorcar manufacture, scores of carbuilders flourished briefly either on paper or in operational fact only to fall by the wayside or to be absorbed in the long line of monopolies which led toward Pullman. What Velie, Stearns-Knight, Peerless and Autocar were in the legend of gasoline, Mann, Woodruff, LaMothe, Lucas, Flower and Hapgood were to the steamcars, names that once adorned ornate letterheads but in time came to be forgotten.

Throughout the seventies and eighties it was a rare industrial community that didn't list a carbuilding shop in its business directory along with the regional brewers, coopers, wheelwrights, carriage makers, iron founders, glass blowers and marble yards.

By the mid-seventies America was getting into fullest stride as one of the most determinedly peripatetic nations in history. The index of national wealth was increasing in geometric progression as the industrial age that had had its primal beginnings during the Civil War swung into fullest production. Rich men, the new possessors of wealth from the expanding West, were setting a pattern of florid and expensive living that was being imitated according to their means by lesser men everywhere. One of the best and most agreeable ways of spending the new easy money that was flowing into bank accounts was travel, an indulgence that had the blessing of the respectable as being cultural and broadening while affording lively new pleasures amidst pastures new.

Greatest single impetus to rail travel in the seventies was the completion of the Pacific Railroad, which made California and the still tolerably Wild West available in upholstered comfort that rolled on patent car wheels in five days where only yesterday the oxen and white tops had taken five laborious and dangerous months. All who could, wanted to board the steamcars, if for nothing more than to put up at William C. Ralston's fabled Palace Hotel in San Francisco. The wonders of the Yellowstone, too, were attracting the adventurous. And the Yosemite, not too remote from San Francisco.

Another incentive to travel in 1876 was the Centennial Exposition at Philadelphia, access to which was almost exclusively by the cars and where the exhibits of the carbuilders themselves displayed all the latest gadgets and decorative splendors of Jackson & Sharp, Pullman, Woodruff and Barney & Smith. To see the sleepers was to feel an urge to board them and go somewhere, preferably as far as possible from home, and the potential now reached 3,000 romantic miles to the Pacific, and through the Deep South almost everywhere but to Florida.

Whole families of Bostonians and Philadelphians, awash with expectations of pleasure and adventure, set their faces toward the railroad depot and boarded the cars with Saratoga trunks and shoebox lunches. They explored the length and breadth of the continent attired in ratcatcher suits and deerstalker caps and often in the frock coats and silk top hats of urban usage. Irreverent plainsmen in Elko and Fort Worth took pot shots at the silk tiles of State Street bankers and were incredulous at the female bustles descending from the sleepers as the fashionable complement to chignons, waterfalls and Empress Eugénie bonnets.

Travel guides, handbooks and vade mecums instructed the unsophisticated in the amenities of travel and listed, largely with honest intent, the scenic wonders and the best station restaurants along the way. Gentlemen required six suits of varying weights and textures to travel from New York to Oakland, and the baggage room and baggagemaster entered the demon-

ology of American folklore. Voyagers were warned against the wiles of the gamblers and prostitutes who held mad Hallowe'en at Promontory as long as that desolate outpost saw the change from the cars of Union Pacific to Central Pacific. They bought bogus mining stocks from slick promoters, who waited for the trains at Winnemucca and Carlin, and mountains of tangible trash from indigent Digger, Shoshone and Washo Indians, all the way across Nevada.

In the Deep South they ate themselves into colics on praline confections hawked by ante-bellum mammy types and addressed every man with a skirted frock coat and string tie in the station lunchroom as colonel. The cars arrived at New Orleans and Natchez in savannahs of waving palm-leaf fans, and the soot of wood-burner locomotives consuming mountains of trackside fuel with turpentine showered alike upon the just and the unjust on the through trains of the Louisville & Nashville, the Old Reliable.

With all this coming and going on a continental scale it was obvious that railroads would have to have cars in ever-increasing numbers and varieties to accommodate their patrons. A few carriers built their own. More awarded their patronage to the carbuilders whose salesmen waited hat in hand or boisterously, as their nature dictated, on the vice-president in charge of operations. At one end of the scale was cool, civil and ingratiating George M. Pullman; his antithesis was brash and glittering Diamond Jim Brady. In between were the whiskered rogue Colonel William D'Alton Mann and a Yankee inventor of the wooden nutmeg school named Asa Hapgood.

Popular belief holds that steel or at least metal car construction came into being well into the twentieth century in the form of products of Diamond Jim Brady's Pressed Steel Car Company, but the shortcomings of wooden cars had been apparent much earlier, and steps to supplant wood with metal construction had been taken before Pullman appeared on the horizon. As far back as 1846 an inventor named H. L. Lewis projected an all-steel passenger coach underslung between its trucks for high-speed operations, but the car never got further off the drawing board than to appear in the pages of *Scientific American*. In 1853 a T. E. Warren of Troy patented an all-metal car of remarkably modern appearance whose structure was based on fifteen wrought-iron columns—similar to the iron pillars then used in building construction—on each side, with plate girders of thin metal between them. Except for small Gothic windows between the columns, the car very closely resembled in outline the coaches that were to be conventional for fully half a century to come. Warren's car, too, stayed on the inventor's drawing board.

A car built largely of metal which went into actual operation in the mid-fifties was patented by Dr. B. J. LaMothe of Paterson, New Jersey. The car was forty-six feet long with thirty seats, and four of them were built for the New York & Erie and the Boston & Worcester. The LaMothe coach was said by its proponents to be proof against the telescoping and overall disintegration that characterized the wooden cars of the period that were involved in collisions and derailments; it was a full century ahead of its time in being liberally padded with cushions and soft insulation at all projecting corners in its interior, much like the crash pads on the dashboards of modern sports cars. If it went into the ditch or participated in a cornfield meet, the LaMothe passengers might be thrown around, but the chances were against their being macerated.

Mention has been made elsewhere in this volume of the curiously built and named Diamond cars (so named because the framework of the car was so trussed internally as to require diamond-shaped windows), which were made in the forties for the Erie Railroad. Archippus Parish—a fine New England name—was master carbuilder of the Erie when the two cars named *Erie* and *Ontario* were delivered from the Stephenson Car Works in Harlem to Piermont by ferryboat. He recalled that they saw brief service between Piermont and Otisville in an equally picturesquely named run known as the *Thunder & Lightning Milk Train*. The cars were too heavy for the motive power of the period and were soon retired.

In 1862 the Erie completed arrangement for running the sleepers designed by T. T. Woodruff both on its own main line and, when construction was completed a few years later, its subsidiary, Atlantic & Great Western Railroad. To build and operate the cars the Erie & Atlantic Sleeping Coach Company was formed as a joint stock association under the laws of New York State with the Erie retaining 1,538 shares of common stock and the remainder, 3,459 shares, divided among a number of individuals, one of whom was Jay Gould. The cars built and operated by this holding company under a number of patents held by the Central Transportation Company were, generally speaking, a Woodruff-type car. Six of them built at a cost of $60,000 each to the Erie's six-foot gauge were named *James Fisk, Jay Gould, Morning Star, Evening Star, Queen City* and *Crescent City*. The cars *Fisk* and *Gould* were, of course, named for two of the evil geniuses of the Erie management and the *James Fisk* had a handsomely executed likeness of the Prince of Erie himself engrossed on a medallion on either side of the sleeper. It is interesting if not profitable to speculate why no car was named for the third member of the Erie wrecking crew, Uncle Daniel Drew.

The Central Transportation Company mentioned above was organized in 1869 by T. T. Woodruff and Andrew Carnegie to operate twenty Silver Palace sleepers over Eastern carriers, including the Erie, and in 1870 George M. Pullman was taken into the firm to operate the newly formed Union Pacific Central Transportation Company whose cars were assigned to lines west of Omaha. In the same year the U.P. Company was dissolved and leased 100 cars to Pullman for ninety-nine years at an annual rental of $264,000 and Carnegie was admitted as a partner in the Pullman Palace Car Company—so called, as recounted earlier in this book, at the shrewd suggestion of Andrew Carnegie himself.

From these brief accounts of the complicated and interlocking associations of only a few of the carbuilding concerns of the period it will be apparent that the railroad equipment industry was churning with excitements and that the profits, already substantial, promised soon to be astronomical.

And while these shufflings and realignments of power among the great carbuilders were taking place, minor firms for the construction and operation of sleeping cars and other passenger equipment were emerging into the light of day, flourishing briefly and disappearing forever in mergers or complete dissolution. There was the Gates Sleeping Car Company named for G. B. Gates and supplying sleeping cars exclusively to the Lake Shore & Michigan Southern

Railroad, which shortly disappeared from the record when it was absorbed by Webster Wagner in 1869. Of the cars it built, only their names survive: *White Pigeon, Golden Gate, Central Park, Garden City,* and *City of Buffalo.* These were all stateroom palace cars. Palace sleeping cars by Gates included the *Adriatic, Coldwater* and *City of Cleveland* on the run between Rochester and Chicago. There was the Flower Sleeping Car Company optimistically incorporated in Maine in 1882 to build cars with a tier of berths down the center with aisles on either side. There were the cars built by the Knight Sleeping Car Company for the Baltimore & Ohio Railroad, and the Lucas Sleeping & Parlor Car Company of Atlanta, Georgia, whose largest backer was William M. Wadley, president of the Central of Georgia, a carrier that absorbed the entire output of the firm. And there was John B. Anderson & Company, which operated all the sleepers on the Louisville & Nashville and was at length, and inevitably, gobbled up by Pullman–Southern in 1872.

One of the most fetching of all names was that of the Harris Palatial Car Company organized at Portland, Maine, in 1889 and whose sole car, built by the Wason Manufacturing Company, was named *Jeanette* and had its picture in the *Railroad Gazette* for 1890. No further mention is to be found of the Palatial except one brief item in 1892, when the *Railroad Gazette* noted sadly that the company was in receivership and advertised for a purchaser for *Jeanette.*

More ambitious and longer lived than the builders of *Jeanette* was the firm reported in *Railway Age* for July 16, 1885, to be organized in New York City with a capitalization of $5,000,000 under the style of the Monarch Parlor–Sleeping Car Company. It was predicated on building a new type of car that could be operated in daytime as a complete parlor carriage and as a sleeper on night runs. Six cars were already in use and more were contracted for by the firm's President A. F. Higgs.

The Monarch Car, which in a general way had adapted the best features of the Leve & Alden Car also contains many improvements suggested by President Higgs [said the *Railway Age* approvingly]. The Gilbert Manufacturing Company of Troy, New York, are building the cars. One car will be run after June between New York and Quebec via the Connecticut River Railroad and its connections and its mate will be run between Boston and Quebec via the Passumpsic Railroad and its connections. The company has connections with the New York, New Haven & Hartford Railway and the Quebec Central and also on days alternating with Pullman cars, between New Orleans and Jacksonville over the Florida Railway & Navigation Company's line via Tallahassee. It also [operates cars] on the Vandalia Lines, the Evansville & Terre Haute, the Cincinnati, Indianapolis & St. Louis and the Cincinnati, Indianapolis, St. Louis & Chicago Railroad, the Louisville & Nashville and the Tavares, Orlando & Atlantic Railroad.

The word Palace in the incorporated title of a carbuilding company throughout the nineteenth century was what Pacific was to the incorporated title of any ambitious railroad, a *sine qua non.* Without it a venture could not hope for an auspicious future.

More shadowy and elusive in the record are the Holland Sleeping Car Company, which in 1903 supplied a compartmented sleeper to the Indianapolis & Eastern Railroad and then faded from view, and the Jones Vestibule Sleeping Car Company of Denver, which in 1892 advertised its intention of building cars whose upper berths were to be so recessed and at such a height in the construction as to add measureably to the space available for the convenience of occupants and their luggage.

Harlan & Hollingsworth, who had the honor of building the first non-railroad-owned private car in California, that of frosty old moneybags Darius Ogden Mills, in 1883 sold a number of cars to the Canadian Pacific, including maroon and gold sleepers finished in Eastlake pattern with such names as *Keewatin, Assiniboin, Kaministiquia* and *Qu'Appelle,* which may well have suggested travel on other carriers to illiterate voyagers.

Far and away the most picturesque of all the carbuilders, themselves a bumper crop of individualists often bordering on the eccentric (Pullman was a determined feudal overlord and labor baiter, Woodruff a hayseed type from Central Casting) was Colonel William D'Alton Mann, father of the Mann Boudoir car and later a seedy magnifico of New York clubdom who earned his living as the town's most explicit and widely respected blackmailer.

Mann's most general celebrity derived from his ownership and management of *Town Topics,* a society *feuilleton* whose masquerade of innocent gossip was a front for the Colonel's lucrative practice of shaking down newly rich millionaires whom his editorial spies detected in moments of imprudence. The Colonel's silk top hat set at a rakish military angle, his flowing white whiskers suggestive of an altogether bogus benevolence and the two bottles of vintage champagne with which he washed down a breakfast of Kentucky ham every morning at Delmonico's were institutional in the New York of a gaslit and hansom carriage era. On such an elevated plane were his blackmailing operations conducted and so exalted the names that paid tribute for his silence in the columns of *Town Topics* that it became, with the passing of time, a mark of distinction to have been shaken down by the Colonel. Cotillion leaders and captains of finance bragged of it when in the company of other gentlemen.

Mann's railroad car was a by-product of his devotion to a property he delighted to invade, namely privacy. The idea of people of quality sleeping in open sections was deeply repugnant to him and on January 7, 1872, he took out patents on a sleeping and parlor car composed entirely of private compartments for single or double occupancy. The distinguishing characteristic of Mann's boudoir cars as he appropriately called them was the extension the full width of the car of the individual rooms and their access solely through side doors as was the practice in Europe.

A great deal of thought and effort had gone into the arrangement of the elements that were included: folding seats, toilets, hand bowls and banquettes that were convertible into berths running at right angles to the sides of the car. The cars were richly ornamented in the taste of the time but, while they appealed to a sophisticated element of the traveling public that took naturally to things English and continental, they found little favor with railroad operators. Their inaccessibility save from a footboard along the outside of the car was regarded as needlessly hazardous in an occupation then none too safe, and the fact that passage through them was impossible to passengers wishing to pass from one car to another while moving, caused railroads to reject them almost everywhere in the United States, although substantial numbers were built in Europe.

Colonel Mann could take a hint, and six years later he came up with a far more practical compartment car in which the private toilets had been eliminated to make room for a corridor extending the length of the car with boudoirs opening off it, while toilet facilities were located at either end of the row of staterooms. An innovation of which other carbuilders and railroad operators approved so enthusiastically that they were at once widely pirated, were enclosed vestibules, at least on later models. The Mann Boudoir Car Company was organized by the Colonel and by 1883 Mann cars were in regular service between Boston and New York, whence their popularity spread into the Middle West and Deep South.

A notable patron of the arts, Colonel Mann liked to name his cars for figures in the world of opera and the stage: *Rigoletto, Il Trovatore, Carmen, Adelina Patti* and *Etelka Gerster*. Traces of the great world marked the goings of travelers in hardware from Bridgeport and Waterbury clocks.

Almost as much as he admired their artistic achievements, Colonel Mann also liked to build very ornate and costly private cars for stage and opera notables, and a considerable body of legend has become associated with the two he built for Lily Langtry and Adelina Patti.

The Jersey Lily at the height of her American and English success as an exponent of the society drama had no more enthusiastic admirer than Freddy Gebhardt, a well-to-do New York wine salesman and promoter. The man of vintages one day encountered Colonel Mann at the bar at Delmonico's and confided that he wanted to give the actress a birthday present, something really super that would indicate the depth and dimension of his devotion. Why not a nice private railroad car, suggested the Colonel brightly? Gebhardt thought it was a perfectly splendid idea and commissioned *Lalee*, which the Langtry said was East Indian for flirt. *Lalee* was an eye-popper and, according to Pierre Sichel, Langtry's biographer, suggested nothing so much as Cleopatra's barge under full sail. It was painted royal blue and the interior decor would have excited Dorothy Draper. Since Gebhardt invariably accompanied the car and its owner on the road, it was probably the most highly publicized rolling love nest of all time.

The car Mann built for Adelina Patti was, somewhat redundantly, called the *Adelina Patti* and it, too, achieved a sort of dubious immortality. For many

215

years the press of the land echoed with feature stories about the luxury and profusion which characterized the diva's private vehicle. On her innumerable "farewell tours" it got almost as good notices as its owner, and its bathtub, richly carved ornamentation of rare woods, elaborate marquetry and inlaid ceiling, not to mention a sliding panel through which breakfast was projected into the owner's private sleeping room, were familiar to all readers of the Sunday press.

Alas, when time at last overtook the old lady and her car alike, it was discovered that Colonel Mann had practiced an outrageous deception upon her. The alleged porcelain bathtub when unsheathed turned out to be zinc, the rare woodwork merely painted canvas, the carved cherubs of the ceiling, images on oilcloth. All was fakement. The news, when circulated, did more to damage Colonel Mann's reputation than being called a fraud by the President of the United States, which is just what Theodore Roosevelt did in referring to *Town Topics*.

Over the years a total of forty-three Mann cars were built and operated in the United States, not counting four that were built by the Gilbert Car Company under Mann patents for export to Australia, where they were reported to have been in use as general service sleepers just three quarters of a century after they were built. If the decor of his private cars was fraud, the Mann underframes, headframes and sidewalls were of the most durable construction.

The discovery of Mann cars still in operation in Australia and New Zealand was made in the year 1960 by Gerald Best, one of the best informed railroad authorities and a bulwark of the Railway & Locomotive Historical Society, of which he is a regional satrap. Two Mann Boudoirs that had been sold to the New South Wales Railways by Wagner were in use in that year as second-class sleepers out of Sydney. Second class in Australia means blankets furnished, and suggested troops or Boy Scouts to Best. A third, still showing traces of a Mann vestibule, was in service out of Orange, where Best's guide volunteered the information that when it went around curves it gave forth a symphony of protesting squeaks, each one tribute to a year in more or less continuous service. When asked why wooden railroad cars dating from the eighties should still be in service on well-to-

do carriers that elsewhere on other runs provided the most modern all-steel equipment, Best was informed that efforts had been made to retire the venerable conveyances, but that sheep farmers, who were important patrons of the runs in which they had been scheduled, protested violently against this manifestation of progress. So vocal had they become that the Mann cars were restored and four such cars were still in service. If the count was accurate, every Mann car sold in Australia has survived since the date of its purchase, although it is possible that more cars were actually shipped out than those included in the sale mentioned above.

It might have grieved the Colonel, who was strictly a de luxe traveler through this world himself, to know that his cherished cars had sunk to the level of second class to be inhabited by sheepherders, who would certainly never have been welcome at Delmonico's, but their longevity would have pleased him.

Eventually Mann sold out in 1889 to the Union Transportation Company, where his patents were combined with those of E. C. Knight and the T. T. Woodruff Company as assets of the Union Palace Car Company, which, in due course and like almost everything else in the field, was absorbed by Pullman. Colonel Mann went on to achieve immortality as proprietor of *Town Topics* and as founder of another magazine, *Smart Set*. Many years later *Smart Set* was the editorial scene of the first of many collaborations by George Jean Nathan and Henry L. Mencken, so that, vicariously at least, the Colonel's name entered into the mainstream of American letters.

During their brief but exotic flowering Mann's boudoir cars got around over considerable geography. They ran in the Boston & Albany between the two terminal cities of its corporate name; they connected the Hub of the Universe with the White Mountains and beyond over the Boston & Lowell; between Cincinnati, New Orleans, Chattanooga and Jacksonville they operated over the rails of the Queen & Crescent Route and between Louisville and Chattanooga over the Louisville Southern; between Atlanta and Birmingham they conveyed sleeping patrons via the Georgia Pacific Railway, and between Atlanta and Shreveport over the Georgia Pacific and Queen & Crescent; between St. Louis and New Orleans they were handled over the Mobile & Ohio; from Chicago to St. Joseph, Missouri, they ran in the consists of the Chicago, St. Paul & Kansas City, later the Chicago Great Western, and in the Northwest between Chicago and St. Paul–Minneapolis on the same carrier. These routes, together with their operating contracts, were absorbed by Pullman, effective January 25, 1889.

The Monarch Company, which appears variously under the styles of the Monarch Parlor–Sleeping Car Company and Monarch Palace Car Company, was an ambitious project, and its cars, built as has been recorded by the Gilbert Works at Troy under the general supervision of Webster Wagner, also went in for jaw-splitting names for its products: *Altoisa, Rhodope, Cleopatra, Bertha, Zenobia, Louis XVI* and *Palatka*. A weakness for royalty showed itself here in *Cleopatra* and *Louis XVI* and again in *Queen Anne*, whose pictured likeness is shown at an appropriate place in this volume.

Monarch was probably the builder of at least some of the open platform observation cars that appeared on the more scenic runs in New England, notably the Connecticut River Railroad and the Portland & Ogdensberg. One, with a characteristically unpronounceable name, *Ymir*, ran to the White Mountains in summer over the Connecticut River route and had a double roof for cooling, two rounded glass ends and was sixty-six feet long, with three private rooms in the center of the car. Its total seating capacity was twenty-eight, and there was a buffet, but its crowning touch was the exterior paint job in brown and silver to represent snow on the mountains, and there were icicles in white paint in the windows and depending from the edge of the roof.

The Monarch parlor–sleepers were equally as grand, being furnished throughout in Honduran mahogany, but none indulged a taste for whimsy comparable to *Ymir*.

Also boasting a New England clientele, including the Boston & Maine Railroad, was the Northern Parlor Car Company, which in 1891 supplied *Fabyan, Franconia, Ammonoosuc, Crawford, Memphremagog, Mt. Washington, Profile* and *Winnipesaukee* for the Yankee carrier. Having delivered this resounding bill of goods it disappeared forever from the Railway Equipment Register, doubtless feeling it had contributed enough to the lexicon of down-East travel.

The vogue for hunting expeditions in the newly opened American West—and one that was in no way abated by the celebrated safari mounted in 1871 by Buffalo Bill Cody for the Grand Duke Alexis of Russia—prompted both Mann and Pullman to build cars for the special accommodation of hunters and fishermen who might wish to live on them for prolonged periods at some remove from the resources and conveniences of cities.

One firm was devoted entirely to the construction and operation of hunting cars. This was the Worcester Excursion Car Company founded in 1877 by Jerome Marble, a first citizen of the Massachusetts municipality of its corporate name. Like Webster Wagner, who was a New York State senator, Marble was a public office holder, having served several terms as alderman of Worcester as well as a member of the Board of Trade and as a director of several banks. A privately organized hunting party of his own which visited the Dakotas in 1875 convinced Marble that there would be a brisk demand for luxury transport and accommodation to the Far West as long as the buffalo, antelope and other wild life lasted, and Jackson & Sharp in 1875 built to his specifications his first hunting car, patriotically named the *City of Worcester*.

Its resources comprised sleeping accommodations for six or eight amidst what was certainly the most elegant decor ever to be seen by the warlike Sioux and Chippewa who still ranged the Great Plains. Its exterior was finished in "lake color," a brilliant purple with infusions of red, and ornamented with gold leaf and silver moldings. Steps of mahogany with brass ferules on the risers led to the platform which housed a refrigerator, a coal box and water tank. Under the car were lockers for food, ice and the storage of game. The interior was rosewood, black walnut and mahogany all decorated with gold leaf, and the furniture was crimson plush with curtains of silk damask and a thick Brussels carpet.

The reading room of this nonesuch of hunting lodges had a sofa bed, and in the combination dining–drawing room was an ample dinner table, six banquette seats, a Needham musical cabinet, portable card tables, two double berths, silver-plated oil lamps and two large French bevel-edged mirrors. There were washrooms with water from gravity tanks, since the air might be bled off for protracted periods, a butler's pantry and galley.

So successful was the *City of Worcester* that Marble at once ordered companion cars to the number of eight, named, among others, *Jerome Marble, Charles B. Pratt, Yellowstone* and *Edwin Forrest.*

The *Edwin Forrest* was, from contemporary accounts, the most stunning of what must have been a very handsome fleet of specialized varnish cars. It came from Wilmington in 1883 and the *Worcester Gazette* remarked editorially: "It is the wonder of all visitors how much comfort can be provided in the space of a railroad car . . . a perfect gem of car construction."

It was sixty-six feet long, exclusive of Miller platforms and Janney Patent couplings, and painted in dark green with gold leaf in abundance. The main salon was twenty-four feet long with a rich green carpet of old Wilton. The woodwork was hand-polished mahogany, and the ceiling was painted in a complicated pattern of birds and flowers centering on a medallion portrait of Forrest himself in the role of Hamlet, flanked by two massive bronze chandeliers.

There were blue plush chairs, an upright "parlor bedstead"—or early predecessor of the Murphy Bed —and, inexplicably, a fireproof "Magneso-Calcite" safe. There were sixteen berths, eight of them finished with detailed marquetry work, and in daytime large easy chairs of different patterns are brought into use, upholstered with the richest Florentine plush of changeable old gold with raised figures. There are chairs of red leather for dining use.

"Metal trimmings are of bronze. The curtains are Turkish designs in red and green, gold threads being woven throughout the odd figures. The glass and numerous doors are decorated with ground patterns showing the varieties of game found in the Western prairies. The mirrors are bevel-edge glass.

"In the library, magnificently carved, is a writing desk which also contains a double bed. It is of the Burr patent and made by Warner & Company of New York and is a very handsome piece of furniture."

The reporter also noted electric bells and commented, "It is almost impossible to conceive of anything that is wanting."

In slack seasons and between Far Western safari, the Marble cars were available to charter by less ambitious private parties and the record shows that in 1883 the *Edwin Forrest* was leased by a party of Lehigh Valley Railroad directors, who presumably had no directors' car of their own at the time, for a junket to Old Mexico. Actors on tour patronized Marble, and the same car was at various times occupied for extended periods by Sir Henry Irving and Helena Modjeska and by Lily Langtry before she had a Mann-built private car of her own.

The Worcester Excursion Car Company under the direction and management of its founder remained in profitable business until well into the nineties, when the game was fast disappearing and the vogue of the hunting car in decline. In 1895 the Pennsylvania refused to accept Marble cars in interchange, presumably for reasons of safety in operation, and after that they disappeared from the record.

The story of Pullman and the New York Central Lines is one of warfare by attrition and of feuding by indirection on a scale representing millions.

From the beginning the Vanderbilt carriers had favored the various carriages built by Webster Wagner and had thrown the weight of their enormous prestige as well as their rich and important patronage in the direction of Pullman's best hated rival. From the very outset of their long-haul operations as interlocking affiliates, the New York Central & Hudson River Railroad and the Lake Shore & Michigan Southern Railroad had run Wagner compartmented parlor cars on their daylight hauls and Wagner Palace sleepers on the New York–Chicago run. The old Commodore himself rode tandem in two of the gaudiest Wagner private palace cars ever seen, *Vanderbilt* and *Duchess,* the former unabashedly boasting colored side panels that were masterpieces of the coachmaker's art depicting scenes, such as Niagara Falls, along the Central's main line. These splendid conveyances were usually drawn by the engine *Vanderbilt,* a classic American-type eight-wheeler of noble dimensions with a likeness of the Commodore—ruddy complexion, stock collars, white whiskers and all—on the great storm headlamps then in use. The engine itself had gold-plated handrails, bell hanger and other ornamental trim until some churl among the Central's stockholders took exception to this elegance, and the Commodore, in a snit, ordered decoration of every sort removed from the Central's motive power everywhere.

The passage through the countryside of a train brigade of this sort was assured a certain amount of notice. It advertised the Vanderbilt Lines and their owner. It also drew favorable attention to the palace cars of Webster Wagner, and Pullman took to kicking at cuspidors and other inanimate artifacts whenever he thought of them.

Not even the great and nationally heralded Boston Chamber of Commerce train from the Hub to California, which in 1872 represented one of Pullman's moments of purest promotional genius, could alleviate the gloom that overtook him thinking of all those Vanderbilts riding in all those Wagner Palace cars.

Now and then Wagner cars participated in one of the frightful railroad accidents that were frequent in the seventies. Two of them were involved in the great Ashtabula holocaust of the Christmas season of 1876. Others were part of the consist of the *Pacific Express* that came to grief at Wappinger's Creek near Poughkeepsie in 1871 when its locomotive sideswiped a passing freight train which included a number of tank cars of petroleum. A commentary on the weight of rolling stock at the time may be discerned in the fact that as the rest of the train was burning on the Hudson River ice, unharmed passengers pushed three Wagner sleepers to safety.

Wagners on the Central Lines became a hereditary fixture and lasted from the regime of the Commodore through the entire reign of his son, William H. Vanderbilt. In 1882 rumors of a consolidation of the Wagner and Pullman interests were rife in the financial world, and reporters asked William Henry if there were any truth in the matter.

"Mr. Pullman knows upon what terms he can combine at any time," Vanderbilt told the press. "The Wagner cars are meeting with great success on our lines and if a consolidation is to be brought about, it must be as much in the interest of the Wagner Car people as of Pullman. The matter is at present in *status quo.*" Mr. Vanderbilt went on to remark to the interviewer that he disapproved most emphatically of Pullman's model industrial city of Pullman, Illinois. "You will never see the Wagner Company building a town of Wagner," he said.

In a small way the Pullman–Wagner feud was reflected in the great railroad war between the New York Central and the Pennsylvania that had its center in the building of the West Shore Railroad, paralleling in its right of way the New York Central's main line from New York City to Buffalo.

This was a nuisance-value project corporately known as the New York, West Shore & Buffalo Railroad, financed by a group of New York and Chicago men of money with the sole expressed intention of harassing the Vanderbilt interests. The project was viewed with good cheer by the Pennsylvania, which was breathing hot on the neck of the Central in competition between New York and Chicago, and, of course, enjoyed the enthusiastic support of Pullman, whose cars went into service on the first West Shore train between Weehawken and Kingston. It began to shape up as a battle between the Vanderbilt and Wagner interests on one side and the insurgent Pennsylvania and Pullman on the other.

For a time Pullman's palace cars rolled grandly up the West Shore of the Hudson, making metaphorical snoot faces at the gleaming Wagners of the New York Central steaming majestically along the other side of the river.

But the younger Vanderbilt was no man to be intimidated. He called a meeting with Andrew Carnegie and the Rockefellers and projected a railroad of his own which would invade the territory until now sacred to the Pennsylvania with a direct line from Reading to Pittsburgh. The line was forty-six miles shorter than the Pennsylvania's main line between the same points and was a bona fide menace. Carnegie put $5,000,000 into the scheme, the Rockefellers $400,000, and Darius O. Mills, without whom nothing of consequence could get off the ground at the time, an even half million. Carnegie's long-standing love affair with the Pennsylvania was cooling. The Rockefellers probably saw in the threat an instrument to demand further rebates from the Pennsylvania in the freighting of their oil products. Mills came along for the ride.

This was the celebrated railroad war that became such a threat to everybody's community of interest in the industrial and railroading pattern of the East that J. Pierpont Morgan had to come home from a vacation abroad and patch up the quarrel in a peace conference held aboard his yacht *Corsair* in Long Island Sound. Progress on the South Pennsylvania, as the Vanderbilt counterattack was known, was suspended. The New York Central took over management of the West Shore; it already had an entrance to Pittsburgh over its wholly owned Pittsburgh & Lake Erie. The dust settled and everybody returned to managing their own affairs. All except George Pullman, who was, perhaps, the most spectacular victim of the affray. His cars, of course, disappeared overnight from the trains of the West Shore, and instead of them, the hated Wagner Palace cars were scheduled.

It was one of the few occasions when Pullman was cast in the role of an unmitigated victim.

Another aspect other than the direct competition furnished by the Wagner organization proved vexatious to Pullman. This was the admiration Wagner displayed for all and any Pullman innovations, regardless of their patent status.

Wagner so much admired various Pullman improvements and patents that with an absolute minimum of elapsed time these same improvements and patents could be observed in the products of the Wagner Palace Car Company. All sorts of components of Pullman cars, brake rigging, the vertical headframes at the ends of cars, vestibule and platform features were no sooner perfected by Pullman engineers and designers than they started making money for the admiring Webster Wagner.

At length Pullman sued Wagner for the sum of $1,000,000 in patent infringement, and the courts found for the plaintiff. Wagner was enjoined to restrain his admiration for Pullman features to comply with the patent laws and from then until 1899, when all the Wagner properties were merged with Pullman, it was more nearly possible to identify a Wagner car from a Pullman, and vice versa.

In all but one respect. When Pullman took over Wagner, its executives discovered that no fewer than 300 Wagner sleepers, parlor cars, buffets and diners had the identical names of their Pullman opposite numbers. There were two of everything from *Ashtabula* to *Zion,* and confusion is said to have resulted. Pullman in this pass, inaugurated the series of names of characters out of classic legend and mythology that were, for years to come, to fill the mouths of travelers who had never before encountered Endymion, Theseus, Heraclitus or Niobe.

It was an important footnote to American culture.

The Pullman–Wagner merger took place in 1899 after all three of the principal participants in the long-standing rivalry, George Mortimer Pullman, Webster Wagner and William Henry Vanderbilt had passed from the scene. It was a deal of considerable magnitude, as may be suggested by the fact that in rolling stock alone, Pullman acquired no fewer than 480 Wagner Palace sleeping cars, 135 parlor cars, nine private cars and combination club cars, diners, buffets and compartment cars in substantial tally. With them, of course, went all the routes then operated by Wagner and the vast Wagner organization for the maintenance, servicing and operation of its cars over railroad lines traversing the entire dimension of the continent.

For the next two decades the magnitude of Pullman operation of sleeping cars was enormous. At one time the company was in a position to boast that its collective beds and berths slept more patrons every night than the combined capacities of all the first-class hotels of the land, a statistic comfortably based on one's definition of first class.

By 1916 the Pullman Company operated a total of 7,500 cars on trains of 137 railroads and 223,486 miles of track. More than 26,000,000 passengers rode Pullman annually, occupying an astronomical 260,000 beds or berths every night.

The acquisitive nature of Pullman's near-monopoly which, by the turn of the century, had absorbed almost all the important competition save that of Barney & Smith and Jackson & Sharp, by now itself part of American Car & Foundry, resulted in the hybrid nature of the Pullman roster for the next several years until the various non-Pullman elements in its tally became obsolete or suffered the mischances of service.

In addition to the great number of Wagner cars, there were still in operation a number of the sleepers and other de luxe cars which had come to Pullman in the Union Palace sale a decade previous. There were parlor cars such as *Evangeline* and its companion *Genevieve* which were pure Union Palace and resolutely refused to change their basic characteristics as long as they were in useful operation. Sleepers like *Juniata* and *Lapland* and combination sleeper–lounge cars like *Montecito* kept green the memory of the resoundingly named Woodruff Sleeping Car & Parlor Coach Company. Vestigial traces of Flower, Mann and Knight patents lurked in the woodwork and brake rigging of scores of cars whose occupants little suspected the involved corporate histories on which they were riding. A few of the original Mann hunting and private-occupancy cars such as *Newport, Davy Crockett, Izaak Walton* and *Pickwick* may still have been on standby service, but they were living on borrowed time, and the ever-stiffening requirements of carriers in the direction of safety and uniformity of equipment soon rendered them obsolete for main-line interchange.

In the blood stream of Pullman there flowed for many years the mingled antecedents of carbuilders long dead and companies that, before they became company assets, had provided the most vexatious and resolute competition. Philosophers may ponder.

One of George M. Pullman's side investments was in the Gilbert Elevated Railway in New York City, a carrier that bought Pullman products and whose construction he is shown inspecting on the Church Street section in 1878. Below is the main building of the shops at Pullman, Illinois, whose grounds were celebrated for beautiful landscaping in an age long before factory sites were known as industrial parks.

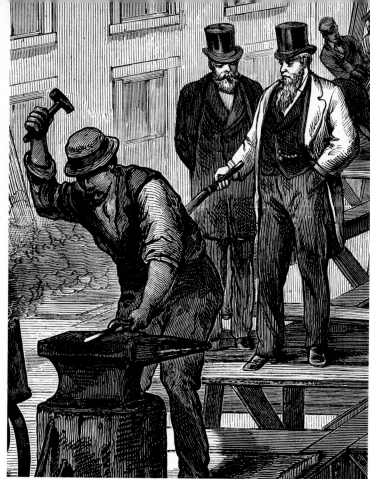

Crown jewel of the feudal township of Pullman, Illinois, was the Florence Hotel, named for Pullman's daughter who later married Governor Frank Lowden. Here railroad presidents and ranking executives gloried and drank deep while placing orders for the incomparable products of the company.

In 1880 this voluptuous congregation of whiskers, dust jackets, derbies and the waistlines of an uninhibited generation at table represented a group of master carbuilders at Weldin, North Carolina, en route to a convention of their peers at Charleston. Cigars were the accepted smoke of grown men, while the silk skullcap was favored by many travelers aboard the cars and had nothing to do with Orthodox Jewry.

OWEN DAVIES

"I met with no silver whatever on the Silver Palace sleeping cars," complained Thérèse, Viscountess Avonmore, in writing of her American experiences in 1875. "The fittings, lamps, bolts, hinges, door handles, etc., are of the white metal called pinchbeck or Britannia metal, and the palaces are fitted up in the ordinary hotel style, the floors carpeted and oil clothed and the seats velvet covered." A decade later the Viscountess would have found the palace cars more sumptuous, but in the sixties and seventies, when the Central Transportation Company was operating such cars as the Silver Palace car Empire between New York and Chicago over the Erie and its connections, sleepers had yet to achieve their Pullman dimension of magnificence. The Central Company was incorporated in 1862 when T. T. Woodruff and E. C. Knight pooled their patents in the venture, as is attested by the nameboards of Empire on the opposite page. Twenty-seven years later the Central Transportation Company, which had in the meantime operated sleeping cars with considerable success on Eastern carriers, was merged with Colonel William D'Alton Mann's boudoir car company to form the Union Palace–Car Company, which in turn was promptly bought up by Pullman, as its stockholders had no doubt intended. The interior of Empire, shown here, might not have appealed strongly to Burke's Peerage, but it sufficed passengers en route to Elmira, Dunkirk and Chicago.

Originally built as a standard twelve-section and one drawing room sleeper by Wagner, Braquemonde was distinguished because when it was taken over by Pullman in 1897 it not only retained its Wagnerian name but many features of Wagner construction and decor such as the wavy finelining on the sidewalls and arched Gothic of opaque glass above the double windows. This photograph from the Dubin collection was taken at the Buffalo Pullman shops in 1897; the car itself lasted in useful service until the twenties. Below is the magnificent Pullman sleeper El Pino, built for the Southern Pacific in 1895 as one of the elements of an all-new Sunset Limited that also includes such famous cars as El Oro and the diner Epicure. El Pino (right) was expensively fitted with mahogany, walnut, oak, cocowood, amaranth, vermilion and tigerwood to make one of the handsomest Pullmans ever to roll across the Southwest.

Like Pullman, Wagner not only built and leased cars to its patron railroads, but maintained and serviced sleeper and buffet cars along Pullman lines, although both firms preferred that individual carriers maintain the catering on dining cars purchased outright from the manufacturer. Some of the regulations governing personnel of the Wagner Palace Car Company are contained in an 1898 edition of the firm's Rules For Uniformed Employees in the Dubin collection and may be worth reprinting here in abbreviated form as a clue to the manner in which the palace cars were conducted in their noontide of public acceptance:

Nuisances: *The washing of personal linen or diapers on the cars not permitted.*

Personal Appearance: *Avoid putting hands in pockets in tails of uniform overcoats in cold weather, giving employees a decidedly loafering appearance as well as spreading the tails of the coat and getting them out of shape.*

Blacking Boots: *Only one pair at a time to be worked on.*

Collars and Cuffs: *White linen only—celluloid are prohibited.*

Passes: *Individuals who, from their large proprietary interests in roads are entitled to ride free on our cars and should not be asked to show their passes.*

Customs re Chinamen: *Canadian officials are to be notified at the frontier when Chinamen occupy space in the cars.*

Uniforms: Barbers: *Trousers must be same as those worn by conductors. Cap with gilt badge with words "Barber, Wagner Palace Car Co." Alpaca coat with small, turn-down collar, five black buttons and "Wagner Palace Co." on lapel in gilt. Standing white collar must be worn at all times. Barbers must be particular to be neat and tidy in appearance.*

Maids: *Maids must be extremely careful to maintain a proper deportment while on duty. Under no circumstances will they allow familiarity on the part of crew or passengers. They will have the following personal equipment: Book of Rules, set of keys, smelling salts, liquid camphor, black and white thread, package of needles and assorted pins for ladies' use.*

This superb builder's photograph of Woodruff's sleeper Juniata was taken at Wilmington, Delaware, after the car was outshopped by Jackson & Sharp, presumably for service on the Pennsylvania system. A rare eleven-by-fourteen-inch collodion plate in the collection of Everett De Golyer of Dallas, it serves as a reminder that in the early years of railroad expansion Pullman had no monopoly on sleeping cars or the patents protecting their manufacture by rival carbuilders. Juniata, which had twelve open sections and no drawing room, later passed into the hands of Pullman as an asset of the Union Palace Car Company.

Women, from earliest times, looked upon the sleepers as immodest and regarded boarding them unescorted by a masculine companion as one of the major hazards of nineteenth-century travel. In the early days of sleeping cars they often refused completely to disrobe and went to bed fully attired. Hatpins were widely advised as suitable weapons to repel masculine advances such as might be encountered by defenseless females, and these two young ladies (possibly aboard Juniata *on the night run to Pittsburgh) found it more prudent to sit up than to risk the nameless perils lurking in the comfortable recesses of a nicely made lower.*

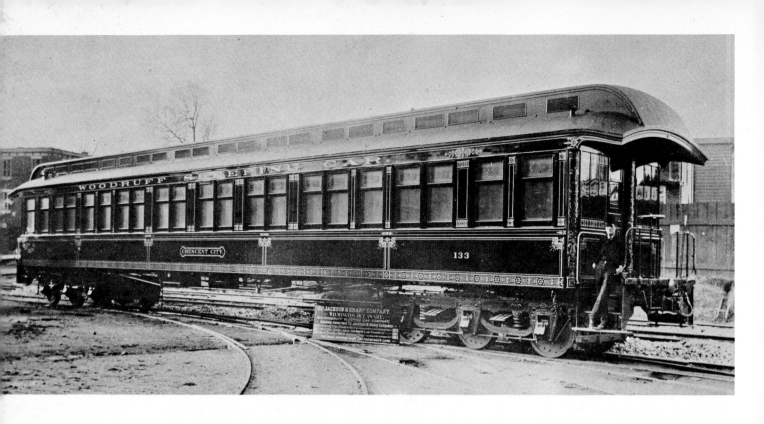

THE WONDERFUL WOODRUFF

Woodruff sleepers such as Crescent City on the opposite page and Berkshire (right) had six sections and a drawing room and were painted in the company livery, seal brown with black end posts and bright yellow roofs, all with liberal gold trim. Interiors were mahogany and marquetry. Crescent City was assigned to the Queen & Crescent Route out of New Orleans.

ROTUNDA

A true sport in the biological sense of the word was the Woodruff Sleeping & Parlor Coach Company's parlor car Ida, *built at Wilmington for the Indianapolis & St. Louis Railroad in the seventies. Known as "the rotunda car" for the domelike extrusion at each end projecting above the clerestory,* Ida *had observation platforms at both ends, Miller platforms, hardwood interiors with French mirrors, reclining seats and observation solariums with curved sidewalls and windows to match. The domes were finished in varicolored panes of glass and formed canopies for the two observation salons.* Ida's *exterior livery was plum- or wine-colored, and it is safe to say that few cars in the record were characterized by such determined individuality. Only its sister car* Nydia, *built to the same specifications, was its peer.*

HOWARD FOGG

Another sport in the biological sense of a spontaneous deviation from established patterns was the magnificently individualistic *Montecito* built by Woodruff in the mid-eighties. Its plan included the usual six sections and drawing room of Woodruff convention, but added a parlor-lounge with brass-railed observation platform at the rear and a barbershop amidships for gentlemen who felt the safety factor favored a professional shave over a straight razor in a washroom of dubious stability. *Montecito* came to Pullman as a Union Palace car asset in 1889 and was assigned to overnight runs, where other equipment complemented its facilities.

TWO PHOTOS: PULLMAN STANDARD

Like the Woodruff sleepers on a previous page, Chicago's floor plan called for six sections and a stateroom and the Woodruff color scheme out- side, which must have made them a glory to behold in any train line.

ARTHUR D. DUBIN COLLECTION

The close similarity of thinking that obtained amongst the major carbuilders of the eighties is illustrated by the two interiors shown here and on the opposite page of Pullman and Woodruff sleepers of approximately coeval vintage. Pullman's ten-section and drawing room–buffet sleeper Ocala (opposite) was built in the pre-Chicago years, probably at Detroit about 1880, with mahogany and oak trim, rounded bolsters with button-ends for arm rests, tufted headboards on the lower berths and flat upper-berth fronts illuminated by oblong panels of frosted glass in a clerestory with a curved roof. It was rebuilt at Chicago in 1901 with a new frame and wide vestibules but retained the original floor plan and sections. It was in service out of St. Louis to Arkansas or Texas in 1914 when it was dismantled. Woodruff's Deerfield is nearly identical in every detail of decor save that its ground plan called for six sections and four drawing rooms. Woodruff's South Side (below) advertises both owner and builder in a single scene.

TWO PHOTOS: ARTHUR D. DUBIN COLLECTION

In the closing years of the nineteenth century and especially, it appears, for carriers in the Deep South Pullman outshopped a number of combination parlor car–diners, one of the more exotic arrangements to which the luxury railroad car was available. Two collector's-item cars in this category are shown here, one built for the Louisville, Evansville & St. Louis in 1889 and the other for service in the Chicago & Nashville Limited, which had its origins on the shores of Lake Michigan on the Chicago & Eastern Illinois Railroad. The first of these boasted the added elegance of an elaborately brass-railed observation platform. On the page opposite, a diminutive cafe apartment seating eight, together with its kitchen offices, complemented a similar compartment with conventional parlor chairs while the ubiquitous Pullman photographer shares in the mirror the immortality he assured so many of the company's products.

FOUR PHOTOS: PULLMAN STANDARD

*Pullman place settings in later years
were less ornate than in the eighties.*

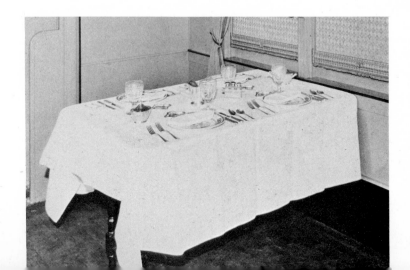

Some idea of Pullman versatility may be gathered from the three interiors reproduced here. At the left on the page opposite is the sleeper–day coach Venus, *a product of the seventies at the Detroit shops, while at the right is a nameless, at this remove, combination parlor car–day coach. On this page is* Jupiter, *a triumph of luxurious utility in the form of a parlor car–sleeper whose sections are visible through the handsomely mirrored doorway. Such hybrid equipment was designed for runs where the density of patronage did not warrant full sleeper or parlor facilities but was sufficient to fill half a car. Elsewhere in this volume will be found other ingenious combinations: parlor–cafe cars, parlor–diners, coach–buffets and buffet–sleepers, each a tribute to the adaptability of the over-all Pullman aim of providing the best in every field where its products were requested.*

THREE PHOTOS: PULLMAN STANDARD

West of Omaha, the Webb party carried their own horses with them in three Chicago & North Western stock cars on the head end of their entire train of private sleeping, buffet and hotel cars. It is shown below posed at Cinnabar, Montana, on the Northern Pacific while at the right Dr. Webb's entourage adorns the observation platform of his personal private Wagner car Ellsmere. Dr. Webb, in riding clothes, sits on the rail. Note the elaborate device on either side for lowering the retracting carriage step when the car was stopped.

TWO PHOTOS: HAYNES STUDIOS

The Webb Special carried a semi-military guard of two riflemen under the command of "Colonel Oscar Edmond, late U.S.A.," and west of Kansas, which Dr. Webb regarded as the last outpost of any dependable social order, there were additional Pinkerton operatives. Colonel Edmond is at the extreme right on the page opposite, looking properly military and grim.

By long odds the most de luxe trip ever arranged by a small private party over American railroads was that organized in 1896 by Dr. William Seward Webb, a Vanderbilt in-law and president of the Wagner Palace Car-Building Company. It started from New York, toured the entire West, Northwest and Rocky Mountain regions and ended in California, having covered the entire distance as a private special train of two private Wagners, Mariquita and Ellsmere, a dining car borrowed from the Lake Shore & Michigan Southern and a combine, in the last of which were space for baggage, sleeping quarters for the kitchen staff, an arms room, a bath, smoking room and an extensive library, wine cellar, cigar humidor and a Chickering piano. To attend the doctor, Mrs. Webb, three children and three guests there was the conventional staff of railway employees supplemented by two chefs, a lady's maid, two nurses, eight porters, a military guard and a number of Pinkerton detectives armed with Winchesters who rode the car platforms between sunset and dawn. West of Omaha additional cars were added for the guards. Three stock cars sheltered horses and grooms for the entire party.

It is, unhappily, impossible to establish the identity of this car interior from the collection of Everett De Golyer of Dallas, as no caption is available to the glass collodion plate from which it was printed. That it was some sort of club car or smoker is suggested by the leather upholstery and bare floor, and the date about 1890 is implied by the presence of both Pintsch gas and coal-oil illumination. A through corridor runs the length of the car behind the partition to the left. Nicely carved medallions in the walls, flowered material for curtains and elaborately painted ceiling, all mark it a luxury car whose antecedents and pedigree must remain forever in obscurity.

242   EVERETT DE GOLYER COLLECTION

The transition, begun in the years of Pullman's most elaborate and ornate appointments, from open sections to all-compartmented sleepers, is illustrated here by interiors of Olesa and Olwein. Olesa, dating from the pre-Chicago era, has open sections whose berth fronts are executed in the pattern known as "Weeping Willow" in white lacquer. Olwein, built at Pullman a few years later, has a through corridor illuminated by oil lamps with folding seats outside each compartment, presumably for occupancy by inmates while their rooms are being made up.

Built in 1897 for the Chesapeake & Ohio, the buffet-sleeping car Mohaska reassured patrons of the line with ball-fringed portières, bevel-edged French mirrors, thick carpets and velour upholstery, while in the galley a chef ran up nutritious collations on trains that carried no diner. The buffet-sleeper was the direct descendant of the original palace hotel car, although the artist's sketch of the chef at work in his galley (right) may seem more ample than is suggested by Mohaska's floor plan, reproduced below.

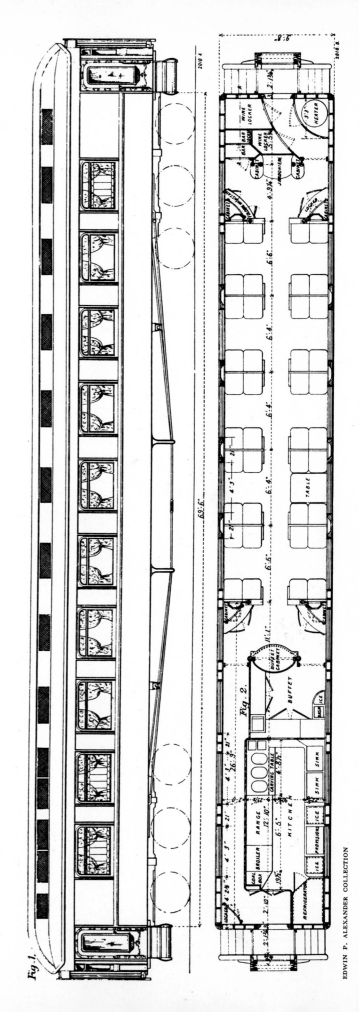

Fig. 1.

Fig. 2.

One of the most elusive of the major carbuilding ventures whose affairs were eventually taken over by Pullman was the Monarch Parlor–Sleeping Car Company which was incorporated in 1883 and whose cars operated largely in New England and Canada, but elsewhere on the Vandalia line, the Louisville & Nashville and the Tavares, Orlando & Atlantic. The Monarch cars were described in company literature as "embracing the novel design of combining in one car elegant revolving chairs for day use and comfortable spring beds for night use," as is suggested by the drawing shown here. A devotee of the good life, and no temperance advocates, the Monarch Company in their insertion in the Official Guide stated in leaded type that all their cars specialized in "Well Stocked Buffets." Less voluptuary, Pullman, Wagner and Woodruff merely stressed the comfort and convenience of their products and, of course, their decor, while the title of Mann's boudoirs in itself contained a hint of perfumed privacy.

The Monarch Patent parlor–sleeping car Queen Anne shows four-wheel trucks in the sketch reproduced below, six wheels in the very rare photograph in service on the Boston–Quebec run of the Quebec Central Railroad from the collection of Andrew Merrilees on the page opposite.

Elsewhere in New England, Monarch cars rode the Boston & Lowell, the Connecticut River, the Passumpsic and the New York, New Haven & Hartford railroads in a pattern of exotic landfaring.

TWO SKETCHES: ARTHUR D. DUBIN COLLECTION

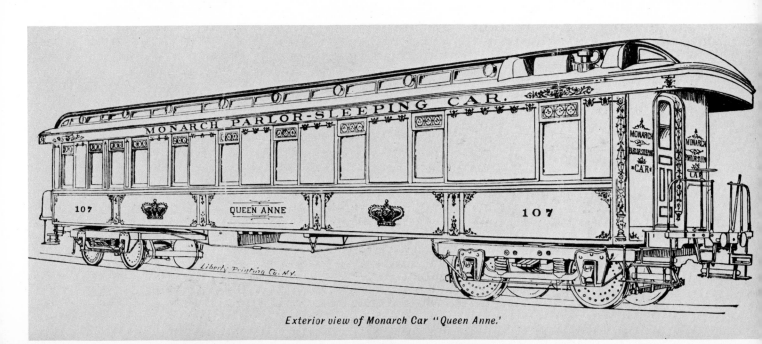

Exterior view of Monarch Car "Queen Anne."

2130   Pullman. Ill. Dec. 7th   5

Two Sleeping Cars   Atlantic Coast Line Ass'n

1066   69' 10"   3' 8⅝"
9' 8"   10' 7/16"   3' 9½"
6' 8½"   none   14' 6"   14' 2½"

20 & 21   none   per plan
Latest Pull. Std.   Dbl diagonal yellow pine 3/4"
Sheathed   Pull. Std for wide Vest.
Pull. Std.   Canvas, Copper flashing
Vermilion
per drawings
3 ply whitewood painted & dead.
2 parts double, Inside each vermilion
3/16" plate   per plan   per plan
Embossed plate
1/4" plate
None. Cro. curtains. Forsythe fixtures.
Pull. Std High Back   Spiral
Vermilion
Pull. Std fawn color plush in body, Blue plush
3 & one ladies toilet.
Three Campbell. No urinals   1 glass, 2 paneled,
3 whitemetal   4 whitemetal
Frumueller double coil & Safety System Steam heat in connection with Penna. return system
Saw, ax & sledge   Pull Std on picts & hooks.
Pull. Std No. 6 Bronze   One bronze in drawing room.
Pull. Std fitted to Pull std Keys.
10 Gordon-Mitchell gas, 4 gas tanks Gordon-Mitchell 22" X 8' 2"
5   2 Gordon-Mitchell gas.
Sessions Steel platform
35'   Janney- Prihary
6 X 8 - 2 coil M.C.C. & T. # 28   Detroit.
Westinghouse, Triple
Hodge   90% of weight
Pull. std wide S both ends.   Beams Nails Yellow, automatic head.
Pull. std.   Pull. Std.
Beveled plate per drawings   Wilton
Westinghouse - 1.   None
Pull. std.   "
     "
Pull. std 5. a
4' 8½"   10' 6" Allen Co.
38" Paper   10
Pull std S. F iron   P. P. C. Co. Detroit
36" Duplex. 5 ply. 4 X 7/16" nail   4 X ⅜ - 13¼"
8⅛ X 10 - 3 Coil   Christie cast
5   Fletcher steel
5 F   Pixcell
5 F Foundry Dept.   Pull. std
Pull. std

     Noble & Hoare
LIFFEY - SEVERN   Murphy
See below.
"Pullman" on letterboard "Atlantic Coast Line" on each end of letterboard.
Name below belt.

82950   85750   118700

No retaining value. 2 old style conductors valves applied
Cars wired for electric light. Deck per ventilators applied.
wheel nos. car Liffey   wheel nos. Car Severn.
P-20932 - P-20937   P-20944 - P-20945
P-20950 - P-20951   P-20948 - P-20942
P-20934 - P-20935   P-20929 - P-20943
P-20930 - P-20931   P-20946 - P-20933
P-20940 - P-20941   P-20949 - P-20928
P-20939 - P-20938   P-20927 - P-20936

Uncounted millions of car miles rolled smoothly from under the laminated paper car wheels that for many years were standard equipment on all Pullman passenger car trucks and one of the firm's most jealously guarded patents. At the left Mr. Pullman himself demonstrates their advantages for a prospective customer, while below is a detail of a No. 5 truck, depicting incidentally the beautifully varnished sidewalls that earned passenger cars of the time the name of varnish cars. On the page opposite is a holograph specification sheet for two sleepers for the Atlantic Coast Line in 1895. Many of the elaborate designs for inlaid woodworks such as the Bird-in-the-Bush and Weeping Willow berth fronts were never committed to paper but executed from memory in the Marquetry Room.

PULLMAN STANDARD

The magnificent whiskers of Colonel William D'Alton Mann together with his boiled shirt and tightly buttoned frock coat (right) concealed the heart of a conspicuous rogue who was better known to his generation as the owner of Town Topics and New York's most elegant blackmailer than he was as a carbuilder. His boudoir cars, nevertheless—many of them named for operas and opera singers—were the first all-room sleeping cars to achieve wide service and pioneered a degree of privacy in travel which was shortly to be available almost everywhere.

In the year 1960, a full three quarters of a century after they had been built, Mann Boudoir cars converted to second class—which is part coach and part sleeper—were still in service, as shown in the above photograph by Gerald M. Best on *the New South Wales Railways at Sydney, Australia. Below, the boudoir car Rigoletto testifies to Colonel Mann's cultural aspirations as a car-builder.*

The drawing room or, as Colonel Mann liked to call it, the grand salon of the boudoir car Adelina Patti was described in company literature as "the richest in decoration, furniture and finish of any car ever built in the world. Decor was by Theodore Hertwig, murals and fresco paintings by Nicholas Rossignoli, as depicted above. On the page opposite, "the fifty-six foot corridor is amply wide for persons to pass freely." The beautiful seventy-foot black and gold Mann Boudoir car Maryland (below) was built by Jackson & Sharp and operated by the Union Palace Car Company under management of Job H. Jackson. In 1889 it passed along with other Union assets into the possession of Pullman.

That the advent of the all-compartmented sleeping car advocated by Colonel Mann was an incentive to extra-marital amour hitherto limited to the Albany Night Boat, the Fall River Line and the Point Comfort steamers was suggested by the drawing from the Police Gazette of 1885 reproduced at the right. It was captioned: "He Was a Traveling Man—How a New York Wife Trapped Her Husband Aboard the Cars of the Erie Line —Love in a Palace Boudoir." Sixty years later in a novel called The Hucksters, Frederic Wakeman was to describe similar scenes of debauchery aboard the even more elaborately perfumed Pullmans of the Super Chief.

FOUR PICTURES: ARTHUR D. DUBIN COLLECTION

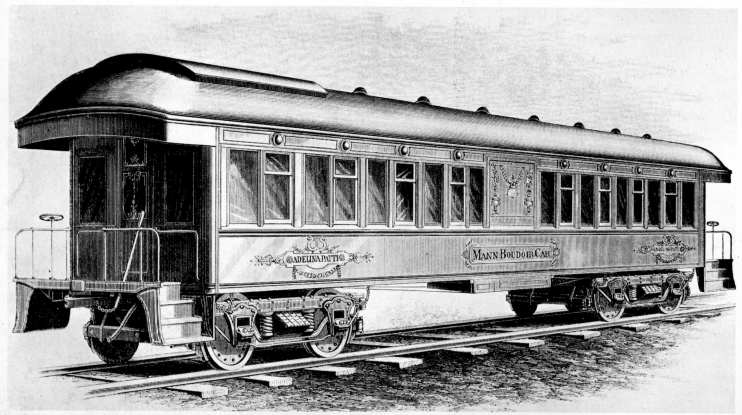

The buffet and smoking room of Mann Boudoir cars boasted "an ample refrigerator chamber in which champagne, beer, mineral waters, milk, etc. may be kept cool . . . also every appliance to enable a substantial breakfast or lunch to be served (say stewed oysters, boiled eggs, cold fowl, hot chocolate, tea, toast, etc.) without the unpleasant odors of a kitchen."

In this "two-place Mann Boudoir" the artist has left the door open to show the corridor arrangement, but Colonel Mann assured patrons that "boudoir doors may be closed and bolted inside if desired, securing absolute privacy." The stepladder formed the legs of a table in daytime. When not in use it was stowed under the sofa. No space was wasted in Mann cars.

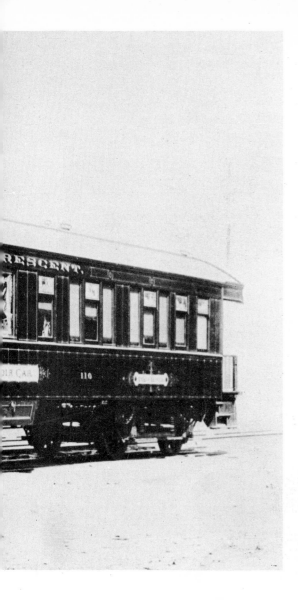

Although the Mann Patent boudoir cars such as *Etelka Gerster (left)*, built for the Queen & Crescent route and named for a contemporary operatic favorite, were not universally acceptable to American railroads, their influence in the direction of private rooms aboard the cars was considerable. Staterooms and drawing rooms, originally conceived by Pullman for occupancy only by invalids, families or unescorted women, soon began to appear, as in the drawing rooms of *Anelo (below)*, in increasing availability for all and any passengers desiring privacy and having the means to gratify it.

AMERICAN CAR & FOUNDRY   PULLMAN STANDARD

Mann Boudoir influence was clearly reflected in the satinwood panels and severe marquetry in the stateroom (opposite) of El Oro, built by Pullman in 1895 for the Southern Pacific's Sunset Limited.

PULLMAN STANDARD

These sleek varnish cars from the collection of
Arthur D. Dubin were built for the Monon route
early in 1900 at Jeffersonville, Indiana, by American Car & Foundry for the Flyer, trains No. 30
and 33 between Chicago & Cincinnati over the
rails of the Chicago, Indianapolis & Louisville
and the connecting Cincinnati, Hamilton & Dayton. They are notable, not only for their characteristic A.C.F. wide picture windows with ornate
transoms, but for having four-wheel trucks instead of the more conventional eight.

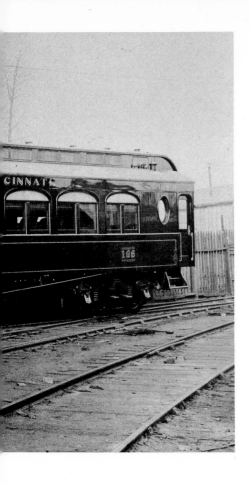

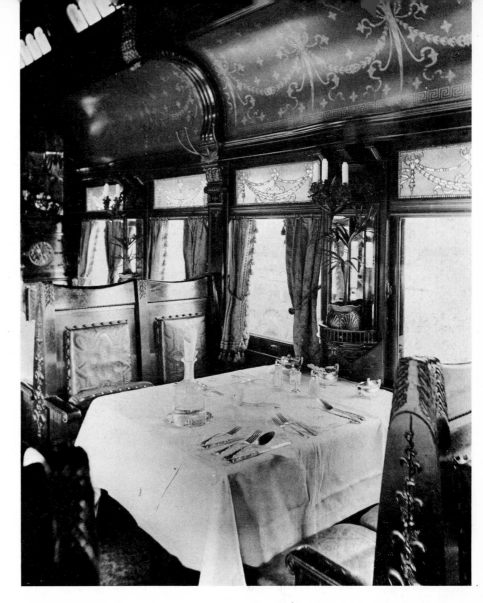

Pullman buffet setup is approximately coeval with the lovely Monon varnish.

PULLMAN STANDARD

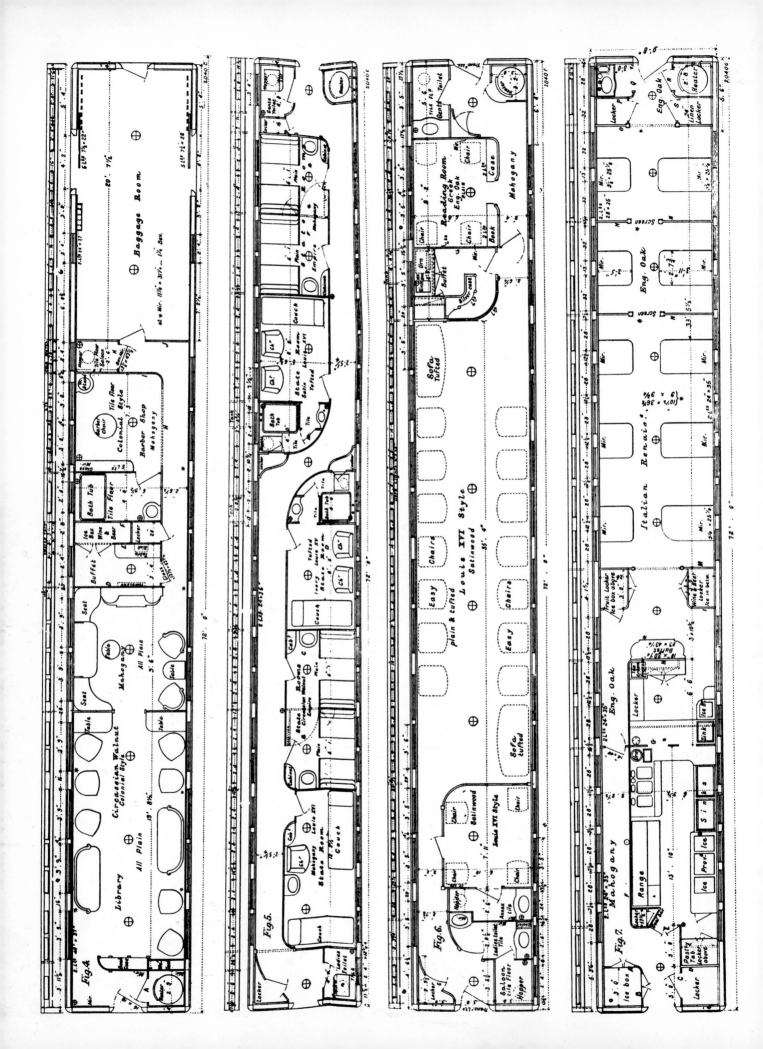

On the opposite page are shown floor plans of four Wagner-built palace cars which the firm exhibited at the Chicago World's Fair of 1893 and which may give some clue to the truly voluptuary dimensions of railroad travel at its apex of luxury and ostentation. At the top is a combination baggage—buffet—library car whose resources include a library paneled in Circassian walnut, a mahogany bar and buffet compartment, a tub bath and Colonial-style barbershop paneled in Honduran mahogany. Next comes a truly sumptuous stateroom car, its various private apartments finished in tufted satin in Louis XVI and Louis XI decor and Empire finish in ivory and satinwood. There is a twelve-foot master stateroom, two bathtubs and couches, built-in berths and other substantial furniture. Next is a club car with a Greek reading room paneled in English oak, a satinwood Louis XVI smoking room and a principal salon with outsize easy chairs and more satinwood panels. The dining car at the bottom is Italian Renaissance in mahogany and English oak with French bevel-edged mirrors above every table and the conventional lockers, pantries and kitchen offices. The doges of Venice, the Medici and the mansions of English nobility in Georgian times all contributed to rail travel in 1893 if you patronized the Wagner Palace cars.

In 1898 the fine dining car Tuileries rode between Montreal and Vancouver in the Canadian Pacific Railway's crack Imperial Limited. It was finished on its exterior with polished mahogany and rolled on wheels and axles of Krupp steel, "not one of which has ever failed." The menu listed Nova Scotia salmon, kippered black cod, English plum pudding, British Columbia peaches, Stilton cheese and Pommery's Extra Sec Champagne for $2.75 the pint. There were Havana cigars, Egyptian cigarets, a number of expensive table waters, and all milk, eggs and other dairy products came from C.P.R.'s own farms.

In the Early Ordovician age of railroading, dry hopper toilets made up with ornate exteriors what they lacked in sanitary satisfaction, but by the eighties they had yielded place to flush toilet facilities on most luxury equipment. Hand bowls in sleeping-car washrooms, even when only cold water was on tap, were usually marble-topped and on the fancier cars the fixtures were silver-plated with mahogany pump handles.

Before the coming of the vapor brakes—as George Westinghouse's patent was at first known —and the train line of compressed air from the engine that activated them, water for domestic uses aboard the cars was carried in roof tanks and distributed by gravity supplemented by hand pumps such as those depicted below and on the page opposite. No magazine editor in 1877, when these sketches appeared in Leslie's, would dream of such commonplace language as "washing up," and the below picture was inevitably and elegantly captioned "The Morning Ablutions." The end result was the same, and more or less unsatisfactory, as hot water had not yet been devised for the cars.

Legend maintains that in the early seventies when he was building the Rio Grande Railroad into the Rockies, General William Jackson Palmer was outraged when the Rocky Mountain News *stated that he had hot and cold running water aboard his private car* Nomad. *It sounded sybaritic to an old campaigner. Time might have mellowed the old gentleman by 1908 when Barney & Smith built the above lady's washroom aboard a Milwaukee sleeper with its assorted homely amenities of hairbrushes, whisk brooms and ice water, and he certainly would have approved the 1937 Union Pacific publicity shot at the right suggesting the pleasures to be encountered aboard the well-remembered* Forty-niner.

Legend emplaces the first bathtub aboard the car of Tom Scott of the Pennsylvania in the sixties. The fundamentals of bathing in transit could not have changed much by 1909 when Barney & Smith built plumbing such as this aboard the Milwaukee's buffet–observation cars Arbor Vitae, Alberton, Alenian, Alaska, Anaconda, Buena Vista, Columbia, Orient *and* Romadka. *They were assigned to Seattle service on the* New Olympian *trains.*

265

The three beautiful Milwaukee cars on the opposite page date from the years in which that carrier was dominated by Alexander ("The Great") Mitchell, Wisconsin moneybags and grandfather of the celebrated Captain Billy Mitchell. Their photographs are from glass plates taken at the Milwaukee shops in 1890 in the possession of Arthur D. Dubin and represent some of the rarest of all car collector's items. America and Alexandria were parlor cars with a single drawing room built at Dayton, Ohio, by Barney & Smith, Alexandria in 1879 and America in 1881. Each weighed 78,000 pounds. Mr. Dubin is of the mind that Alexandria was named for Banker Mitchell. Marion was a ten-section sleeper, built by Harlan & Hollingsworth at Wilmington, Delaware, in 1881 and weighed 71,600 pounds. The dining car interior so nicely set up on this page is one of a series numbered 4505 to 4516 built by Pullman in 1911 for the Milwaukee. They were lettered on the nameboards C.M. & P.S. and were designed for service in the New Olympian *trains over the road's new West Coast extension the Chicago, Milwaukee & Puget Sound.*

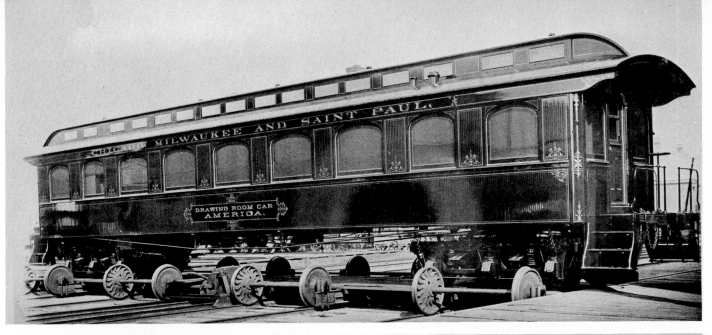

This fine equipment was built for the New Haven's all-Pullman, extra-fare Merchants Limited in 1905 with wooden sidewalls. When the first all-steel cars replaced them in 1913 they were painted to suggest wooden sheathing because passengers feared electrocution in case of accident on the newly electrified section west of New Haven.

268

Patrons of the New Haven's buffet cars in the era following 1905 when the equipment shown on the opposite page was built by Pullman for such crack Boston–New York runs as the Knickerbocker, Merchants, Colonial and Shore Line Express found a wine card recruited from the resources of the Boston firms of S. S. Pierce and Cobb, Bates & Yerxa and Park & Tilford in New York. There was Medford rum made by the Lawrence family and Krug's Private Cuvée champagne at $2.75 a half bottle for those afflicted with carsickness. Periodicals available included such devotional reading of the proper Bostonians as the Atlantic Monthly and Boston Evening Transcript and profane periodicals such as Munsey's, Scribner's and Puck. Hot filament light bulbs, the "hairpin in a bottle" of rural jest, activated by whimsical generators were supplemented by Pintsch. lamps. Passengers taking meals aboard the comely diner Lenox naturally found Boston scrod, Deerfoot sausages and Cotuit oysters staples of the menu.

NEW HAVEN RAILROAD

269

Let us for a moment turn back the hands of time to July 1921 at Forest Park, Illinois, a Chicago suburb, when Alfred W. Johnson took this photograph of a Minneapolis, St. Paul & Sault Ste. Marie northbound train on the Twin Cities run, No. 5, with an open observation car, it being the vacation season. Overtones of railroad romance, fixed in silver bromide, are implicit in the semaphores at the clear board, the straw hats of summer and the girl in white skirts and a cloche hat running for the train.

ALFRED W. JOHNSON

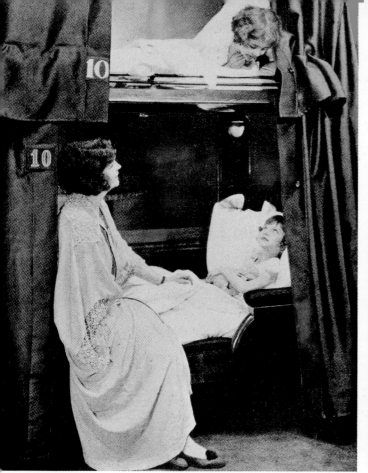

Early in the century, the Soo made a pitch for the North Woods vacation trade with travel folders depicting the joys of domestic occupancy of open berths and venerable gaffers reading from Youth's Companion *to* Buster Brown *types.*

The massively proportioned Barney & Smith–built parlor–observation car Fernie, *which ended its days on the* Redwing *on the run between Boston and Montreal, started life on the same Soo Line run as that shown on the page opposite.*

THREE PHOTOS: ARTHUR D. DUBIN COLLECTION

A new departure in sleeping car construction in an age when all-stateroom cars
were still in the unforeseeable future, was the Chicago, Burlington & Quincy's
home-built car No. 150. On one side of its aisle was a series of conventional open
sections with uppers and lowers, while across the way on the other side of the car
was ranged a suite of private staterooms for double occupancy enclosed in windows of frosted glass with leaded panels. The date of this novelty is unknown, but
the early eighties would seem probable.

273

THE WAGNER PALACE CARS.

EXHIBITED BY THE WAGNER PALACE CAR COMPANY, NEW YORK.

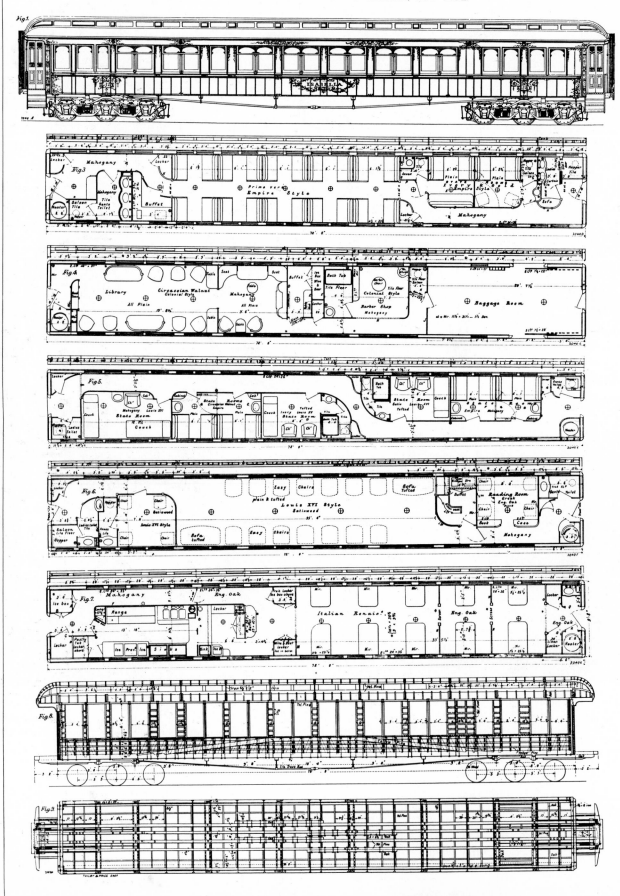

In 1891 Dr. W. Seward Webb, as president of the Wagner Palace Car-Building Company, as well as a Vanderbilt in-law, was important enough to rate the entire front page of the April 25 issue of Leslie's *as shown in this sketch. On the page opposite are elevations of* Isabella *and other Wagner luxury cars shown two years later at the Chicago World's Columbian Exposition in direct competition with the stunning exhibit of the Pullman Company.*

When the Virginia & Truckee Railroad in Nevada, one of the most celebrated and picturesque short lines of the Old West, discovered an old tool car in its shaded yards at Carson City (above), the management was inspired to rebuild it at the company shops as the club car Julia Bullette. It was probably the only short line in the record with a bona fide club car, and certainly it was the only one named to honor a woman of easy virtue, for Julia had been the leading courtesan in bonanza days of the Virginia City of the carrier's corporate name. On the opposite page is the Denver & Rio Grande's fine diner San Juan, as it came from the builders, and a dining car of coeval vintage, reduced at last to the estate of a wrecking-equipment car, a melancholy example of the downgrading that is the eventual fate of even the finest equipment.

PLUSH AND ORMOLU

WHETHER the palace car when it reached its fullest flowering in the eighties and nineties reflected the taste of its period or was instrumental in shaping it is a matter for the deliberations of The Moot, but it may be said with certainty that their first experience of luxury for many Americans was aboard the cars and that the first encounter with tangible beauty for many more was in viewing the diners, sleepers and parlor cars that the various carbuilders placed on view at Philadelphia in 1876 and Chicago in 1893.

That these two exhibitions exerted a profound influence on the national taste and manners is a truism, and there is no reason to doubt that the railroad exhibits that were an important and integral part of both did not in some measure find themselves reflected in the consciousness of the American people.

By the time the first Silver Palace cars and Pullmans were in service on the Overland route to California, the American people were already riding the steamcars to destinies of ever-increasing national opulence.

The Civil War, which antedated the Pacific Railroad, had already created some of the millionaires who in a few years were to be thick as autumn leaves on Vallombrosa, and the national tastes in splendor were being shaped by the New York mansions of Vanderbilts, Goulds, Belmonts and Stewarts. Men of substance liked to be surrounded with substantial things, and massive brownstone façades, marble mausoleums, ponderous mahogany furniture, splendid grand staircases and table services of heavy-gauge silver and gold were the order of the day for those who could afford them.

The time was yet in the future when Charles T. Yerkes, the traction magnate, was to plate the bronze doors of his Fifth Avenue residence with platinum and J. P. Morgan was to establish entire carpet factories to weave the rugs for his yacht *Corsair,* but good times were everywhere, now and then punctuated by roaring depressions. Wealth was making itself conspicuous, if not always comfortable, and the carbuilders, Pullman, Wagner, Mann and Woodruff, were not men to ignore a trend.

The sources of inspiration to which the manufacturers of palace cars turned for interior decor and outer appearances were two: the Mississippi River packets whose splendor had already given birth to the term "Steamboat Gothic" and the Victorian homes and their furnishings of the well-to-do element of American society.

With some justification it has been claimed by students of American folkways that, antedating the coming of the palace cars by roughly three decades, the Mississippi River packet with its magnificence of Gothic decor and luxurious appointments first pointed the way for all classes to live amidst rich and ornate surroundings. Undoubtedly there is a degree of validity in the claim. To be "as beautiful as a steamboat" was a commonplace comparison in the mid-nineteenth century vernacular. An admirer of P. T. Barnum's oriental palace at Bridgeport, Connecticut, reported it to be "as elegant in its appointments as a steamboat." A writer in *Harper's* in 1858 protested against the steamboat influence in domestic architecture. "The white and gold gorgeousness of the salon may be appropriate to the steamboats," he wrote, "but when it invades the sanctity of the domestic hearth, is it not time for the conservative classes to pause?" "The steamboats of the great American rivers are floating palaces" was a cliché among foreign travelers and commentators as early as the twenties. Undoubtedly the splendid interiors of cabins and salons with their crystal, grand pianos, gilt trim and brilliant illumination had an enormous impact on those who encountered them on the rivers, but the number of such impressionable travelers was microscopic when compared to the uncounted thousands who rode the palace cars daily in the noontide of railroading.

Obviously the differences in clearances and functional organization of railroad cars inhibited their designers from taking a leaf bodily from the book of the river steamers, but that they looked at them with longing eye and appropriated what they could is abundantly evident in the record.

What was undoubtedly the first of the long line of palace cars to come—it never got off the drawing board, but, no matter, it showed where the thinking of the time was directed—was in actual fact a steamboat to ride on wheels. In 1829 there was exhibited in Faneuil Hall, Boston, under Deacon Shem Drown's celebrated grasshopper weather vane, a land barge in model form that still staggers the imagination with its spacious concept. R. F. Morgan of Stockbridge, Massachusetts, sired this monster which had two decks or levels, on the bottom of which were a number of open berths while a spacious promenade occupied the top. There was also toward the stern of the top deck a sort of caboose or wheelhouse from which the captain would direct operations, and a handsome flagstaff with the American flag fixed to it rose another twenty feet or so.

The specifications called for a beam of Morgan's car of better than twenty feet and it was soon forgotten in a flood of more practicable projects, but it contained the seeds of the sleeping car, the observation platform and the way car for freight trains.

A certain number of Gothic details were actually incorporated in primeval cars that saw useful service. Gothic windows appear in the picture of many early day coaches and in 1867 Henry Hull, master carbuilder for the Chicago & North Western Railroad, came up with a director's car right out of one of Tennyson's moated granges or the Hudson River school of Gothic novelists. The directorate of the North Western was largely English at the time and English capital financed the road and Hull wanted his backers happy with a decor as suggestive as possible of Westminster Abbey. It had tall, narrow, pointed windows like a cathedral and leaded panes of colored glass let into the clerestory to diffuse a dim, religious light. From the two ends of the car, matching staircases led down to a main salon countersunk below the axle level of the trucks. The stairs had silver risers and the carpet was thick Axminster. On the exterior, Gothic lettering on the nameboards proclaimed the car's identity, and a sort of sheathing, forerunner of streamlining, concealed the running parts like a bishop's apron.

On a center table in the salon was a heavy silver service for ice water, strongly suggestive of sacramental vessels. The British milords who owned the North Western used the service for Scotch.

On the whole the pattern of early carbuilding was almost precisely that which was later to characterize the early years of the automobile. Impetuous individuality ran riot. Carbuilders were men of strong character and pronounced notions and they incorporated in their products all the evidences of individuality that were practicable and some that were not. It was possible to tell the product of one carbuilder from another just as it was to be possible at a later date to tell one make of motorcar from the next.

As late as the eighties the then flourishing Woodruff Sleeping & Parlor Coach Company built a double-ended parlor observation car for the Indianapolis & St. Louis Railroad that became known as "the rotunda car" because in the salons at either end it embellished the ceiling with a dome that extended a foot or so higher than the clerestory. The domes were lined with many-colored panes of glass.

Colonel William D'Alton Mann's cars, as related elsewhere in this volume, were characterized by sleeping compartments called "boudoirs," some of which contained original oil paintings by Italian artists and woodcarvings by artisans from the Black Forest.

The Silver Palace cars built for the Central Pacific by Jackson & Sharp had a patented mechanical brake which was wound up with a spring and which, when released, snapped the cars to such a sudden stop that passengers complained of injuries and carmasters of flattened wheels.

In the eighties, too, a ranking executive of the Old Colony Railroad out of Boston was a confirmed Anglophile and ordered two cars on the English model with side entrances to their several compartments and no through corridor. Train crews worked the car from footboards on the outside. The rear compartment on each of them was curved remarkably like the observation end, half a century later, of the *Empire State Express* and the *Forty-niner*.

Both Woodruff and American Car & Foundry outshopped observation cars whose solariums or observation salons were characterized by curved bulkheads as a variation on the conventional square car ends of Pullman and Wagner, and everyone tried to outdo the competition in the matter of splendid platform rails, tail gates and brake handles.

An authentic *rara avis* and collector's item among luxury passenger cars of the nineties was the Allen's Patent hotel car, specially designed to transport Bostonians to the Chicago World's Fair of 1893 and to house them while viewing the exposition. The cars were designed by E. G. Allen, general superintendent of the Old Colony Railroad, and were intended for charter under management by William H. Church

of Boston. The originating carrier was the Fitchburg Railroad, whence cars were routed west over a variety of connecting lines.

The arresting feature in Allen's car was the presence in the car's center of a galley, pantry and kitchen offices, so located to facilitate the service of meals in the eight staterooms accommodating thirty-two passengers at the car's either end. The compartments rode at conventional level on the top of six-wheel trucks, while the galley and its adjacent area were countersunk to the level of the journals in a manner reminiscent of the classic Gothic cathedral director's car on the Chicago & North Western in the sixties. The Allen hotel coaches were seventy-seven feet long over buffers and ten feet three inches wide and cost $20,000 each to build at the Jackson & Sharp works at Wilmington, Delaware. Probably they were the first appearance of split-level design in railroad cars for general occupancy and antedated the first Pullman duplex sleepers by more than forty years.

Each room had a lavatory with hot and cold running water, an icing tank for drinking water, a Pintsch gas light, incandescent electric light, then a great novelty, together with an electric fan, and a truly offbeat feature in the form of a "footbath set into the floor of each apartment." the last is a novelty that must have aroused envy in the breast of Colonel Mann, who designed many conveniences for his boudoir sleeping cars, but whose bathing facilities were limited to conventional tubs in his private hotel cars.

How the individual footbath functioned or, indeed, precisely what may have been its useful function was not disclosed in Allen's literature, but it is pleasant to envision the westbound Bostonian threading the snowy passes of the Berkshire Hills, his eyes fixed on the distant prospect of the Great White City, while with rolled-up trousers he rode with his feet immersed in thermal waters set in the floor of his compartment.

The resourceful Allen of footbath immortality also designed several compartment sleeping cars for service on the New Haven's Shore Line run between New York and Boston, but unhappily neither floor plan nor photograph has survived. The all-room sleeping cars of both Pullman and Wagner were finding wide acceptance by the early nineties, and undoubtedly the New Haven was happy to patronize home talent in

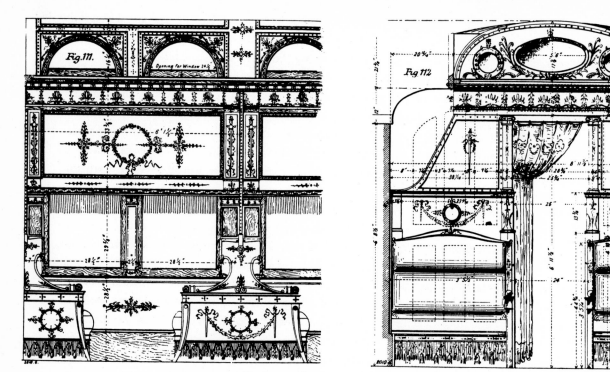

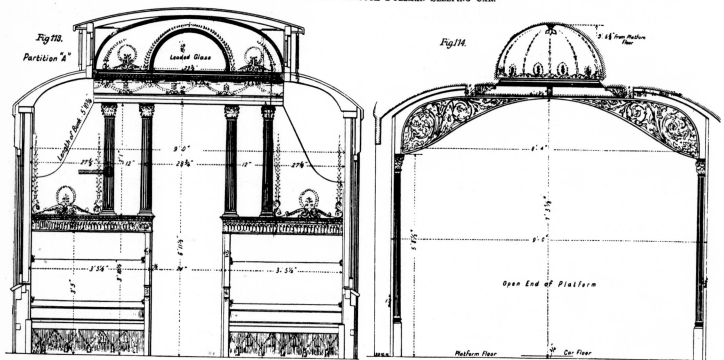

TRANSVERSE SECTIONS THROUGH PULLMAN SLEEPING CAR.

TRANSVERSE SECTIONS OF PULLMAN OBSERVATION CAR.

the person of the Old Colony's versatile superintendent.

The Monarch Palace cars, many of which saw service on Canadian carriers, were boldly marked "First Class" on either platform in defiance of the edict that railroad travel in America was a classless society.

Pullman equipped its best cars for many years with laminated paper wheels, and the cars built by E. C. Knight had an upper berth with cords at its four corners which snapped the entire arrangement up to the ceiling, sometimes with the occupant in it.

In exterior decor, cars had as much individual personality as they possessed inside. Although the practice of painting animals and landscapes on the sidewalls had largely disappeared before the palace cars came along, the private Wagner of Commodore Vanderbilt, well into the sixties, had Niagara Falls in full color on one of its outside panels and the Hudson River by moonlight on another.

The aforementioned Monarch cars were painted a rich chocolate brown with white trim; Mann Boudoirs were seal brown with black end posts and brilliant ochre roofs; vehicles of the Jerome Marble Hunting Car Company of Worcester, Massachusetts, were wine-colored with lavish gold trim and lettering; Woodruff painted his cars in several two-tone combinations, but the most frequent was plum color and old-gold lettering. Various individual railroads contributed to the diversity of color schemes, the Milwaukee with its traditional orange and black, the Baltimore & Ohio with royal blue and gold, the Pennsylvania with Tuscan red and cream, and the New York & New England with its "White Train," which the photographs show to be something less than snowy.

But if private enterprise asserted itself in a variety of individual characteristics, there were certain basic or fundamental considerations which held the undivided attention of one and all the carbuilders, and the greatest of these was elegance. Almost all the manufacturers of luxury equipment had "Palace" in their incorporated title and most of them did their best to live up to its implications. Colonel Mann's marquetry work might turn out to be merely applied patterns of paint and, as critical travelers sometimes commented, the silver on the Silver Palace cars was usually just plain white metal, but topnotchers in the business, notably Pullman, Wagner and Jackson & Sharp, had no traffic with shoddy. The materials they used were superlative, the workmanship expert and the luxury authentic.

Cabinetwork was the basic excellence upon which all other de luxe appointments depended; for its executing, a great variety of woods, some rare and exotic, others relatively commonplace but specially suited, were brought from all over the world—mahogany, cedar, cyprus, olivewood, primavera, rosewood, satinwood and vermilion wood. The crowning glory of the Pullman plant both at Detroit and later at Pullman was the famous Marquetry Room where a corps of about twenty skilled craftsmen that Pullman himself had recruited in the Black Forest produced the remarkable berths, panels, ceilings and doorways for which the product of the firm was famous. For many years no two Pullmans were built to exactly the same pattern and every sleeper and diner was a masterpiece of unique design.

After the turn of the century this scheme of things, of course, came to an end and the assembly line took its place, but for many years the hallmark of Pullman and, to a lesser extent, Wagner carbuilding was the individual character imparted to every car outshopped.

Legend at Pullman maintains that no preliminary sketches or blueprints were used by the artisans in the Marquetry Room, but that each car interior was fashioned extempore, with the individual talents and special expertise of the workers fused and gathered in the completed product. Be that as it may, the fame of Pullman's cabinet department was world-wide and when Fred Bonfils, the Colorado newspaper publisher, wished to build himself a new and specially opulent mansion in Denver, he journeyed in person to Chicago to ask the Pullman management for the loan of a team of woodworkers. Gene Fowler, who vouched for the story, did not add if the favor was granted.

Once the basic woodwork had been evolved, skilled upholsterers took over installing Brussels, Axminster and Turkey carpets underfoot and an almost incredible variety of fabrics and designs for seat covers and headboards. On special and exhibition cars this was sometimes rare petit point, cut velvet, plush or velours, tufted, roached and pleated. Elaborately hand-tooled leather, occasionally white or eggshell, went into smoking car and dining car seats and banquettes. Curtains in passageways, portières to the various compartments and window drapes were of richly colored velvet trimmed with ball fringe or tassels. Valances around the bottoms of the berths were equally expensive and enduring. In the earlier Pullmans the night curtains separating berths—which came in later years to be a uniform green baize—were frequently wine-colored or royal blue with gold borders, fit for a senatorial toga. They were supported by rods of burnished brass in ornate designs and with intricate functional aspects.

Ceilings and transoms were enlivened with beautifully executed patterns in harmonious colors and lighting fixtures, as long as coal oil or Pintsch gas was used, and came in an amazement of designs in crystal, etched and frosted glass. Conductors' signal cords running through the cars were of woven material depending in ornate catenaries from hangers made of multicolored fabrics.

Period designs in which the entire decor of a sleeper or lounge car re-created a classic style were frequent: Chinese and English Chippendale, Romanesque and Byzantine, English baronial, Egyptian, Renaissance baroque, Spanish mission and Provincial. Elaborate grillwork provided ventilation at strategic places, and the hallmark of Wagner sleepers for a sequence of cars was a little colonnade of exquisitely turned onyx pillars with Doric pediments supporting the clerestory at each end of the car.* Winged lions formed the endboards of lower berths, and French mirrors abounded. For a time there was a vogue for mirrored recesses in the car walls of diners in which ferns and flowers were placed. Some Pullman buffet cars in the most rococo period housed collections of expensive delft chinaware in locked glass breakfronts and sideboards.

In the washrooms the fixtures ran the gamut of the plumbing manufacturer's art. Toilet bowls were fres-

* The early nineties saw a considerable vogue for onyx for decorative and structural use, and in his cars of 1893 Wagner was very much *au courant* with public taste. Sumptuous effects were achieved with great expanses of Mexican onyx in soda fountains, barrooms and other de luxe public premises. The most opulent surviving example today is probably the lobby of the Brown Palace Hotel in Denver.

coed with floral wreaths and had mahogany seats and seat covers. Open plumbing was partially concealed behind gold-painted grilles. On a few general service cars there were silver plumbing fixtures, and gold and silver were commonplace on private cars. Hand bowls were of travertine, Carrara and occasionally onyx. Adjustable mirrors were a boon to masculine shavers in the days of the open straight razor. Kitchen lucifers were handy in heavy bronze matchsafes.

The evolution and eventual acceptance of private stateroom space aboard the palace cars followed with remarkable fidelity the same progress from common sleeping accommodations to cabins for limited or family occupancy on the Mississippi River packets that antedated the universal railroad by several decades. In the original steamers that plied the Mississippi in the early years of steam navigation, from 1814 to 1820, common cabins for ladies' and gentlemen's nighttime occupancy were the nearly universal rule. Two tiers of berths, almost precisely like those of the first Woodruff, Wagner and Pullman sleepers, were screened off for a degree of privacy in retiring and dressing, and common washrooms served for the niceties of both male and female toilet.

Shortly, however, the luxury trade began demanding private sleeping rooms. On the Mississippi run between St. Louis and New Orleans, staterooms and individual cabins began appearing in ever-increasing numbers. In 1814 the packet *Buffalo* boasted four private staterooms; the second *New Orleans* in the following year advertised thirteen staterooms with two berths each, and in 1818 the *Volcano* and the *General Pike* contained fourteen private cabins each. The luxury of appointments and fittings in these comfortable apartments kept pace with their increasing availability. Fine linen served as bedding. Gay printed material was at the windows. Coal-oil lamps in expensive crystal swung in gimbals, and Axminster carpets were underfoot.

By 1841 the open berth or sleeping section on boats with any pretentions to quality had virtually disappeared and staterooms were as commonly accepted as they were to be years later on the steamcars.

The pioneer role of the river steamers in establishing the amenities of public travel may further be discerned in the circumstance that, as aboard the cars, it was found necessary to admonish the first river passengers against retiring with their boots on.

Beyond all doubt the boudoir cars of the versatile Colonel Mann paved the way for all-room cars on the drawing boards of Pullman, Wagner and American Car & Foundry. The Mann cars were nicely designed to take advantage of the available space and provided a degree of privacy that had hitherto been available only in the single drawing room carried on conventional open section sleepers.

By the time of the 1893 World's Fair at Chicago both Pullman and Wagner were promoting all-room cars as well as compartmentent cars in various combinations, often observation sleepers with four or six staterooms ahead and an observation or smoking salon at the platform end. These were invariably equipped with standard upper and lower berths that were retractable for daytime use and made down for night occupancy. The permanent built-in berth or brass bed was still exclusive with private cars and the first all-bedroom car with a fixed single lower berth did not appear until 1910, when the New Haven introduced a Pullman-built corridor sleeping car, each room of which had a fixed bed, night table and movable chair.

Over the years and as long as open sections were being built, one single property of the sleeping cars remained immutable in its original form, without change or improvement either in style or function. This was the green net hammock the porter strung across the windows to contain the occupant's possibles, his shirt and collar, underwear and socks and perhaps his trousers. They were subject to no improvement and maintained continuity with the past while all around them changed. It may be noted that the same item of furniture remained static over the decades on ocean steamers and that suspended net hammocks, handy to berths, bunks and bedsteads, were part of the *Titanic* when it sank in 1912.

The palace sleeping cars of the Victorian or Chester A. Arthur period might be thought fussy by today's standards no matter how their elegance might fascinate contemporaries, but what shall be said of the public or non-revenue cars of the age, the diners, club cars, lounges, smokers and buffets? Here the decorative imagination of carbuilders ran most uninhibitedly amok amidst arcadian bowers, booths, alcoves, opera boxes, barricades, and compartments, in thickets of potted plants and jungles of palm trees, pouffed, quilted and tasseled, decorated in parquetry and marquetry and with a profusion of *bibelots* and *boiseries* to make the head swim and the senses reel.

The dining cars of the nineties were really something and so were the lounge cars. Here the carbuilders drew most lavishly for their inspiration on the Mississippi River steamers and the wealthy properties of the private mansions of the period with liberal infusions of hotel decor and the appointments of Delmonico's and the Fifth Avenue Hotel.

Baths, both tub and shower, barbershops, manicures, lady's maids, valet service, news tickers, libraries, current periodicals and hotel and railroad directories, smokers accessories and, of course, the fullest possible facilities for sluicing and gentling the patrons with wines and strong waters were taken for granted on all luxury trains of the era. The presence of full hotel service was the accepted thing and the only difference between individual trains was the degree of its excellence and comprehensive scope.

On some of the earliest transcontinental trains there were parlor organs, presumably dedicated to devotional music on the Sabbath but as often as not devoted to profane compositions executed by musical passengers. Pianos appeared in a few private cars, notably those rented by opera stars and theater performers such as Paderewski and Fritzi Scheff, but until the age of radio, music was generally in abeyance on the cars.

Parlor cars, since they presumably were dedicated to feminine travelers, the elderly or ailing, were pervaded by genteel touches of decor and convenience. Here the cuspidor, elsewhere universal, was banished in favor of tufted hassocks and footstools. The elegant antimacassar was spread against the prevailing hair oil of male patrons, and ball fringe draperies and portières flourished in particularly rich profusion.

For a time there was a vogue for specially sequestered sections for parlor car patrons of uncommon diffidence or retiring nature and all sorts of opera boxes, paddocks and alcoves shielded by potted verdure and velvet curtains from the common gaze appeared on the *Pennsylvania Limited,* the *Albany Day Express* and the *Colonial.* In them starched parlor maids served tea at the appropriate hour and women in Gibson Girl hairdos reclined on overstuffed sofas in attitudes of well-bred relaxation while perusing the *Atlantic Monthly* or, daringly, *Collier's*. Here, too, gentlemen of refined taste might be expected to wear gloves against the possibility of soiled hands. Traveling caps of risible pattern replaced the top hat, which was carefully deposited in a frilled metal baggage rack of frivolous design and inconsequential capacity.

Gentlemen might not smoke in the principal apartment on the parlor cars, although there were smoking rooms specially provided on most, and if they took whisky it must not be in quantities calculated to encourage boisterous conduct. Poland Water and other mineral beverages were more recommended.

Smokers, in the days of the palace cars, were obviously for men and massive in the grand manner of Eastlake or the Union League in New York. Perhaps

the finest example of its kind was *Marchena*, which Pullman exhibited at the Chicago Fair of 1893 and which boasted what was probably the most resolutely splendid barbershop anywhere outside Potter Palmer's hotel, where the floor was inlaid with a mosaic of silver dollars and ranch hands in Montana and Texas dreamed of the day when they might visit Chicago and see for themselves the wonders of "The Garden of Eden" as the proprietor of these tonsorial parlors sometimes called them.

The barbershop on *Marchena* was conducted under a dome of many-colored glass, while mirrors at all angles reflected the patron in his every aspect and façade as whiskers were singed and Florida water applied. Customers reclined in a Kochs Patent chair upholstered in finest tan leather, and the chalice in which shampoos were achieved was sheltered under a mosque-like pagoda with arabesques in beaten copper. The shelf where unguents and patent hair restoratives were arrayed when these palatial premises were activated was inlaid with gold marquetry work and might have served in a queen's boudoir. The entire domed superstructure was supported at the corners of the apartment by pillars of Honduran mahogany capped with pediments of black onyx. It seemed nigh to sacrilege to commission so trivial a service as a mere once-over-lightly from the graduate of the Harvard of barber schools who presided over this cathedral of Ed Pinaud.

Elsewhere, *Marchena* was equally as splendid. Its armchairs upholstered in the finest product of the tanneries of Peabody, Massachusetts, might have served as ducal *fauteuils* or the cural chairs of Roman proconsuls. Underfoot was an Axminster of special design as thick as a stockyards *filet mignon*. Mazda electrical bulbs gleamed on the carven beams that shaped a noble ceiling like lights on a theater proscenium. Handsomely leaded circular lunettes lined the clerestory like portholes, giving the conveyance a nautical air that would have had the approval of J. P. Morgan, a notable yachtsman of the time.

As a matter of fact, it did. Morgan chartered the car on one occasion, along with several sleepers and a diner, to take a number of clergymen to an Episcopal congress in San Francisco. He took the precaution, having heard about Utah, of having the baggage compartment fitted with wine bins for his favorite Rhine, a Schloss Johannisberger Auslese 1872 that his agent had picked up for him at auction in Berlin for $35 a bottle, gold. The *San Francisco Chronicle* when confronted with this statistic figured that each glass of the stuff set the old gentleman back $4. To supervise its proper service and that of other refreshments for the ecclesiastical outing, Morgan took along as his personal major-domo Louis Sherry. Altogether it was a safari that lived up to *Marchena's* every implication of magnificence.

The impact of the palace car on the general imagination is not only reflected in the newspaper and periodical press of the time, but also in the accounts of their American experiences of foreign visitors of importance. There were certain American institutions to be experienced, and a trip of short or long duration on one of the nation's crack railroad trains was emphatically one of them. Many cultivated foreigners overlooked more salutary aspects of a young and growing country to take a dim view of American society, American hotels and American culinary habits. Rudyard Kipling was especially outraged by the Palmer House, which he found to be "a huge hall of tessellated marble crowded with people talking about money and spitting about everywhere," but he had nothing but admiration for the great transcontinental flyers which took him to California swiftly, surely and in much the atmosphere of a London gentleman's club.

"The train is what is called a limited," wrote another visiting Englishman of the *Pennsylvania Express* in 1892, "which means that it consists of four Pullman sleeping cars, a smoking car, a dining car, an observation car and a composite car, the last named having a compartment for mail, luggage and sleeping berths for the conductors. The smoking car has a reading room for the passengers, library, easy chairs, writing and card tables and a barber's shop. The traveler can have his hair cut, curled and shampooed for half a dollar, a shave for a quarter or a bath at the rate of forty miles an hour for seventy-five cents. The cars are designated palace-cars and fully deserve the title for they are indeed traveling palaces where one can obtain all the comforts of home. . . . The conductors who rendered me great service are smart and dignified in appearance, courteous in their behavior and what is most surprising, proof against tips, the offer of which would be regarded as an insult."

That George M. Pullman, and to a somewhat lesser degree, his imitators and competitors, contributed materially to the national well-being and taste for comfort is an inescapable conclusion to any survey of the part the palace cars played in the noontide of their riding. That they may have been overdecorated is only the sterile judgment of an era that has produced nothing half so fine in any field of transport, decor or the amenities of living. Or, it may be added, a dimension to the language.

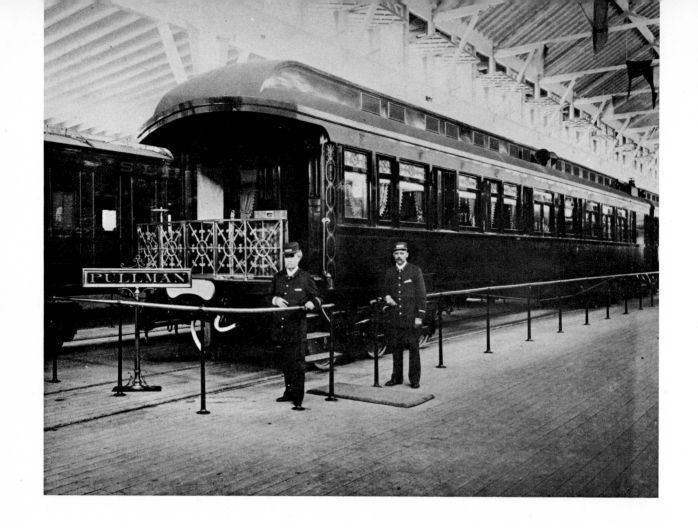

Portrait Gallery From The

In 1893 the World's Columbian Exposition, celebrating the four-hundredth anniversary of the discovery of America, turned the eyes of the nation to the shores of Lake Michigan, where "The Great White City" had arisen to give the lie to the widespread belief that Chicago was merely a pandemonium of commerce or porkopolis of profit devoted exclusively to "cash, cussing and cuspidors." It has remained a golden memory in the American consciousness ever since; the giant Ferris Wheel, the Court of Honor, the Midway Plaisance, the gyrations of Little Egypt, Edison's Kinetoscope and the architectural innovations of Louis Sullivan have become part of the national lexicon of happy yesterdays. Of all the exhibits

Chicago World's Fair 1893

mounted there, none overshadowed those of the railroads then at what may perhaps be termed the high-water mark of their picturesqueness, prosperity and prestige. Both Pullman and Wagner were aware of the rich potentialities of the Chicago Fair as a setting in which to display their finest merchandise and most voluptuous devisings to the best possible advantage. The year 1893 also marked the spring tide of ornate decor in passenger equipment and some of the cars that were admired by millions in that now distant time are shown on the following pages.

PULLMAN STANDARD

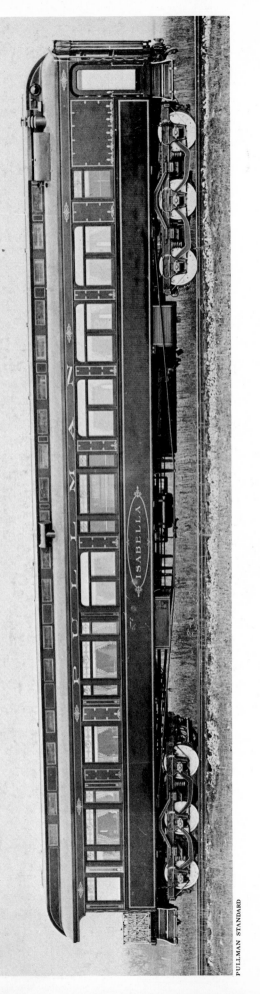

Confusion reigned supreme at the Chicago World's Fair of 1893 as a result of the decision of both Pullman and Wagner to exhibit a car named in honor of the royal husband of Queen Isabella, as well as a car named for the Queen of Spain herself. Two Isabellas, therefore, and two Ferdinands were on view to addle the wits of visitors who knew nothing of the rivalry of the two carbuilding firms or of the admiration at Wagner which prompted the close and sometimes slavish imitation of everything that Pullman did. Let

the reader take a firm grasp on himself and know that on these two pages are depicted the exterior, an interior and the ground plan of the Pullman combination sleeping–observation car Isabella, one of the most ornate palace cars ever outshopped and one which gloried, among its other wonderments and conveniences, in a full-length bathtub. The car was later renamed Pacific for general service and carried McKinley's body to Canton, Ohio, after his assassination.

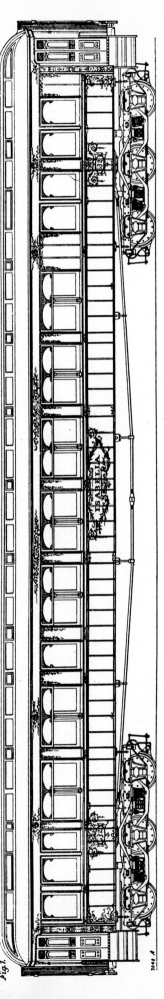

Fig. 1.

The page opposite is devoted to details from the collection of Arthur D. Dubin of the Wagner sleeping car Isabella *shown at the Chicago Fair of 1893 and not to be confused with Pullman's* Isabella *on the preceding pages. The Wagner sleeper embraced ten open sections, two staterooms and a buffet, and was as ornately conceived, in its own Wagnerian style, as its opposite number on the Pullman tracks. On this page is the interior of another, but unidentified, Wagner open section sleeper, the hallmark of whose manufacture is the little colonnade of exquisitely turned onyx pillars in the clerestory at the far end of the car. In addition to the two* Isabellas, *Wagner and Pullman each had a* Ferdinand *at the Fair, but here confusion was lessened to an appreciable degree because Wagner's* Ferdinand *was a dining car, Pullman's, an all-compartmented sleeper.*

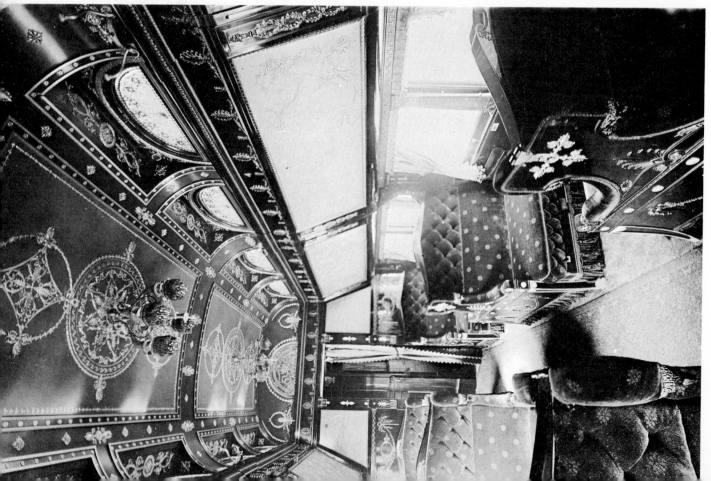

Both exhibits at Chicago in 1893, Pullman's and Wagner's, represented the high-water mark in ornate and lavish decoration of the palace cars of the rival firms. Opposite, on the left, are the open berth fronts of the sleeping sections of Pullman's combination sleeper–observation car Isabella, *while at the right is a vista of the staterooms, opened en suite, of the same company's all-compartmented sleeper* Ferdinand. *On this page is a suite approximating in decor the furnishings usually designated as "bridal" from the Pullman sleeper* America, *a splendor of quilted upholstery, fringed valances and bevel-edged mirrors.*

Throughout the latter half of the nineteenth century in America the bridal suite was the feature of all but commercial hotels, and those at resorts favored by the newly wed such as Niagara Falls and Atlantic City had several. Railroads, too, scheduled bridal accommodations on through trains, specially ornate bowers that could be occupied by drummers or less romantic patrons when a bridal couple wasn't available. Vanderbilts and Whitneys usually managed a private car, but less exalted lovers were happy with stateroom suites such as that of the Pullman sleeper Gladiolus shown opposite. In time bridal suites became so much a property of humor and their occupants so conspicuous that they fell from favor and became presidential or executive suites. Today they have almost disappeared from the hotel keeper's lexicon. On this page the irreverent Police Gazette has fun with the dilemma of a newly married couple aboard the cars who were sundered by a broken stateroom lock.

296

PAGE OPPOSITE: PULLMAN STANDARD

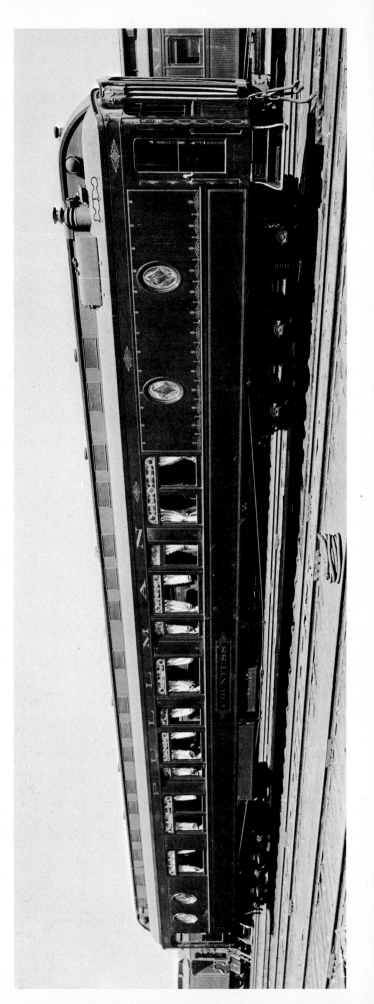

Among the most opulent parlor cars ever out-shopped by Pullman were Maud and Countess, the latter having started life as the Chicago World's Fair car Santa Maria. The truly staggering interior decor of Countess, shown here, recommended it to a generation of travelers to whom luxury was accustomed and who wanted the best of everything in outsize lots. It ran on the Baltimore & Ohio between Washington and Jersey City for many years.

Here is another and
full-length interior
view of Santa Maria,
Pullman's parlor
car exhibit at
the World's Columbian
Exposition of 1893
at Chicago.
Santa Maria *cost*
a staggering $38,365.85
and later, renamed
Countess, *went to the*
Baltimore & Ohio
to run in that
carrier's princely
limited,
the Royal Blue.

PULLMAN STANDARD

Just to show what it could do in the way of investing the lowly baggage car with grandeur, the Pullman Company for the Chicago Exposition of 1893 built Marchena, which was paneled in primavera and, in addition to more conventional appointments, included a tub bath, buffet for bar service and perhaps the fanciest barber chair in the record under a dome of multicolored glass in the center of the car.

Fig.1.

Fig.2.

SMOKING ROOM

BARBER SHOP

TILED FLOOR & WAINSCOT
BATH ROOM

BATH TUB

Dome

BAGGAGE ROOM

HEATER

LOUNGE

SETTEE

CHAIRS

SEAT

SEAT

SEAT

BUFFET

GENTLEMENS
TOILET

Anything in the decorative line omitted from Marchena *by the woodworkers at Pullman's Marquetry Room was purely accidental. When placed in general service the car so fetched the elder J. P. Morgan that, after prudently building wine racks in its baggage compartment for the transport of his favorite Moselle, he included it in the consist of a five-car private train he rented to take a group of Anglican bishops to an Episcopal conference in San Francisco.*

303

In the golden age of rail travel almost every main-line through train with any claim to distinction advertised maid and manicure, valet and barber service. On the page opposite is undoubtedly the most ornate train barbershop ever designed. It was a feature of Pullman's car Marchena, exihibited at the Chicago Fair of 1893, while at the left is an only slightly less handsome equivalent built by Pullman in 1911 in a club car for the Chicago & North Western. Below: in a more modern decor, the barber of the Burlington's Aristocrat practices his calling on the run between Chicago and Denver in the thirties.

PULLMAN STANDARD   IVAN DMITRI

Even after seven decades it is possible to see why the dining car La Rabida *bugged the eyes of visitors to Chicago where it was part of the Pullman exhibit at the World's Columbian Exposition of 1893. Its Edison Mazda electric lights were sensational and, in the picture on this page, taken later than the one opposite, it had been found expedient to use even more of them in the wall brackets originally intended for supplementary use of Pintsch gas only. So successful was* La Rabida *as a prestige leader that Pullman outshopped several closely similar diners immediately thereafter.*

After its success at the Chicago World's Fair in 1893, Pullman's diner La Rabida was made available to private charter and one of the first to hire it was George Gould whose sister Anna was being courted by the French adventurer Boni de Castellane. Dinner en route during a protracted tour of the United States and Canada was a function, de Castellane noted in his diary, for which all members of the party scrupulously dressed in full evening attire.

PULLMAN STANDARD   DON BUZZARD

Over the years, Illinois Central diners have been staffed by chefs genuinely schooled in the expertise of *Deep South* cuisine and travelers seldom forgot a dinner aboard the Panama Limited or Green Diamond. *The cafe–smoker of the twenties between St. Louis and Chicago (below) reflected the individuality and nice appoints also found in the cafe–parlor cars, as suggested on the page opposite.*

TWO PHOTOS: ILLINOIS CENTRAL RAILROAD

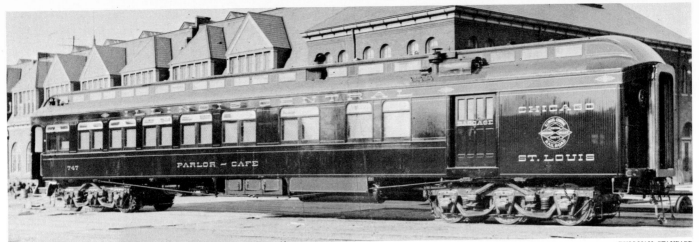

Strongly reminiscent of the interior decor of Pullmans built for English and Continental railways rather than conventional cafe cars on American carriers, the Illinois Central's parlor–cafe cars by Pullman for use on the Chicago–St. Louis daylight runs were distinctive and stylish showpieces for an uncommonly stylish railroad.

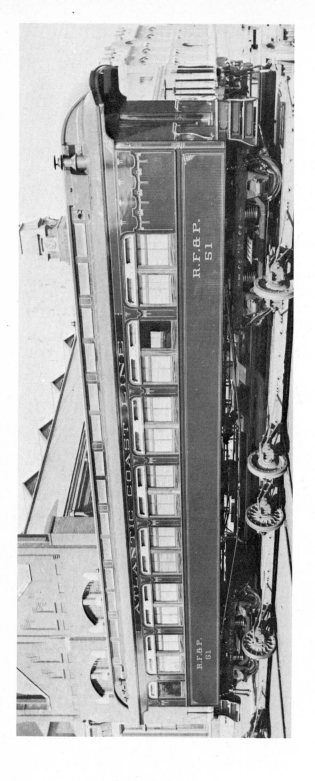

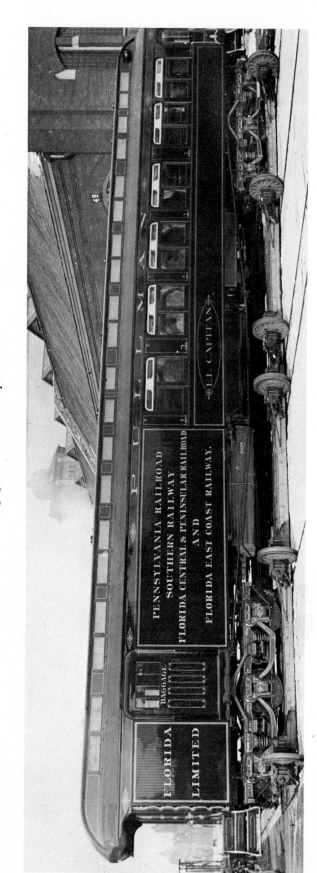

Venetian blinds, rattan seats and other concessions to tropical climate were part of the equipment of through coaches of the Florida East Coast in the nineties. This one had its Washington connection over the Richmond, Fredericksburg & Potomac.

With the opening up of Florida in the nineties, resorts along the Flagler system were soon serviced in winter by through trains from New York—such as the Florida Limited running over the connecting lines listed on the combination baggage–smoker El Capitan.

Three full decades before air conditioning was thought of, trains in the Deep South and especially the luxury runs to Florida resorts during the winter months did what they could to encourage keeping cool. The seats on this Florida East Coast parlor car assigned to the Florida Limited out of Jacksonville had rattan-covered armchairs instead of the conventional plush of other climates. It was the heyday of the palm-leaf fan.

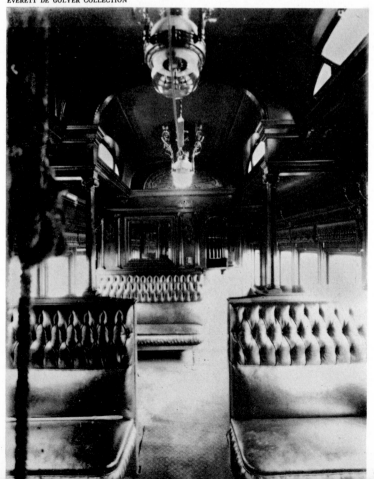

The beautiful parlor–observation car Undine built by Pullman and assigned to service on the Eastern division, was finished in Honduran mahogany with fourteen chairs, seats for nineteen and restorative facilities at a richly paneled buffet. Below it, at the far left, is an unidentified club car interior from the collection of Everett De Golyer and next to it the smoking compartment from the Pullman parlor car Maud. On the top at the right is another unidentified club car interior, known to be by Pullman, however, and at the right the lavish smoking compartment from the combination baggage and buffet car Minneapolis.

FOUR PHOTOS: PULLMAN STANDARD

Between 1883 when Pullman foresaw a trend and outshopped the all-room palace sleeper Herkimer (see opposite page) and 1912 when it built Piute (opposite and above) for assignment to the Santa Fe's extra-fare De Luxe of fragrant memory, carbuilding had seen much change. Companion cars to Piute, named Pima, Pampa, Ponca, Pinto and Prado and known as "the brass bed cars" were ordered for the De Luxe between 1912 and 1918 and, excepting only the New Haven's similar cars on the Boston–New York run, were the most luxurious general service sleepers ever built in the United States. When the De Luxe with its $25 service charge and free

orchids was suspended, the Piute series cars were used in the same carrier's California Limited, which, until the advent of the Chief, was flagship of the Sante Fe fleet. The original six stateroom cars were supplemented by eight additional all-stateroom varnish in 1920, named in a burst of patriotism for battlefields in the First World War: Belleau Wood, Meuse, Montdidier, Soissons, Somme, St. Mihiel, St. Quentin, and Vimy Ridge. The first six were dismantled in 1939 and the remainder of this remarkable series were used in special movements until 1943. They had made much railroad history.

317

Few properties of nineteenth-century travel assumed the dimensions as status symbols of the railroad parlor car for well-placed persons on daylight journeys. On the page opposite, from the collection of Everett De Golyer, is the fine parlor car Delaware *built in the eighties for the Chicago & Atlantic, the western extension of the Erie, by Jackson & Sharp.* Delaware *boasted gas illumination, to judge from the tank, and the proud imprimatur of the builder on each truck. On this page is the interior of the parlor car* Maud, *a Pullman masterpiece of the nineties whose every fringe and tassel bespoke travel à la mode and genteel elegance. Wide windows, thick rubber springing and expensive carpets made it comfortable as well as stylish.*

EVERETT DE GOLYER COLLECTION   PULLMAN STANDARD

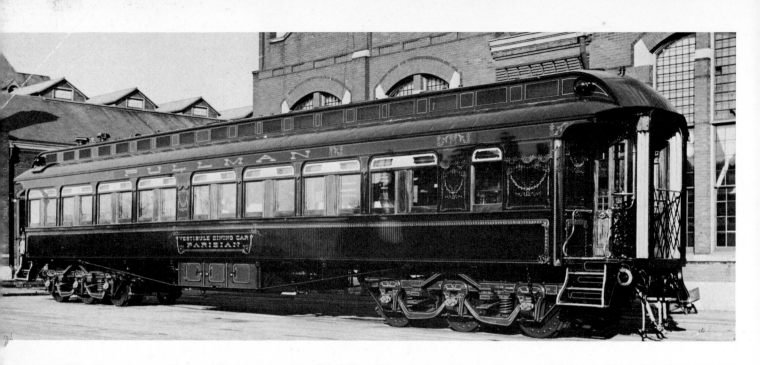

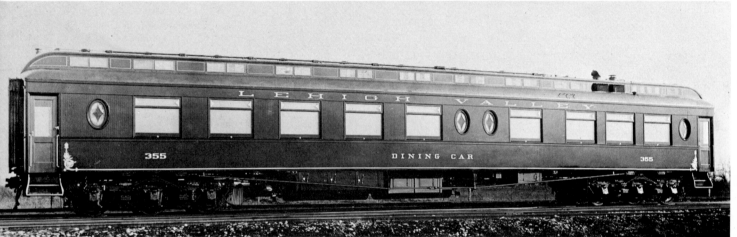

The diner Parisian, *shown here in its interior and on the page opposite, was Pullman restaurant car decor at its most sumptuous. Its white upholstery proved impractical and was later replaced by elaborately tooled Spanish leather, as shown elsewhere in this volume. Above: the chef of the* Chief *presides at a buffet of true Santa Fe bounty.*

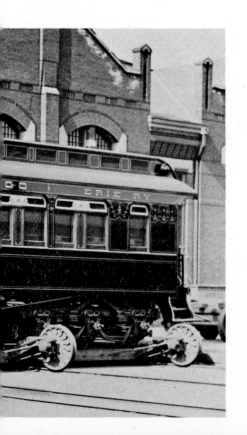

The dining car Shohola *was built by Pullman specially for service in the Erie's flagship on the New York–Chicago run, the* Erie Limited, *while the competing Lehigh Valley between Jersey City and Buffalo ran diner No. 255 in its crack* The Black Diamond. *The car seated thirty patrons, five tables of four each and five of two; the photo shows the car as it was originally built. Later the vestibules were closed in at both ends to make it accessible only from adjoining cars. The car was remarkable among diners of its period because it had a washroom, a convenience that included a washstand but no water closet.*

321

The stately sleeper Majestic (left) built by Pullman in 1899 contained six sections, a drawing room and four staterooms and immediately went into service on the Chicago & Alton's Midnight between Chicago and St. Louis, passing partly over the right of way that had carried Pullman's first experimental sleeper half a century earlier.

Pullman built the parlor car Czarina as Lot No. 2258 to the specifications of the Baltimore & Ohio, where it was placed in service between New York and Washington in the Royal Blue *wearing the royal-blue and gold livery favored by the "Mother of Railroads." The beautiful observation–compartment sleeper* Louisiana *(below) was built by Pullman specially for its exhibit at the St. Louis World's Fair and was reportedly among the most costly ever outshopped for general service anywhere. Twenty years later* Louisiana *turned up in Cuba, where, together with a number of other observation sleepers, it was part of a luxury tour train available to parties wishing to see the island in the grand manner without putting up at hotels for the night.*

PULLMAN STANDARD

ARTHUR D. DUBIN COLLECTION

For fully two decades after they were first placed in service on the railroads of the land, dining cars and every detail of their conduct and management made fascinating reading for patrons of newspapers and magazines. Editors sent their best reporters to ride aboard them and their ranking artists to depict interiors and the passengers who peopled them. Here a staff artist for Leslie's was inspired to draw "The Chef in His Glory" while riding aboard a Union Pacific train to the Far West. The two beautiful Pullmans on the page opposite suggest that granger-state passengers admired to take the air and view the countryside while waiting for a table.

325

Visitors to the Centennial Exposition at Phila-delphia in 1876 arrived in style aboard Pennsyl-vania Railroad parlor cars such as this.

The splendid vestibuled library–compartment car Tryphena was built by Pullman at a cost of $17,034 as sister to Tryphosa and promptly went into service on the Colorado Midland between Denver and Salt Lake–Ogden. It had eight sleeping sections, an elaborate observation lounge with four sets of bayed windows through which to admire the Rocky Mountain scenery up Ute Pass and some of the most ornate luggage racks overhead ever to be devised by Pullman artisans.

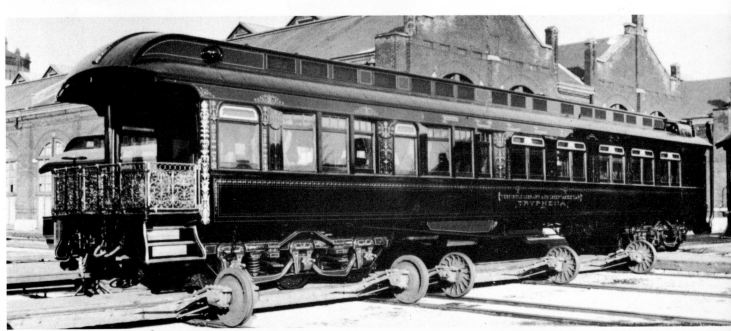

Pullman's bridal suites had no monopoly of cream and gold decor as is suggested by the truly magnificent stateroom suite aboard a New York Central Wagner sleeper at the Chicago World's Fair of 1893, while the winged lions (right) on berth ends were known as the Columbian Motif and used by both firms of carbuilders. On the facing page is a Wagner parlor car interior at a time when box seats at the theater or the Diamond Horseshoe at the Metropolitan represented the ultimate in splendor and ostentation, and this drawing, when it appeared in a popular periodical of the nineties, bore the caption: "An Opera Box In a Parlor Car." It probably was one of the cars of the Empire State Express.

The sleeper Hebrides, *shown here in profile and platform elevation, was built by* Pullman *in 1892 for general service on the company's Eastern division and shows the narrow vestibule construction in its most classic dimension and also its nearly final hour.*

The open section and drawing room sleeping car America, *part of the Pullman exhibit at the Chicago Fair of 1893 was perhaps the most resolutely elegant car designed and outshopped by the most celebrated of all carbuilders for public availability. Its upholstery was royal-blue and old-gold plush, electricity supplemented its nicely designed Pintsch gas fixtures, berth fronts were of Honduran mahogany ornamented with a classic* wreath and love-knot motif at Pullman's Marquetry Room, and its transoms were of leaded art glass let into a curved clerestory with intricate marquetry and gold inlay. Tufted headboards framed the lowers and velvet corded portières set off the doorways. It was a conveyance to ennoble the humblest passenger who ever occupied Upper Ten.

Three reasons why entire successive generations were awed by Pullman grandeur are to be found in the open sections of the sleepers Titania *and* Rockbridge (*page opposite*) *and in the ladies' retiring room of* Mohaska, *shown here. The design on the bunk fronts of* Titania *was "Bird in the Bush," one of the most celebrated and widely admired creations of the Marquetry Room at Pullman.*

333

Perhaps the most opulent equipment ever designed for general service were the library-observation cars such as Courtier, built by Pullman in December 1890 at a cost of $15,992.50 and immediately placed in service on the Richmond & Danville Limited, which connected the Deep South with New York via the Pennsylvania. A glory rode aboard palace cars, where perfectionism shone in the ornate platform grille, the finelining on the sidewalls and in bowed windows in the two rear window sections, the better to view the scenery in the Blue Ridge Mountains.

The nineties, when train speeds were only infrequently great enough to pick up fragments of the roadbed in the slipstream, was the golden age of travel on the platform of the observation car. In 1893 the noted illustrator Childe Hassam depicted these passengers, perhaps aboard Courtier itself, on the cover of Harper's "On the Way to The Exposition—All Roads Lead to Chicago."

Throughout the closing decades of the nineteenth century, when Boston was at the apex of its social and economic importance, the carriers serving New England ran luxury equipment to all points of the compass as a matter of course.

In the days when Boston was a consequential focus of rail travel and the Boston run was a prestige symbol, access to Chicago was provided aboard the Pullman vestibuled sleeper Sabara, as shown opposite, via the Grand Trunk connection at Niagara Falls, and Boston to Washington travelers arrived at the Federal City in comfort on the parlor car Barbara in the Shore Line Express maintained jointly by the New Haven and the Pennsylvania. Grandest equipment of all was the seasonal equipment that rolled over the Boston & Maine (below) to Troy and then Saratoga Springs with summer patrons for the United States Hotel and Grand Union. Here, fringed, mirrored and upholstered to the nines, passengers could look forward with bright anticipation to taking the waters, playing the races and disapproving of the gold-plated bicycles with which Diamond Jim Brady provided his friend Miss Lillian Russell.

In the mid-nineties, Pullman flattered local sensibilities by naming its cars for the places they served, as is suggested by the twin sleepers *For Benton* and *Billings* leased to the Northern Pacific for service on the transcontinental run of its crack North Coast Limited.

The interior of Fort Benton *did nothing to ensmall Pullman's reputation for giving its patrons their money's worth of eye-compelling opulence as the car and its companion sleepers,* Billings, Oriole *and* Heron *rolled on their occasions between the twin cities of St. Paul and Minneapolis and the Northwest over the rails of Henry Villard's proudly maintained Northern Pacific, the second transcontinental.*

For many years the Chicago, Milwaukee & St. Paul Railroad made a practice of lettering its diners rather than naming or numbering them, and the beautiful Dining Car C shown here in exterior and within was built in 1882 by Harlan & Hollingsworth at Wilmington. It was seventy feet three inches long, weighed 86,000 pounds and reportedly served the finest filet of Lake Superior whitefish you could find anywhere.

In March 1890 readers of the Police Gazette in a thousand poolrooms and bar-bershops from Sarasota to Seattle were made glad by the drawing reproduced here purporting to convey the veritable low-down on Twin Cities infidelity in terms of the high life which was the Gazette's asset in most request. It was cap-tioned: "The Old Dodge; He Took His Typewriter With Him; How a St. Paul Merchant Prince Set Up an 'Office' in Palmer's Hotel in Chicago; They Drank Wine on The Palace Cars." Wine, of course, meant only champagne and it is possible that the stirring scene depicted here actually took place on one of the several other railroads that furnished the Milwaukee's competition on this run, the Wisconsin Central, the Père Marquette or the North Western, but it is pleasant to imagine it was aboard the gilt-edge varnish of the Milwaukee. Nobody, at this remove, can say it wasn't.

THREE PHOTOS: PULLMAN STANDARD

The transition from open platform sleepers to the new and widely advertised vestibules is illustrated on the page opposite by Pullmans Neva *and* Avis, *the first built for the Atlantic Coast Line in 1889, the latter for general service the year following. The picture of two Pullman palace cars in train line (above) was widely circulated to illustrate the safety factor involved and the firm's progressive attitude generally. Approximately a decade later the two women in a Pullman lady's room suggested the complete propriety with which unaccompanied women might now travel aboard the cars.*

ARTHUR D. DUBIN COLLECTION

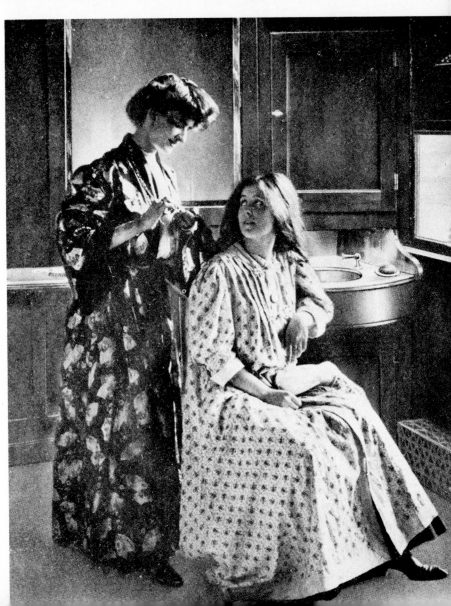

Ontonagon and Onalaska were private drawing room cars of the Milwaukee's 1905 edition of the Pioneer Limited and a contemporary advertising folder proclaimed that "Neither words nor pictures can begin to convey to the mind the thorough artistic excellence, the quality of elegance and delightful harmony of the finish and furnishing of the entire train . . . as bright hued as the yellow butterflies that flutter over the golden dandelions in early spring."

Of Omaha and its twin Des Moines when they were delivered by Pullman to the Milwaukee Road in 1900 the Chicago Tribune commented editorially that their "longer, wider and higher berths ought to prove a gold mine for the coffers of the road." Reason for this approval were the six-foot-three-inch berths inaugurated at this time on Milwaukee sleepers which had fourteen sections and a drawing room and were in the carrier's Chicago–Omaha service. They were painted Milwaukee yellow and were owned outright by the railroad instead of being leased from Pullman.

Executive grandeur in the Milwaukee's glory days is suggested by the flowered upholstery of its business car Milwaukee *with a bathtub presumably for the highest official use only.*

Among the most venerable of all cars in point of service on any de luxe run must have been the Milwaukee's library–buffet–lounge cars Wauwatosa *and* Winneconne, *which were built for assignment to the road's* Pioneer Limited *in 1909 by Barney & Smith and were still in service nearly forty years later. They survived two World Wars, a major depression and much other history, as well as complete rebuilding with steel sidewalls and a change of name to* Chicago *and* Minneapolis *in 1927. Their lounge compartments were paneled in mahogany with Turkey carpets, leaded glass in small, highly spaced windows with the universal cuspidors. Passengers sank deep in armchairs upholstered in Spanish leather and commanded drinks from a morocco-bound wine list. Of special interest were the exterior nameboards of these two durable cars which indicated ownership by the Wilwaukee's subsidiary, the Chicago, Milwaukee & Puget Sound Railroad over whose rails the* Pioneer Limited *never ran for a single mile.*

The love affair between imaginative travelers and the railroad dining car, although occasionally marred by lover's quarrels, is of long standing, dating from the first oysters and champagne that George M. Pullman served newspaper reporters aboard Western World in 1867. Dining on the cars at once became a delightful preoccupation and the cars themselves increased in magnificence to match menus that bristled with antelope steak, Scotch grouse, Maryland terrapin, Mallard duck, rabbit pie, quail in aspic and sparkling wine in double bottles for breakfast. "The demand for rapid travelling, to gratify which a struggle has been made by the railroad managers to save every possible delay, has led to the abandonment of many stops at lunch rooms and stations," declared Harper's Weekly for August 25, 1888, the year dining cars celebrated their twenty-first birthday. "The cry: 'Wilmington, fifteen minutes for refreshments!' is no longer heard, but instead the passenger enjoys his soup, his fish, his joint, Clicquot and coffee while the train runs fifty miles an hour. In fact, dinner ordered at Newark is scarcely finished by Trenton, and the stump of a cigar lighted shortly before completing it is often thrown away to the gamins of Broad Street, Philadelphia."

PAGE OPPOSITE: PULLMAN STANDARD

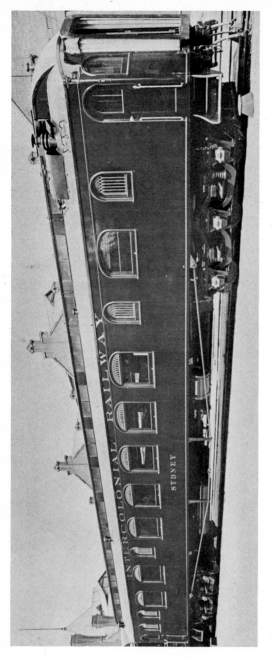

The beautiful observation—sleeper Mount MacDonald, built for the Canadian Pacific's crack Imperial Limited was sheathed throughout in teakwood in its natural finish. The Intercolonial's Sydney was a vestibule sleeper almost as stylish with arched and leaded windows and gold-leaf finelining.

Few if any sleepers south of the Canadian border were peers in ornate *boiserie, intricately designed pillars, berth fronts and paneling of Moosehead, which Barney & Smith built for the Canadian* Pacific *in 1895. Malahat (below) was rebuilt as a parlor observation car from the sleeper Palgrave for the Esquimalt & Nanaimo, a 131-mile subsidiary of the Canadian Pacific.*

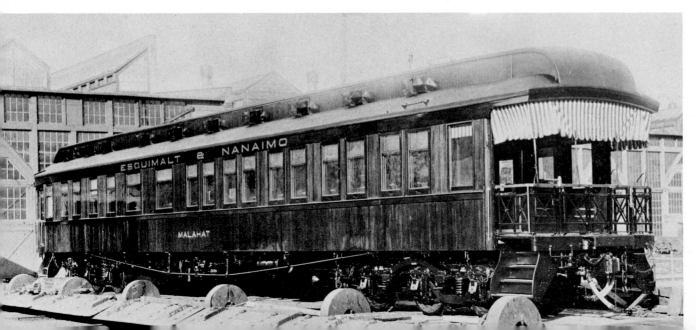

A PORTFOLIO
OF
PRIVATE VARNISH

I**T IS DIFFICULT** in a generation in which any sort of rail travel is regarded as faintly exotic and many of whose members are not even familiar with the once commonplace amenities of travel aboard the steamcars to imagine the position occupied in the scale of material assets and luxury appointments by the private railroad car.

In an age when the phrase "status symbol" had yet to be invented, the private Pullman was probably the most exalted and enviable of all available indexes of economic preferment and social inaccessability. Beside its implications of wealth and exclusiveness such recognized properties as a Fifth Avenue address, titled sons-in-law, social recognition at Newport or Palm Beach, galleries of old masters, English servants and entire garages filled with Rolls Royces and Bentleys paled to insignificance. Only the ocean-going steam yacht of acceptable dimensions and the maintenance of a top-flight racing stable possessed comparable connotations of grandeur.

The reason for this supremacy in common acceptance and the general imagination of a comparatively inexpensive artifact lies in the hold that the entire business of railroading held on the minds of the American people for three quarters of a century. A château on Bellevue Avenue or Nob Hill might cost from $3,000,000 to double that amount at a time when the most princely of private cars could be built to the owner's specifications for no more than $50,000. The dowry that went with a Vanderbilt heiress when she married an English duke could come to $2,500,000. A seat in the United States Senate at a time when it was the most exclusive club of rich men in the world might carry a $1,000,000 tab and often did. The price tag on a single art masterpiece such as Gainsborough's "Blue Boy" when acquired for an American collector by Sir Joseph Duveen could come to $620,000, but Henry E. Huntington who bought "Blue Boy" maintained no fewer than four private railroad cars whose total value was the merest fraction of this sum.

At the period of its greatest costliness a private Pullman stood its purchaser $500,000 and in the period of its greatest multiplicity in the twenties $150,000 would get something extremely nice from American Car & Foundry. The private car was very far from being the most expensive evidence of upward mobility in American society and finance, but as a symbol of success it had few peers and was topped by nothing.

Its possession combined luxurious convenience with the romantic hold railroading had for the popular imagination and the combination exalted it above ownership of the Hope Diamond or a claim on the favors of the ranking Hollywood Cyprian of the moment. Swimming pools were for successful greengrocers and electrical contractors. Palm Beach and charge accounts at Cartier were for well-placed stockbrokers. The private Pullman, its dark green varnish and brass-railed observation platform headed for Florida or Del Monte or the Adirondacks, was for grand seigneurs and the feudal overlords of the American economy. Each lent a dimension of magnificence to the other.

By proper definition the private railway car in America fell, in the golden noontide of its splendor, into three categories: cars owned, maintained and occupied by private individuals for their personal occasions; the official cars of ranking railroad executives, owned by the carrier itself or its stockholders and designed for use only on railroad business; and cars maintained by various carbuilders or railroads and available to private rental for whatever occasions of business, pleasure or necessity their temporary occupants might indicate. In this last category there were not only hotel cars to be occupied as complete living accommodations by their lessees, but also hunting cars, parlor cars, funeral cars and specially constructed horse palace cars for the transport—usually in connection with a private hotel car—of the horses and carriages and sometimes the grooms and stable attendants of wealthy travelers.

In actual practice the private car seldom fell into any of these neat compartments to any reassuring degree. Official cars of railroad executives were for many decades conspicuously devoted to the private convenience of important shippers, politicians, newspapermen, relatives, in short, anybody who might have a claim on the special attention of the management. In other cases, to add to the confusion, railroaders of towering authority, Goulds, Vanderbilts, Hills and Harrimans were the actual owners of the carriers so that an official business car of a president or chairman of the board might well be also his personal property. There are numerous cases in the record of railroad presidents who ordered private cars to their personal specifications, paid for them out of pocket and boldly designated them as private cars on the rolling stock roster. The

private car soon became the most ambiguous of properties, its precise status of ownership and occupancy impervious to all but the most searching inquiry.

Private cars for railroad executives began appearing soon after the Civil War and kept pace with the general and parallel improvement of living facilities on the palace hotel cars of the time. Tom Scott of the Pennsylvania had a hotel car of his own in which the kitchen was designed to ride at the rear to obviate the smells of cooking. The directors of the North Western rode proudly in a miraculous Gothic car with baronial overtones (see Plush and Ormolu chapter). Engineers in charge of construction on the Union Pacific lived on special equipment as the rails went westward across the Great Plains and at Promontory Point, where the railheads met; Leland Stanford of the Central Pacific and Thomas Durant of the U.P. arrived at the historic site in the Utah uplands aboard private varnish whose comforts, especially their resources of things to drink, astonished the natives.

The first private car for a non-operating railroad man in the Far West appears to have been built by Harlan & Hollingsworth for Darius Ogden Mills, frosty satrap of the all-powerful Bank of California, early in the seventies, and thereafter no San Francisco nabob of consequence failed to command the services of a private car, either of his own or for his disposal and pleasure, from the Central Pacific. The C.P. and its connecting Southern Pacific maintained perhaps the largest fleet of private cars anywhere, ostensibly for the use of company officials, but in practice for directors, major stockholders, important politicians and friends of the railroad in general, a category that included big shippers and West Coast business men of all sorts.

Throughout the rest of the country private cars began appearing in ever-increasing numbers and ornate splendor, at first as the property of railroad directors, who had some claim to official use of such conveniences, and then among men of wealth and importance with no railroad connections whatsoever.

By the year 1895 the list of private car owners embraced almost every top-ranking industrialist and banker and a good many at some remove from the upper brackets of finance. Small-town squires in the West and South and factory owners in the Middle

West got themselves elected to the directorate of railroads of small or no consequence in order that their private cars might receive the courtesies of free transport and parking, then extended to all other railroaders by short lines and transcontinental carriers alike. All railroaders from the rank of division superintendent upward had their own cars, which were not known in the strict latter-day terminology as "business cars" but explicitly as private cars. They varied in resources of splendor, but the connotation of the private railroad car was always superlative. It was the grandest property to which any American could aspire.

As the ultimate symbol of upward mobility in a society desperately competitive, it became imperative for the wives and families of the socially exalted to travel by private car. It might be borrowed, rented, scrounged or owned outright, but to arrive at Palm Beach, Saratoga Springs, or Louisville for the Derby, by private Pullman or Wagner was *de rigueur* not only among Vanderbilts, Whitneys, Belmonts, Wideners, Fricks and Stotesburys, but amongst far smaller fry to whom social façade and keeping up with the Joneses was a way of life in itself. Patent medicine kings in upstate New York, owners of coal in West Virginia and timber in Wisconsin with no other claim to recognition achieved a cachet of distinction by having their private varnish spotted in terminals adjacent to that of Edward H. Harriman or James Ben Ali Haggin. More than any other single carrier in the land, the Florida East Coast serving the princely resorts erected by Henry M. Flagler trafficked in private varnish on a wholesale basis and its correspondence files for the nineties could provide lush source material for a chronicler of the vanities, ambitions and petty subterfuges of men and women clamorous for special favors and preferred treatment.

In few other tangible properties—excepting homes and steam yachts—could the whims, prejudices and taste for the exotic of the well-to-do find expression in such a dimension as the design and construction of a private railroad car. He was inhibited only by the standards of the American Association of Railroads, the clearances of individual carriers and the limits of his bank account, and within these limitations his imagination could and did run riot.

Furniture and interior decor generally followed the fashion of the time but ran at all periods to a synthesis of comfort and ostentation designed at once to gentle the occupant and to impress the beholder. Since woodwork and cabinet building were the original basis for all railroad car construction, private cars reflected these skills in the rich and exotic wood employed in their finishing. Mahogany was standard; olive wood, primavera, satinwood, Circassian walnut and curly maple abounded. Marquetry, as long as this special *expertise* was in favor, was highly esteemed. The variety of fabrics employed in upholstery, drapes, carpets, portières, bed linen and table service represented the combined looms of Brussels, Axminster, Manchester, Milan, Belfast and Haverhill, wherever satin, velour, velvet, linen, plush, silk and hammer cloth were manufactured.

In general, the ground plan of one private car closely resembled that of any other. It included a dining room, usually seating eight or ten, an observation salon whose dimensions might vary at the whim of the owner, a master stateroom usually with its own bath, three or four slightly smaller staterooms for guests, a galley and kitchen offices and quarters for the crew which traditionally numbered two and were known as cook and waiter. To call them chef and butler would be a departure from accepted railroad usage of a parvenu.

The galley with its storerooms, ice boxes and repositories of linen and other necessities was traditionally located at the head end of a private car, while the rear end was devoted to a brass-railed observation platform from which occupants might take the air or enjoy the view. The number of staterooms and size of the drawing room depended on each other. It was possible to have more private sleeping space and less room for general assembly, or the reverse. A corridor along one side of the entire length of the car gave access to its various apartments and to the rear platform for the members of the crew working the train.

It was in its special appointments that the tastes of private car owners found their fullest gratification. Marble bathtubs, gold-filled plumbing, jewel safes, cedar wardrobes, king-size beds and other built-in equipment was fairly standard. One car of recent record had a steam bath activated by the main train line. The private car *Adolphus* of August Busch, Jr., reportedly had beer piped to all its rooms. The first air

conditioning on any railroad equipment was incorporated in Major Max Fleischman's *Edgewood*.

When Mrs. James Paul Donahue set out for Palm Beach aboard her celebrated *Japauldon*—the abbreviated name of her husband—a conventional stateroom sleeping car traveled ahead for her retinue of personal servants, and meals were served by an English butler and footmen in the Donahue livery. Cissie Patterson, the Washington newspaper publisher, was bored with seeing the same furniture every day on *Ranger* and seven sets of slip covers made it possible to redecorate the car every day in the week. She also admired quantities of cut flowers and these her major-domo telegraphed ahead for and had put aboard at strategic points along the route. When J. P. Morgan hired a special train of Pullman Palace cars, his major-domo was Louis Sherry, as recounted elsewhere in this volume. Valets, ladies' maids, secretaries and paid companions went with their employers by the score, and a total of six bedside pushbuttons in mother-of-pearl in her personal bedroom on her husband's *Loretto II* testified to the number of domestics at the call of Mrs. Charles M. Schwab. Its predecessor, *Loretto I,* had but five, but the United States Steel Corporation had come into being in the meantime.

Henry Ford took a dim view of the tensile strength of any vehicle not manufactured at his own River Rouge plant and when he commissioned *Fair Lane* from Pullman, double weight of steel was ordered at all points of structural strain with the result that *Fair Lane,* while safe as Fort Knox in the event of going into the ditch, rode like a military tank, and a subsequent occupant, Daniel Upthegrove, president of the Cotton Belt Railroad, remarked that he always emerged from a business trip bruised and smelling of arnica as though he had been in a prize fight.

Jay Gould was troubled with dyspepsia, and his entourage when he boarded *Atalanta* or another of the several private cars owned by or available to him in his lifetime, included not only a personal physician but a French chef specially skilled in the preparation of ladyfingers and other featherweight pastry allowed by his regimen. Sometimes he was accompanied on long trips by his daughter Helen who brought her own car *Stranrear* along for the ride.

The son of James Jerome Hill of the Great Northern and famed as an empire builder, known to intimates in St. Paul as "Pooch," maintained a Great Northern car with a garage that occupied its forward portion, access to which was achieved by a ramp that could be let down like a drawbridge. In the early days of automobiling, Hill was a Rolls Royce addict and, in a time of few and uncertain highways, traveled with a Park Ward tourer on board. There was sleeping space too for a chauffeur.

The private car of one Georgia nabob with a taste for mushrooms had a mushroom cellar slung from the underside of his car between a storage locker and the batteries.

It was aboard Mrs. Donahue's *Japauldon* while it was spotted at Palm Beach in the early twenties that an invited guest strayed from the observation salon to investigate the resources of the rest of the car and returned awe-struck to tell a friend in a stage whisper: "You ought to get a load of the dining room; all the silver's solid gold!" Another gold table service of railroad legend was that manufactured by Shreve, the great San Francisco silversmiths, for *Salvador,* Pullman-built palace car of James Ben Ali Haggin which traveled between California and the owner's vast stock farms in Kentucky with a chef from Foyot's in Paris in the galley. The crew on August Belmont's private electric car in which he used to ride from the Belmont Hotel in New York to the races at Belmont Park were attired in dress uniforms from Wetzel, the costliest of all gentlemen's tailors, and there was a parlor organ on Car No. 100 of the Kansas City, Pittsburgh & Gulf occupied by its sanctimonious President Arthur E. Stilwell, around which he was in the habit of gathering the train crew for Sabbath devotions.

These are the merest samplings from the rich folklore which surrounded the private railway car in its golden noontide, a body of legend which the author of this volume has explored at greater length in an earlier essay, but it will indicate the spacious ways that were characteristic of membership in the private car club.

Largely, of course, private Pullmans and Wagners were assigned for their maintenance and storage to a major carrier serving the region in which their owners lived or roads with which they had business associations. These supplied crews when cars were seasonally activated and to their auditors went bills for repairs, fuel, food, laundry and other services when the car was off the rails of its home railroad.

Not a few cars of legendary splendor were in the custody of short lines of less resounding names than the great transcontinentals and as a curiosity of the private car story it may be worth while to devote a few moments' time to their contemplation.

To the informed railroading intelligence, the idea of a costly and elaborate business car for a short-line carrier must seem at first consideration a gratification of extravagance or delusion of grandeur on the part of the management.

Sometimes it was.

The function of an office car is and was, even in the golden age of railroading, to provide living and occupational facilities for executives at remote and inaccessible points along the railroad's property. That of a private car of bona fide non-railroading ownership was to provide luxury travel and prestige for the owner whilst traveling far away from home. Neither of these useful or luxurious functions were served by hauling or spotting a business and/or private car along a carrier only a hundred or at best two hundred odd miles in extent. The very nature and existence of a private car presupposed a wider range of usefulness, geographically speaking.

And yet special equipment flourished mightily along the short lines of the land no longer ago than the turn of the century, and even the years that saw the gradual decline of rail transport as a passenger medium witnessed ownership or custodianship of some remarkably opulent private cars by short lines or railroads other than the great carriers of first-class category.

The answer is a divided one. In the case of purely official usage, a business car was a prestige symbol on a short line's roster of passenger equipment; it gave a modest railroad a dimension of splendor at least comparable to the luxurious practices of the Pennsy or Union Pacific. A business car, especially in the days when the difference between business cars and private varnish was purely academic, was a fine thing to have around even if you couldn't really afford it, the peer of Rolls Royces and other affluent properties and prerogatives.

A railroad president or director, even if his road was only a country carrier running between rural nowhere and suburban noplace, needed a private car the way he needed a Prince Albert coat and gold-headed walking stick. Without one there was some doubt as to his bona fides.

Private cars assigned to short lines as their home railroad by simon-pure private parties with only remote railroad connections or none were something else again. A short line was glad of the track rental and storage as well as being the originating carrier for safaris of interchange. It was nice to see its insigne on nameboards on the private car tracks at Palm Beach and Louisville at Derby time. Shippers and business connections with private car ambitions gratified them to mutual advantage by assigning their private varnish to the local or home-town carrier. One way or another it was a good deal for everyone concerned.

And overall in this discussion it must be remembered that the touchiness of railroad executives about the sharp demarcation between private car and business car is of comparatively recent origin. In the nineties special equipment was a great deal more ambiguous. Railroad presidents and general superintendents had no least hesitation about speaking of their official cars as private cars. Many of them were so designated on doors and nameboards. Jay Gould or Jim Hill would have scorned the implications of subservience in calling their private varnish a business car, even though it was. Cheap gestures of democracy on the part of big business were yet in the unforeseen and deplorable future.

Often enough a railroad president owned his fine Pullman outright as a personal chattel in fee simple. He wasn't responsible for its conduct to directors or stockholders, and what was to be gained by the evasive euphemism of "business car"? Only in comparatively recent times has it been possible to induce apoplexy in railroaders by the mere use of the words "private car." Before then, a private car was a fine thing to have and nobody who owned or rated one was overwhelmed with embarrassment by it.

In the eighties special equipment began to lend a glory to short lines, sometimes disastrously.

Take, for example, the San Antonio & Aransas Pass running some 200 miles from the Texas capital to Aransas Bay, a vicinage still noted for its tarpon fishing. Right off the bat the directors commanded a splendid mahogany car with two open platforms, as was the style of the time, from Pullman, and to show an awareness of progress they named it *Electric*. Then nothing would do but that General Manager B. F. Yoakum must have something nice in the varnish line and Pullman obliged with *Rubio,* the builder's photograph on that distant day showing it at Pullman with a large black dog.

Enchanted with the social acclaim accruing from these splendors, and learning that the neighboring Pecos Valley Railroad had ordered an even more magnificent private car named *Hesperia,* the Aransas Pass management commissioned Pullman to build a hunting car, the *Fern Ridge. Fern Ridge* took a page out of the book of Jerome Marble of Worcester, Massachusetts, who was at this time building and renting hunting cars for use in the West with such success that he numbered among his patrons the Grand Duke Alexis of Russia and the Duke of Sutherland. The Aransas Pass sports model p. v. was plainly furnished, with four cast-iron beds at the corners of its principal apartment, and had wide baggage-type doors for easy egress of occupants with fishing gear and guns.

To haul this opulent multiplicity of special equipment, the Aransas Pass also ordered liberally in the field of motive power from the New York Locomotive Works at Rome, New York, and presently the San Antonio & Aransas Pass Railway was broke. It defaulted on its bonds in 1891. Failure to pay for its engines hastened the bankruptcy of the New York Locomotive Works. General Manager Yoakum went to greater destinies with the Frisco. With such a name on its nameboards, Jay Gould couldn't resist acquiring *Electric* for his Western Union Telegraph Company and sheriffs' writs against such Texas names on the board of directors as Sam Maverick and Reagan Houston put the snatch on *Fern Ridge* and *Rubio.*

Eventually the Southern Pacific picked up the pieces of the S.A. & A.P. but the glory was gone and its decline was pointed out as a monument to the folly of too much private varnish on a 200-mile carrier.

Well to the north of the Rio Grande at about this time and operating in much more flourishing circumstances was the rich and well-managed West Virginia Central & Pittsburgh Railway, whose seventy-odd miles of right of way between Piedmont, West Virginia, and

Elkins is now part of the Western Maryland. The W.V.C. & P. was a fine example of a short line that boasted two magnificent private cars, one carried on the company books and the other the property of R. C. Kerens, a well-to-do director from St. Louis. Kerens in 1894 commanded Pullman to build him *Katharyne,* an all-mahogany car with enclosed front platform in the new style and looped and fringed drapes, inlaid woodwork and silk portières beyond counting. The W.V.C. & P., in order that its President H. G. Davis might travel in fashionable privacy, maintained also the p. v. *West Virginia* whose ancestry is unknown, at least to the writer. That coal-haul presidents traveled in the best society is indicated by the books of the Florida East Coast which on March 16, 1894, accepted *West Virginia* in interchange with "H. G. Davis & Party" aboard and delivered them to Palatka, Florida, a resort of contemporary fashion at a time when Palm Beach was just getting under way.

All the Florida lines of the period including the Florida Southern and the Plant System's Savannah, Florida & Western had private cars on their roster of varying degrees of magnificence, most of which turned up at one time or another as guests of the F.E.C.

For geographic coverage we may turn briefly to the Munising Railway, which in 1895 was chartered to run thirty-eight miles from Munising to Little Lake, Michigan, with twenty-four miles of branch lines. This microscopic outfit was controlled by the Cleveland–Cliffs Iron Company, which had immense iron interests in the region and could well afford the extravagance when, in 1901, it ordered from Pullman a nice private car for the use of its President William G. Mather of Cleveland. No. 21 was upholstered in tufted pigskin with silver lighting fixtures, and its interior accommodations, generally speaking, were comparable to those of the cars of William C. Whitney, Charles M. Schwab, James Hazen Hyde and Thomas Fortune Ryan which Pullman outshopped in the same vintage year for private varnish.

In the Far West where distances were greater and millionaires more spectacular, short lines in Nevada, California and Utah with mining backgrounds flourished green-bay-tree-like and produced a notable quota of private cars and special equipment, much of it homemade in company shops. In time to show it at the railroad pavilion at the Centennial Exposition at Philadelphia, Peter Donahue of the California Pacific Railroad in Northern California had a "private palace car" built by the Union Iron Works at San Francisco. Milton Latham's narrow-gauge *Millwood* was the glory of the North Pacific Coast, and over in Nevada the by now swaggering Virginia & Truckee was building at its main shops in Carson City a similar conveyance for its general manager, Henry Yerington, possessor also of the finest whiskers in Nevada, saving perhaps those of Senator William M. Stewart. The V. & T.'s private varnish was rebuilt from a coach purchased from the Central Pacific in 1876 for $2,500 and came onto the railroad scene shrouded in mystery and departed the same way. That it existed at all is shown by part of a letter from Yerington now in the Nevada State Museum: "My private car is now in the East at the disposal of John Mackay, the richest man in the world." Nobody knows what happened to the V. & T. official car after that.

Nearly three quarters of a century later the V. & T. was briefly and in its final year of operation home railroad for *The Gold Coast* owned by Charles Clegg and Lucius Beebe, a car that had been purchased from another short line nearly 3,000 miles away, the Georgia Northern.

The V. & T.'s narrow-gauge subsidiary, the Carson & Colorado running from Mound House in Nevada to Owens Valley in California, possessed in its years of teem an official car, the *Esmeralda*, which finally ended its days on the ground as a summer house in Owens Valley. When the Southern Pacific acquired the C. & C. shortly after the turn of the century, it also boasted a second three-foot official car that somehow had strayed from the Nevada–California–Oregon Railroad.

Still another narrow-gauge private car, this one unusually eccentric in that for all its august ownership it was nothing more than a slightly more than usually elegant passenger coach, was the conveyance of New York millionaire Anson Phelps Stokes, owner of the Nevada Central Railroad connecting with the Central Pacific at Battle Mountain and with the booming silver town of Austin at the other end. The *Silver State* was pressed into service whenever owner Stokes chose to come West to survey his properties and survived the vicissitudes of time to play the role of the Central

Pacific's *Stanford* in the railroad pageant staged by Gilbert Kneiss at Treasure Island in 1938. It, like *The Gold Coast,* now reposes among the historic properties of the West Coast Chapter of the Railway & Locomotive Historical Society.

In the Southern deserts, the Tonopah & Tidewater is known to have had a business car, although, like properties of so many departed carriers, its origins and details of construction have vanished over the years. The nearby Ludlow & Southern running seven and a half miles from Stagg Post Office, California, to Steadman possessed a business car that has become a legend of magnificence in the region it once knew. No. 100 was popularly reputed to have been at one time the presidential car of Chauncey M. Depew on the far-off and lordly New York Central, but since it is hard to conceive of Mr. Depew using on his business occasions a combination baggage car and coach, this seems improbable. That the furnishings, including a mahogany roll-top desk and finely wrought brass lighting fixtures, were uncommonly beautiful and ornate was admitted by all who saw it.

At least two California short lines have had a p. v. on their equipment rosters in recent years. The Santa Maria Valley, a fifteen-mile-long feeder for the Southern Pacific, picked up the Espee's once splendid business car *Arizona* that had been built by Pullman years before for the El Paso & Southwestern, while the McCloud River Railroad, a still operating lumber carrier, in 1913 ordered from Pullman a business car conventionally numbered 100.

Prize collector of varnish equipment in the Far West, however, was the Nevada Northern, a rich copper-haul railroad once dominated by the Guggenheim interests. Its insignia has variously ornamented the nameboards of Solomon Guggenheim's strictly private car *Nirvana*, the Pullman-built company business car *Ely*, and two gorgeous also-Pullman-built p. v.'s each named *Cyprus* and owned at various times by Colonel Daniel C. Jackling of Utah copper fame and one of the legendary tycoons of the industry. *Ely* was sold to the Gulf, Mobile & Ohio in 1937. Colonel Jackling's first *Cyprus* passed into the hands of Julius Fleishman and is now the business car *Hopedale* of the Pittsburgh & West Virginia, which also owns the one-time p. v. of Henry Frick, the celebrated *Westmoreland.* Second

Cyprus went to the War Department during the Kaiser War.

Perhaps the ranking contemporary private car short line is the Georgia Northern, a feudal property of the Pidcock family, which owns two other short lines in the neighborhood of Moultrie, Georgia. Until a few years ago Mr. Pidcock's private varnish was an authentic veteran *Moultrie* that in primeval times had been the property of Henry M. Flagler and named the Indian River Railroad as its home carrier. When *Moultrie*'s wooden underframe rendered it not available to main-line interchange, Mr. Pidcock purchased from the Central of Georgia its office car No. 98, which had been built in the company's Savannah shops in 1907. This eventually became Lucius Beebe and Charles Clegg's Virginia & Truckee–maintained *The Gold Coast* and is now the property, by their gift, of the Pacific Coast Chapter of the Railway & Locomotive Historical Society. Finding that he couldn't live without a private car, Mr. Pidcock then purchased from the Chicago & Eastern Illinois its Pullman-built office car *Mount Vernon*, which now adorns the Georgia Northern as the second *Moultrie*.

Other short lines within the memory of the oldest inhabitant have had business cars of varying degrees of elegance and austerity. The forty-six mile Mississippi River & Bonne Terre, operating in mining country south of St. Louis, had American Car & Foundry build for its directors an uncommonly comely wood-sheathed palace car, the *Linares*, which popped the eyes of Ozark rustics for many years.

The Tennessee Central rejoices in the Pullman-built car *Palm Beach*, built at Pullman in 1916, Lot No. 4422, Plan No. 2502 B, reported once to have been under lease to Mary Pickford in her days of silver screen ascendancy.

The Atlanta & St. Andrews Bay Railway some years ago purchased a Florida East Coast official car and subsequently sold it to Mike Duffey, general manager of the Central Indiana Railway of Anderson, Indiana.

For a brief interregnum, while the Chesapeake Western Railway was without a depot or offices at Staunton, Virginia, the general manager, D. W. Thomas, directed the company's operations from the former *Moultrie* of the Georgia Northern, which before that had belonged to Henry M. Flagler, and finally set the venerable relic on the ground as his summer house at Harrisonburg.

The Mississippi Central has an old-time business car stored in the company shops at Hattiesburg, Mississippi, and the Georgia & Florida, perhaps not a simon-pure short line, is generally reported to have maintained a car of some elegance until recent years, while the Cincinnati, Indianapolis & Western at one time maintained Indianapolis No. 07 for its ranking personnel and directors.

And to bring to a conclusion this brief and by no means definitive survey of short line private varnish, let us pause to salute Charles M. Schwab's second private car *Loretto,* built to the ironmaster's personal specifications by Pullman in 1916 from Plan No. 3316 after Schwab had retired his first car by the same name. *Loretto II* became the personal, private conveyance of Colonel Elliott White Springs, president of the Lancaster & Chester, a short line serving the vast Springs cotton mills in South Carolina, and a carrier with a board of directors that included James Montgomery Flagg, Lowell Thomas, Gypsy Rose Lee and the author of this chronicle and occupies half a page in the *Official Guide.* Because of its outmoded draft gear and brake rigging, *Loretto II* never left the rails of its home railroad, but Colonel Springs had a great deal of pleasure out of it.

Nobody can say that short line private varnish doesn't get around.

Over the years Pullman estimates that it has built between 450 and 500 private cars and its records make no slightest distinction between business and official cars for railroads, those outshopped for corporations and their officers and simon-pure private varnish built to the specifications of private, non-railroad people of means. American Car & Foundry, whose records do not exist at all in this field, may have built a quarter this number, some of them celebrated, such as Harry Sinclair's *Sinco* and Mrs. J. P. Donahue's *Japauldon*. Several score at the least have been built in the shops of individual railroads for their official occasions, Union Pacific, the Central of Georgia and Illinois Central being prominent among the do-it-yourself carriers. Conversions from general service equipment to private cars are infrequent but not unknown, an example in this category being Charles Clegg and Lucius Beebe's *Virginia City,* which began life as *Golden Peak* on the Great Northern.

Changes of ownership which saw the private cars of millionaires pass to railroads and vice versa were the rule and a constant occurrence in the noontide of railroading. There was a lot of mileage in Pullman Standard and some private varnish is in the record as having lasted through three successive generations of owners by inheritance. Almost all private cars changed names when they changed owners: A. C. Burrage's *Alicia* became *Helma* when purchased by Bruce Dodson, a Kansas City insurance magnate; A. A. McLeod's first *Alexander* turned up on the Southern Pacific as *Emalita*; the Georgia Northern's No. 100 made its final appearance on the roster of the Virginia & Truckee as *The Gold Coast*.

Like the names of yachts, country estates and race horses, the names of private cars reflected the affections, whims, aspirations, occupation, erudition or sentimentality of their owners. Charles Crocker's *Mishawaka* was the name of the Indiana town where his wife was born; Major Max Fleischman's *Edgewood* was the name of his country estate, as was Henry Ford's *Fair Lane*; John Ringling's *Jomar* was a synthetic abbreviation of his own first name and that of Mary Ringling; Edward F. Hutton's *Hussar* duplicated that of his ocean-going steam yacht; William F. Kenny's *St. Nicholas* was also his patron saint; John S. Craven's *Nomad* caused confusion with no fewer than two cars so named

by General William Jackson Palmer of the Rio Grande Railroad, and variation on these themes is endless.

A few of the owners with the names of their private cars over the decades would include:

David Moffat	*Mascotte* and *Marcia*
Collis P. Huntington	*Oneonta I* and *Oneonta II*
John McLean	*Ohio* and *Enquirer*
Edward H. Harriman	*Arden*
James Hazen Hyde	*Bay Shore*
William C. Whitney	*Wanderer*
Charles M. Schwab	*Loretto I* and *Loretto II*
Daniel C. Jackling	*Cyprus I* and *Cyprus II*
Thomas Fortune Ryan	*Oak Ridge* and *Père Marquette*
Joseph Widener	*Lynnewood*
Bruce Dodson	*Helma I* and *Helma II*
James B. Duke	*Doris*
Edward S. Harkness	*Pelham*
Mrs. Henry Flagler	*Whitehall*
Mrs. C. B. Stocker	*California*
Mrs. Cissie Patterson	*Ranger*
Harry Payne Whitney	*Adios* and *Wanderer*
William H. Woodin	*Berwick*
Walter J. Salmon	*Mereworth*
E. G. Grace	*Bethlehem*
John Raskob	*Skipaway*
E. Palmer Gavit	*Anacalpa*
Paul Block	*Friendship*
A. K. Macomber	*Seminole*
William B. Thompson	*Alder*
Nicholas F. Brady	*Adventurer*
Harry Payne Bingham	*Pawnee*

Almost invariably, private cars have been impervious to upward mobility and their course of status has been downward. The car once sacred to the president of the railroad is inherited, when the president gets a new one, by the general manager and thence is downgraded until it ends as the dormitory of a maintenance-of-way gang. In private circles the resale value of palace cars was never strikingly high and at the turn of the century the trade periodicals listed in their classified sections numerous bargains in old-time private varnish that might have cost up to $50,000 when they were built but whose going price was about $5,000. Many of these were bought up by dog and pony show proprietors, patent medicine vendors and evangelists. When changing standards made cars no longer available for interchange between main-line carriers they sometimes passed to short lines from whose rails they never ventured, or were sold as restaurants and lunch wagons. The roadside diner of tradition had often been a private car of distinction only a few years earlier and a notable example of this transition was *El Fleda* built by Pullman shortly after the turn of the century for John Bunting, "The Millionaire Brakeman" of the Southern Pacific. *El Fleda* a few years later turned up as *Sunrise* on the Colorado & Wyoming Railroad. Still later it was the official business car of the president of Toledo, Peoria & Western and today is an element in a regionally celebrated restaurant on the outskirts of the Toledo of its ultimate corporate name.

Many factors contributed to the eventual decline of the privately owned railroad car, taxes, the difficulty in obtaining trained railroad servants, the hard times of the thirties, but most of all the decline of railroad travel in the face of competition from motorcars and airplanes. Other status symbols came to take its place. Railroads, of course, maintain official cars in numbers depending on the magnitude of their operations, some, like the Santa Fe and Union Pacific, numbered in the scores. Almost any carrier of pretentions has at least one for its chief officer, but only a short time back the Rutland's president declared he could no longer finance a business car and the road's sole remaining private varnish was sold to a Canadian lumber company. It was a notable car, too, having been once the private car *Ellsmere* of Dr. William Seward Webb, president of the Wagner Palace Car-Building Company and a Vanderbilt in-law. It was probably the last Wagner Palace car in operating use anywhere.

But although the sun has set on the ownership of private cars, its setting was untarnished by cheapness or mediocrity. No property ever commanded the envy, respect and admiration of the private Pullman and it is unlikely that, in a world of ever-changing values, anything ever again will occupy its position of unchallenged magnificence.

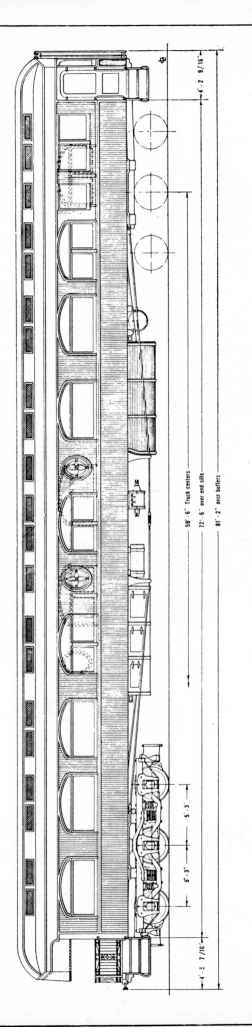

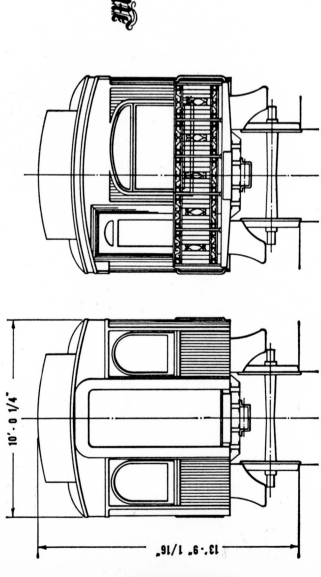

A.C.f.

Mississippi River & Bonne Terre

Railroad

Private Car

Linares

PULLMAN STANDARD

A Portfolio of Private Varnish

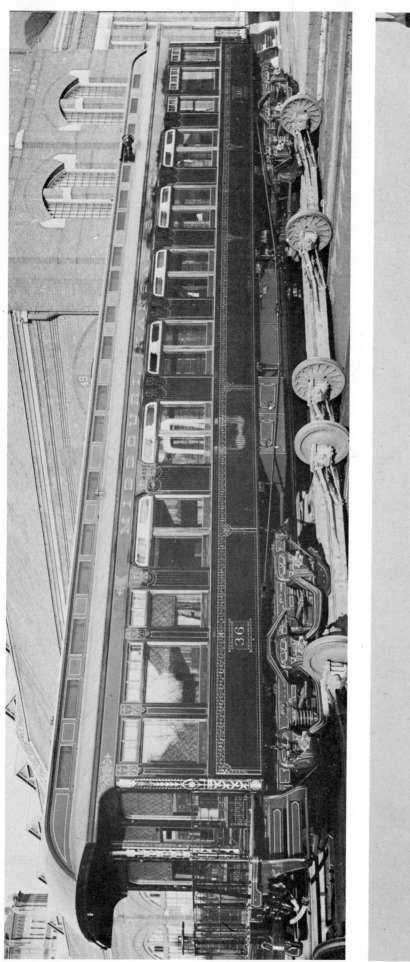

The late eighties produced some of the most enchantingly decorative private cars in the entire Pullman record, among them the opulently gilded No. 36 for the Missouri–Kansas–Texas and the International Great Northern's celebrated Cleopatra, *both shown on the page opposite, and* Hazelmere, *which appears here. Like most private varnish of the period,* Cleopatra *and the Katy's pride were more or less available to friends of the company as well as to its executives, while* Hazelmere *was altogether at the public disposal as an element of Pullman's per diem pool of private cars available for rental.*

365

CAR STANFORD
BUILT AT C. P. R. R. CAR WORKS,
SACRAMENTO, CAL., OCTOBER, 1882.

O. V. LANGE, Photo.   BENJ. WELCH, Master Car Builder.

Leland Stanford's beautiful private car *Stanford* annually carried the railroad builder and his wife and friends over thousands of miles of the Central Pacific and its connecting railroads in what Oscar Lewis, biographer of "The Big Four" described as "a Roman triumph." "Word went through the organization that when the Governor traveled he liked to receive the attention due him as president of the company," wrote Lewis. "Consequently news of his approach was telegraphed ahead so that groups of employees could be in evidence at crossroads stations to salute the passing of his car. . . . Section crews stood at attention when the special roared past in a swirl of hot dust; engines of freight trains standing in sidings sounded long salutes, and the crews of roundhouses and repair shops were marshaled at points sure to be visible from Stanford's window." Below it on the opposite page is the well-groomed exterior of the Southern Pacific's second *Stanford,* dedicated to the occasions of General Manager James Corbett and spotted in the New Orleans Union Depot in the spring of 1959. Shown here is the interior of the Southern Pacific's *Sunset,* built in the late fifties for occupancy by President Donald Russell.

PULLMAN STANDARD

Old Moneybags Darius Mills Rode In Private Splendor

There was no democratic nonsense or affectation of folksiness about Darius Ogden Mills of the all-powerful Bank of California and a gold-rush millionaire who had no hesitation about listing his occupation as "capitalist" in the San Francisco directory. Side whiskers, frock coat, flowered vest and congress gaiters, he looked the part he played throughout a long, powerful and acquisitive life. His was the first private car to be owned west of the Missouri by a tycoon with no explicit railroad connections. Its only known photograph, shown on this page, is from the collection of Roy Graves and shows it on the transfer table at Harlan & Hollingsworth in 1872. Opposite, it has been re-created in operational glory by Howard Fogg on a Central Pacific train in the High Sierra, bound for the Comstock Lode in Nevada which was one of the most fruitful sources of Mills's multiple millions.

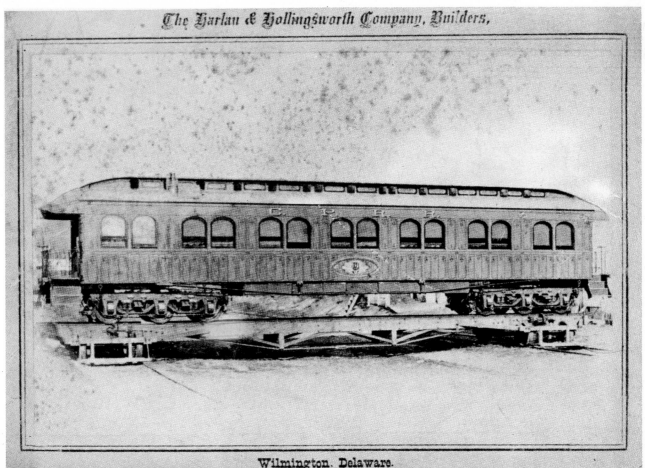

The Harlan & Hollingsworth Company, Builders,

Wilmington. Delaware.

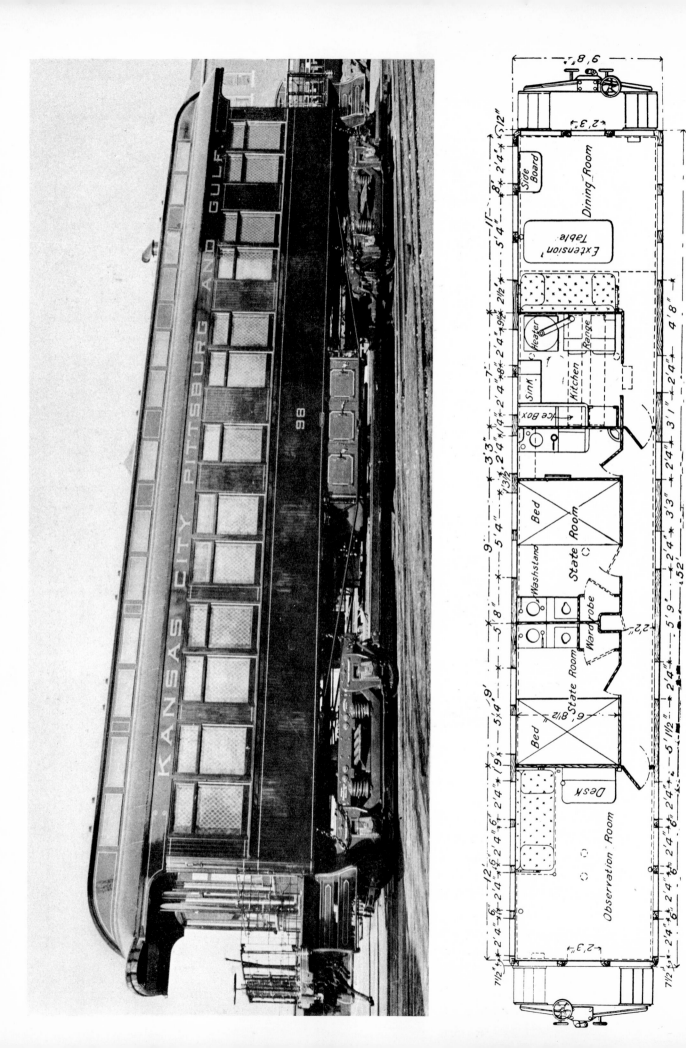

Not all business cars in the spacious years were characterized by the palace car decor favored by A. A. McLeod, Robert Garrett and other swaggering magnificoes of the main line. Some were mere pint-size châteaux of modest appointments, such as No. 98, which Pullman built for the Kansas City, Pittsburgh & Gulf in 1895 before that carrier's affairs were dominated by Arthur Stilwell who eschewed such Spartan simplicity and rode one of the fanciest private cars of his age. The floor plan on the page opposite and the interior shown here were of a Burlington official car of comparable proportions and the same general era. Snug and warm against the elements and night on the Great Plains, these diminutive house cars possessed a charm lacking in the ornate palaces in which vice-presidents of Union Pacific and the New Haven rode to greater destinies.

371

PRIVATE RAILWAY CAR NO. 120
Built For Thomas Scott
The Pennsylvania Railroad Car Shops
ALTOONA, PENNA. 1871

One of the first of all private cars and one in which George M. Pullman took a marked professional interest was No. 120 on the Pennsylvania, built to the personal specifications of Pullman's close friend and associate in many business deals, Tom Scott. Its innovations and improvements over the primitive private cars then in process of evolution gave the carbuilder many pointers. No. 120 was favored by many celebrities ranging from General Grant, the Emperor Dom Pedro of Brazil and Samuel Tilden to James G. Blaine, John Hay and the Grand Duke Alexis. It was often borrowed by President Chester A. Arthur (left) himself a notable fancier of good living. In the rare old-time photograph shown below of a Pennsylvania inspection train in the days when division superintendents still wore top hats, No. 120 is shown in the train line, awash with executive dignitaries and the powerful Bourbon whisky for which Scott was celebrated.

To the connoisseur of private varnish it sometimes seems that short line carriers had fully as exacting tastes in special equipment as the mighty transcontinentals and trunk lines with multiple vice-presidents and corporate titles ending in the magic word Pacific. Two of them, belonging to the Cleveland, Lorain & Wheeling and the Elgin, Joliet & Eastern, respectively, are depicted on the page opposite, while the interior of the Wheeling road's austere yet stylish No. *10* is shown on this page. Short lines of the period favored official cars with two open platforms, which eliminated the necessity of turning at the end of an abbreviated run. The C.L. & W. ran *157* miles from Lorain, Ohio, to Bridgeport with a branch to Bellaire and was dominated by Cleveland ownership and management. In *1902* it was absorbed by the Baltimore & Ohio, which already owned *75* per cent of its stock and is now the B. & O.'s Cleveland branch.

375

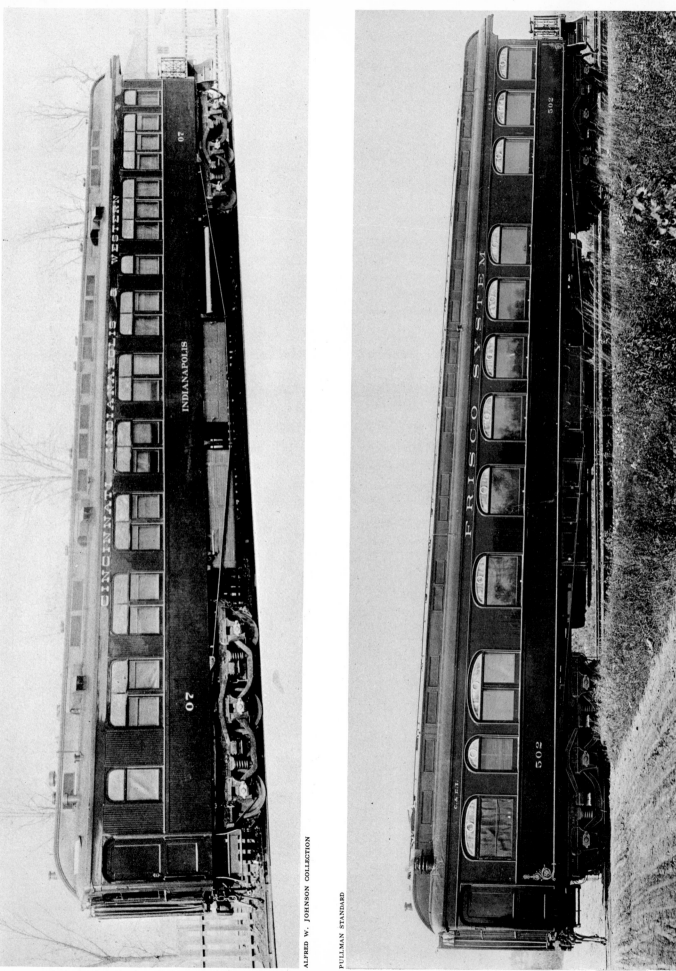

Geographically various as the carriers they served might be, the official cars shown on these two pages, the Cincinnati, Indianapolis & Western and the St. Louis–San Francisco shown opposite, and the Oregon Short Line on this page all possessed the hallmark of Pullman excellence. In the case of the Short Line interior excellence was translated in terms of comparative austerity, evidence of the pervading personality of Edward H. Harriman at the time the car was built for the Harriman-dominated affiliate of Union and Southern Pacific.

PULLMAN STANDARD

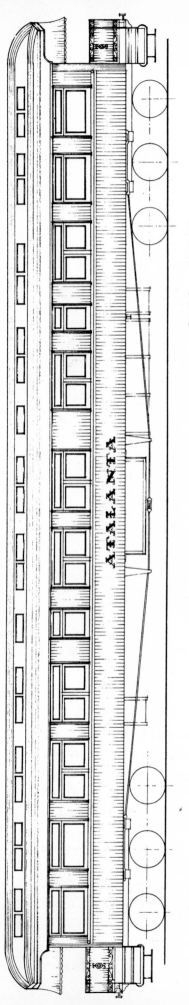

SIDE VIEW

ATALANTA

PRIVATE RAILWAY CAR
Atalanta
For Jay Gould, Esq.
Missouri Pacific Railroad

AMERICAN CAR & FOUNDRY CO., BUILDERS
ST. CHARLES, MO.

END VIEW

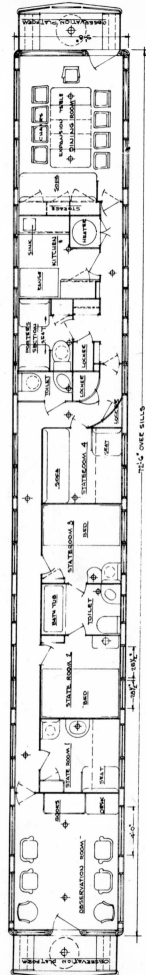

PLAN VIEW

OBSERVATION PLATFORM

DINING ROOM

EXPANSION TABLE

CHAIRS

SOFA

STORAGE

HEATER

KITCHEN

SINK

RANGE

PORTERS SECTION SEAT

LOCKER

LOCKER

LOCKER

TOILET

SEAT

STATEROOM 4

SOFA

STATEROOM 3

BED

BATH TUB

TOILET

STATE ROOM 2

BED

STATE ROOM 1

SEAT

BOOKS

DESK

OBSERVATION ROOM

OBSERVATION PLATFORM

Of all the business and private cars built for and occupied by Jay Gould in an age when the difference between privately owned varnish and the official cars of the carriers was purely academic, the one most closely associated with his name was Atalanta, the fleet-footed huntress of Arcadian legend. Built by American Car & Foundry in 1888 with two open platforms according to the ground plan reproduced on the opposite page, Atalanta was occupied on innumerable safaris across the continent over the Gould railroads by the man of disaster who was also one of the greatest operators of them all.

Always with him aboard Atalanta was the private Gould physician and special Gould chef in the galley, and often his favorite daughter, Helen, for company or traveling en suite in her own car Stranrear. On truly epic jaunts a private Gould cow rode in a baggage car ahead ready to give just the right amount of butterfat for the ailing titan. The entourage thundered at top speed through the Southwest with all the implications of the progress of a Roman proconsul, for Gould had but little time. As a daily ritual the Gould chef prepared the ladyfingers that constituted an important article of the financier's diet.

The change on the nameboards of this car representing new ownership was a reflection of one of Newport's more epic social vendettas.

TWO PHOTOS: PULLMAN STANDARD

The two views of the same Pullman-built private car depicted on the page opposite represent "before" and "after" one of the celebrated social engagements in the record of American upper-case plutocracy. The Illinois Central car No. 15 was ordered from the master carbuilder in 1906 for the occupancy of that carrier's aristocratic Stuyvesant Fish and was completed as shown in the official builder's photograph with the I.C. insigne on its nameboards. Before delivery could be made, however, a social error of the first magnitude on the part of the impetous and acidulous Mrs. Fish intervened. Mrs. Fish, momentarily the acknowledged queen of Newport, failed to invite E. H. Harriman and Mrs. Harriman to a particularly exalted social affair at Crossways, *the Fish estate in Bellevue Avenue, and a few days later Mr. Fish was discovered to be no longer president of the Illinois Central. Mr. Harriman owned the railroad and, while he probably couldn't have cared less for himself, Mrs. Harriman had wanted to go to the Fish entertainment. Before he had a chance to occupy it, Fish's fine car was reassigned, this time as Union Pacific No. 99, where, as an alternate to his car* Arden, *it was sometimes used by Harriman. Innocuous in appearance, Harriman was in reality no man to tangle with and a tough customer in the in-fighting. He is shown on this page at a Newport coaching party whose hostess was apparently better advised than Mrs. Fish.*

At the turn of the century and in the golden noontide of the fortunes of railroading, when railroad presidents were frock-coated potentates and the peers of bankers as the proprietors of everything in sight, the private cars of the lordly Rock Island were of legendary magnificence and suited to the exalted status of their occupants. No. 1901, a Pullman masterpiece of varnish, is shown on these two pages as testimony to the style in which the lords of creation rode at the end of the train.

For many years No. 1901 was reserved for the occupancy of Judge W. F. Moore, one of the group of Pittsburgh millionaires who had taken over the carrier's affairs after their properties had been purchased by Andrew Carnegie. Moore was anxious that his oldest son should become a railroader and to this end had him appointed station agent and telegraph operator at an obscure tank stop along the Rock Island main line at $50 a month and no allowance. The youth countered this Spartan parental decree whenever his father's splendid car with its French chef was routed over his division by handing up along with the train orders for the rear brakeman the dinner menu for the day at the $15 a week boarding house where he lived. The judge's heart was not softened. He had the boy reassigned to a lonely branch over which his car never passed.

Gold finelining on trucks and sidewalls, plate-glass windows with art glass tran-
soms, a neatly folded carriage step and brightly polished brasswork elements of
the observation platform on the Chesapeake & Ohio's presidential car No. 5
all bespeak the devoted expertise of a generation of artisans long since dead that
made the name of Pullman in the railroad world what Rolls Royce was to be in
a later time of motoring. The interior of another C. & O. official car, No. 9,
shown on this page, details the meticulous cabinetwork and upholsterer's care
which went into the private cars of a carrier whose prudent management was
matched by its dividends for many decades.

385

Two of the most celebrated private cars of archmillionaires and titans of American industry are depicted on the page opposite in Charles M. Schwab's Loretto I and Cyprus I of Colonel Daniel C. Jackling, Colorado gold miner and Utah copper king. Each was to be followed by a Loretto II and Cyprus II. The dining salon of Loretto, on this page facing its banquette end, reflected the opulence of its time and owner in its spray of electric bulbs prudently supplemented by Pintsch gas, marquetry and rare boiseries, rich hangings and splendid upholstery. In its confines the affairs of United States Steel traveled in circumstance and privacy appropriate to its billion-dollar capitalization and the patronage of John Pierpont Morgan the Magnificent.

387

Massive leather upholstery characterized the observation salon of Loretto, cushioned ease for the moneyed nates of Henry Clay Frick, James R. Keene or even the sanctimonious Judge Elbert H. Gary who disapproved of card playing as "undignified in one of the partners of United States Steel."

The master stateroom of Loretto, *however, which was reserved for the personal occupancy of Schwab or possibly J. P. Morgan upon occasion, reflected every refinement of comfort and elegance that money could afford and ingenuity could contrive within the confines of standard car construction. The equivalent apartment in a subsequent* Loretto *built more than a decade later was to be painted in cream and gold, but in 1902 the convention of opulence decreed rich, dark woodwork and the Marquetry Room at Pullman was never in better form.*

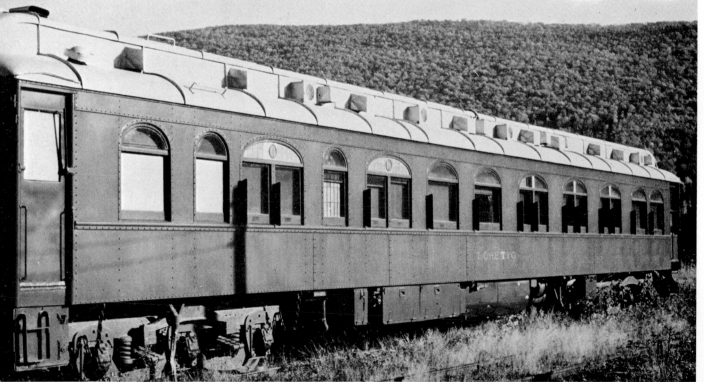

On these two pages are shown the dining salons of Charles M. Schwab's Loretto I *(page opposite)* and Loretto II, *evidence that, so satisfactory was the decor of the steelmaster's first private car, the second very nearly duplicated it. The ornamental vase went from one car to the next. Opposite, too, is Loretto I as it finally came to rest at a girls' camp in upper York State, a classic commentary on the mutations of time and the transient qualities of glory.*

Blue days and fair came to the Rock Island Railroad when J. P. Morgan, in the course of evolving United States Steel, paid the Tin Plate Trust composed of Daniel G. Reid, William B. Leeds and the Moore brothers $140,000,000 for their various rolling mills and amalgamating plants. The new group of millionaires promptly bought control of the affairs of Rock Island and became known as the Rock Island Group, an operation with money to throw at the birds and uninhibited by other stockholders. The Rock Island overnight became one of Pullman's best customers for private varnish. Throughout the opening years of the century a stunning series of private cars were outshopped to the Rock Island's order, among the most princely of which was Rockmarge built in 1902, a vintage year for palace cars generally on the still flowing tide of McKinley prosperity.

TWO PHOTOS: PULLMAN STANDARD

Some of the advantages of being Dictator of Mexico are suggested by the interiors, on these two pages, of the two-car private train built by Pullman in 1898 for Don Porfirio Díaz. The decor, according to the Presidential specifications, was of Honduran mahogany overlaid with gold ornamentation and dominated by the eagle and snake of Mexico at frequent intervals.

In the spring of 1886 the nation was pleased to learn that President Grover Cleveland, hitherto a confirmed bachelor, had taken a bride and the press followed the details of his wedding trip with avid interest. Both of the important illustrated weeklies, Harper's *and* Leslie's, *sent staff sketch artists to report on the Presidential wedding trip, which was spent at Deer Park, Maryland, where Cleveland indulged his favorite relaxations of hunting and fishing. His return to the capital city was made by special train over the Baltimore & Ohio on the private car of the carrier's President Robert Garrett. On this page* Harper's *depicts the happy couple at breakfast aboard Garrett's* Baltimore. *On the page opposite,* Leslie's *shows the president in the time-honored pose of public men as the train paused for fuel at Piedmont, Maryland.*

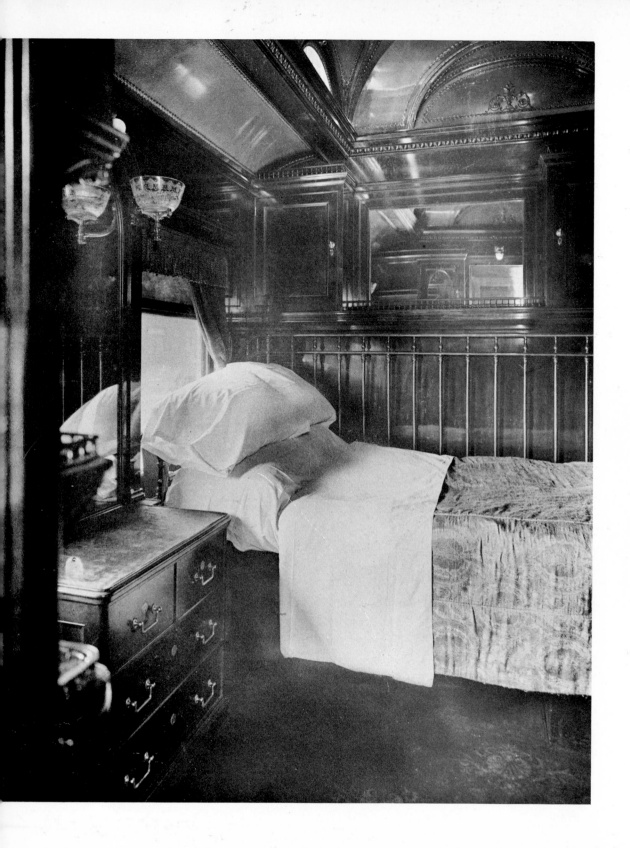

A good night's rest was assured the fortunate occupant of the Chicago & North Western's official car No. 60 on his occasions of travel through that carrier's far-flung empire of traffic. Mahogany panels, a king-size brass bed, broad picture windows and ornate gas illumination provided the finest that money could buy and that Pullman could design in the nineties.

In its original incorporation, David Moffat's Denver & Salt Lake Railroad was known as the Denver, Northwestern & Pacific, and for this carrier and the occupancy of Moffat himself, Pullman built the handsome private car Marcia in 1906. Notables who rode aboard Marcia and shared Moffat's hospitality read like a Denver Who's Who of the time: W. G. Evans, D. C. Dodge, Charlie Boettcher, Gerald Hughes and Spencer Penrose. The car was still in service long after the Denver & Salt Lake had been absorbed by the Denver & Rio Grande Western and was for many years assigned to the carrier's famous General Manager Al Perlman, later president of the New York Central in the regime of Robert Young.

THREE PHOTOS: PULLMAN STANDARD

The closing decades of private cars saw the outshopping by Pullman and its rivals of some uncommonly fine conveyances for the significant few who could afford them. One was Mrs. James Paul Donahue's *Japauldon* (below), built for the Woolworth heiress by American Car & Foundry with gold plumbing fixtures and a salon paneled in rarest boiseries with a ceiling of quartered oak beams. Paul Block's *Friendship* bespoke subdued elegance for a wealthy publisher who liked nice things.

HOWARD FOGG   PULLMAN STANDARD

The repercussions of Elia J. Baldwin's good fortune in Comstock mining shares, which first caused him to be known as "Lucky Baldwin," extended far and wide in California real estate, racing stables, hotels and ultimately in the Rancho Santa Anita that is today the West's most celebrated race track. Approximately $50,000 of Baldwin's multiple millions were used in 1912 by his daughter, Mrs. C. B. Stocker to have Pullman build her a fine private car, California, *whose cream and gold owner's stateroom is shown here, a pioneering gesture in decor in an age more given to mahogany than to pastels.*

PULLMAN STANDARD

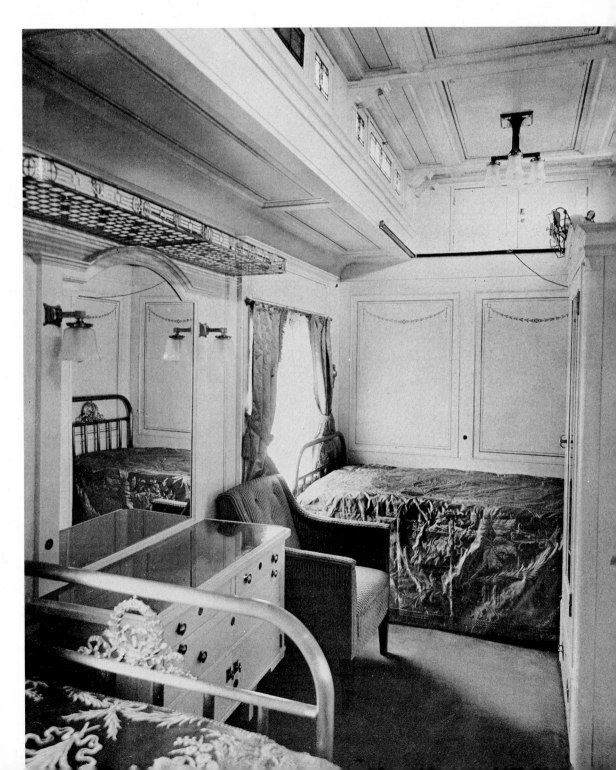

A promotional genius well in advance of his age, George M. Pullman disproved the adage that a rolling stone gathers no moss when he put his own private car *Monitor* on the road as a super de luxe sample and showcase of his palace car line. Built at Pullman in 1877 and known everywhere the rails were laid, its elegant appointments proved irresistible to rich men and executives and orders poured in to Pullman's books in its wake. A shrewd understanding of the value of publicity suggested that its owner place it at the disposal of every public figure of consequence for nearly three decades.

THREE PHOTOS: PULLMAN STANDARD

Happy times in old Carson City when the Virginia & Truckee still ran found Irene Simpson, Ruth Teiser and Katharine Haroun of the Wells Fargo History Room guests at luncheon of Charles Clegg and Lucius Beebe aboard The Gold Coast in the V. & T. yards. On the page opposite, the last of the long tally of private varnish to roll through Washoe Meadows finds immortality of a sort in a likeness in pastry from the kitchens of the Palace Hotel in San Francisco from the hands of the great Lucien Heyraud and on a gold cigaret box by Cartier in the possession of Charles Clegg. Ignorant of accepted railroad practice, the engraver portrayed the car with four-wheel trucks instead of the more conventional six.

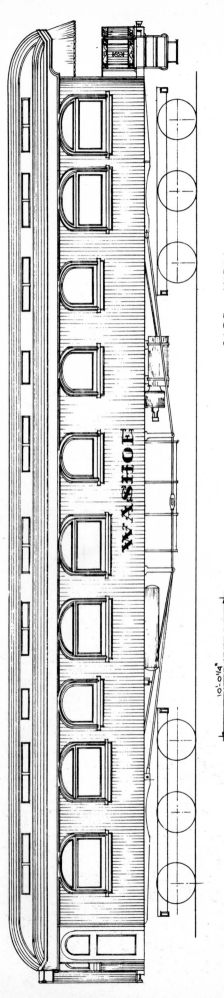

SIDE VIEW

WASHOE

BUTTE, ANACONDA & PACIFIC Ry.

Private Car WASHOE

PLAN NO. 1395

AMERICAN CAR & FOUNDRY CO., BUILDERS

ST. CHARLES, MO.

END VIEW

10'-0 1/4"

14'-1 5/8" OVER SMOKE STACK

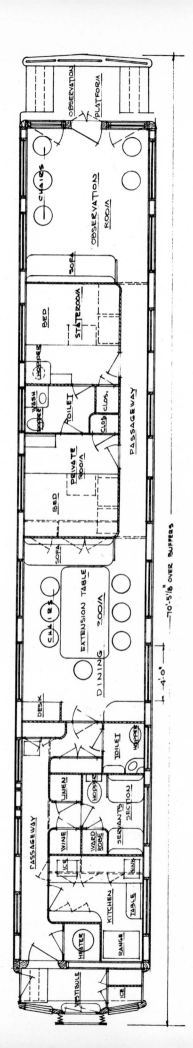

OBSERVATION PLATFORM

CHAIRS

OBSERVATION ROOM

SOFA

LOCKER

BED

STATEROOM

WASH

LOCKER

TOILET

CLOS. CLOS.

PASSAGEWAY

PRIVATE ROOM

BED

SOFA

CHAIRS

EXTENSION TABLE

DINING ROOM

DESK

TOILET

HOPPER

LINEN

HOPPER

PASSAGEWAY

WINE

WARD ROBE

SERVANTS SECTION

ICES

BUNK

KITCHEN

TABLE

HEATER

RANGE

VESTIBULE

ICE

70'-5 1/8" OVER BUFFERS

4'-0"

The New York, Ontario & Western, a railroad dogged by disaster until its abandonment in 1957, in its tired lifetime owned two official cars, Warwick, and No. 25, a Pullman-built business car that eventually passed to the Detroit & Mackinac. It is shown attached to inspection engine No. 26 as a special outside the carrier's Middletown depot in 1911 with a loving cup for retiring President Thomas P. Fowler. On the page opposite, the builder's plans of the Butte, Anaconda & Pacific's fine car Washoe suggest that, in the golden age of railroading, even a short line in the howling wilderness of Montana could afford the elegance of private varnish.

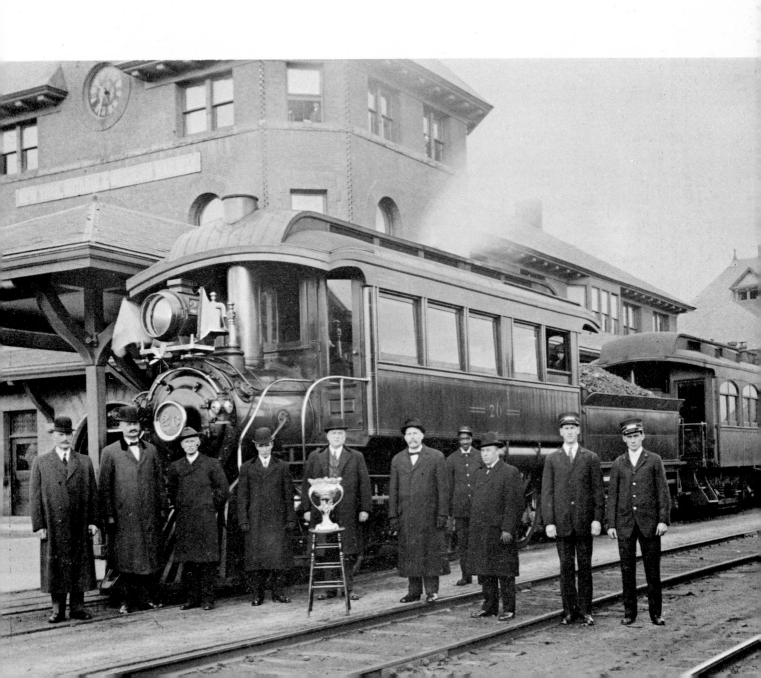

When, in 1878, a reporter for the Rocky Mountain News *mentioned in a news story the fact that aboard* Nomad, *private car of General William Jackson Palmer of the Denver & Rio Grande Railroad, the General's personal apartment boasted hot and cold running water, the old gentleman was enraged. Such details were an invasion of his privacy and reflected on his reputation as a seasoned campaigner. In letters to his wife, the General spoke of* Nomad *as "our nice house car" and for many years after the hot water matter had been forgotten he rode comfortably aboard it through the Rockies, guiding the destinies of his ever-crescent railroad empire. In 1959* Nomad, *still in operable repair, became the property of William White, president of the Minnequa Bank of Pueblo, Colorado, and on these pages it is shown restored with loving care to its Victorian elegance of decor by Mrs. White. It is stored at Durango and frequently rides at the end of the consist of the* Silverton *between Durango and Silverton via the spectacular Canyon of the River of Lost Souls.*

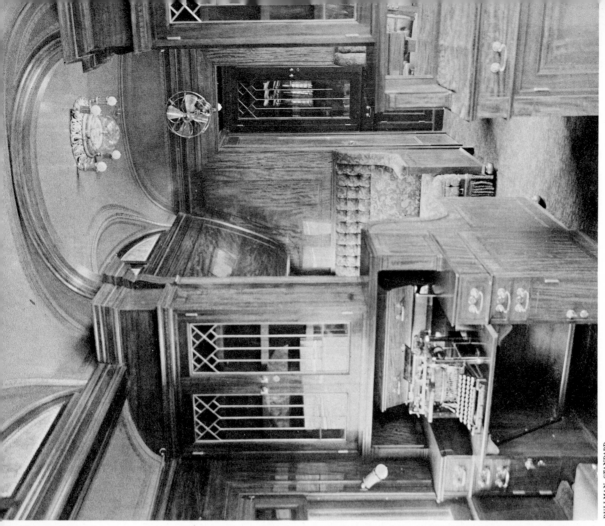

Changing times and typewriters are reflected in the half century of business car fittings represented by the 1905 Remington aboard Cape Girardeau and the secretary's office aboard the Southern Pacific's Sunset fifty years later.

Among the multiple functions of the official car, which include living accommodations for executives while on line and the entertainment of influential notables, is that of mobile office. From times primeval, business cars have been built with a combined stateroom and diminutive office for the occupancy and occasions of the secretary of the vice-president or division superintendent to whom the car is assigned. Both tradition and the proprieties have invariably suggested that the secretary be a man. On this page, aboard the New York Central's official car No. 5, built by Pullman in 1930, is the secretarial cubicle, whose decor nicely embraces both the era of roll-top desks and a later age of metal lock-cabinets and streamlined lighting fixtures.

PULLMAN STANDARD

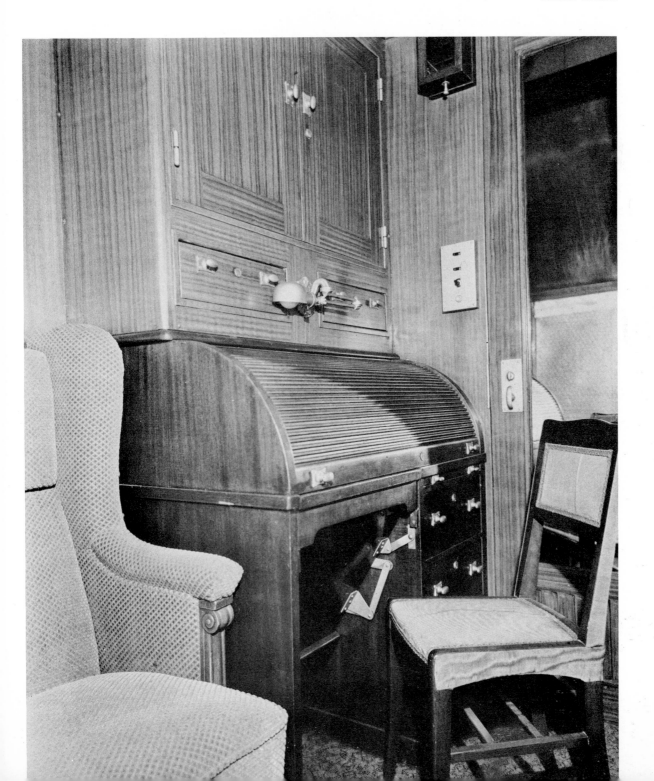

The Private Car *Black Hawk*

Built For Charles E. Perkins

of

The Chicago, Burlington & Quincy Railroad

At Pullman, Illinois

1902

One of the celebrated official cars of the railroad West in its great days was Black Hawk, built by Pullman in 1902 for the Burlington's aristocratic Charles Elliott Perkins and depicted on the page opposite and at the left. The Burlington purchased a second Black Hawk, shown below, in 1944 and modernized it with air conditioning in 1951. Black Hawk II had originally been built by Pullman as Robert Peary in 1927 and its new name lent continuity to one of the venerable traditions of a far-flung system of railroads.

PULLMAN STANDARD   RON CHRISTISON

Described by Railway Age as "a dealer in railroads," Newman Erb at one time controlled, among others, the Ann Arbor, the Père Marquette, the Wisconsin Central, the Denver & Salt Lake and the two railroads represented on the opposite page, the Minneapolis & St. Louis and the St. Louis, Memphis & Southeastern. Aboard the beautiful car Cape Girardeau, whose interior is also shown on this page, he rode comfortably in his lifetime; on the M. & St. L. No. 300 he died. No. 300 was originally outshopped by Pullman to the specifications of Cowin Hawley, president of the road and a partner in the firm of Hawley & Davis, 25 Broad Street, New York City. A member of the so-called Waldorf crowd, which included Diamond Jim Brady, John W. Gates and Bernard Baruch, Hawley had the car delivered to New York and it was four years before it ever touched M. & St. L. iron. In 1916 Erb took over the carrier and changed the name of No. 300 to Twin Cities. Shortly thereafter he was dethroned and committed suicide while a guest aboard the private car that had once been his own. Twin Cities is the only varnish in the record to achieve this morbid distinction.

THREE PHOTOS: PULLMAN STANDARD

When Alamogordo, *shown on this and the page opposite, was built by Pullman for the El Paso & Northeastern, later to become part of the Southern Pacific, the high-water mark of fine cabinetmaking for railroad cars had been achieved, as had the zenith of their exterior beauty and symmetry of design. From then on, gold finelining, art glass windows and shaded lettering on nameboards were to be in decline. A quarter of a century after the vintage year 1902 that saw* Alamogordo *outshopped, in an age of all-steel construction and austere decor, the Magma Arizon Railroad in 1926 ordered* Alder *just to show that a short line railroad could still afford the elegances of the grand manner.*

THREE PHOTOS: PULLMAN STANDARD

Although miles apart in social philosophy, James Hazen Hyde, whose Pullman-built private car Bay Shore *is shown on the page opposite, and* Henry Clay Frick, whose Westmoreland *is beneath, had this much in common: each liked a nice train ride aboard a fine private car. Young Hyde, whose taste in knee breeches, French actresses and $200,000 dinner parties was equally Corinthian, got into trouble when it was discovered that he was financing many of these with policyholder's funds from the Equitable Life* Assurance Company *of which his father was president and he an officer. Frick, the implacable foe of the steel unions, was finally remembered as a great public benefactor through the agency of the Frick Museum in New York City. On this page is the comparatively simple interior of Thomas Fortune Ryan's private varnish* Père Marquette, *tangible evidence of its owner's profitable association in New York streetcar franchises with Peter A. B. Widener and William C. Whitney.*

THREE PHOTOS: PULLMAN STANDARD

In modern times there is no counterpart to the workmanship of Pullman's palace cars, save possibly Rolls Royce, and only Abbot Downing, the Concord coachmaker, was the contemporary peer. Abbot Downing lasted barely into the Pullman age, its last great shipment of coaches to Wells Fargo having been made in 1869. Rolls Royce, founded in 1905, was a contemporary of the later, but by no means declining, years of Pullman craftsmanship. It would be difficult to conjure more glittering paradigms of Pullman perfectionism as they came from the paint shops than the Chicago Great Western's No. 101 or the Colorado Midland's No. 100, built in 1901 and 1898, respectively. Both were in the superb tradition of exterior finish that justified the name of varnish car. No. 101 is still in service on the Great Western sixty years after it was delivered; the C. M. No. 100 achieved later celebrity when it was named Cascade for occupancy by Bert Carlton, the Cripple Creek millionaire who took over the road's management in its final years. The time that produced them was an age of dedicated craftsmen that the world has only infrequently seen since.

THREE PHOTOS: PULLMAN STANDARD

Winner, hands down, in the elegance sweepstakes for private cars of the nineties were two successive cars named *Alexander*, built by Pullman for Angus Archibald McLeod, president of the Philadelphia & Reading Railroad in Pennsylvania. *Alexander I, built in 1890, is shown in its exterior elevation on the page opposite. The master* stateroom of *Alexander II is depicted here. Both were paid for out of his personal pocket by McLeod and were in no sense either railroad property or business cars. In fact, Alexander II bore the word "Private" boldly engrossed on the nameboards of the car and on all its exterior doors. It was just that.*

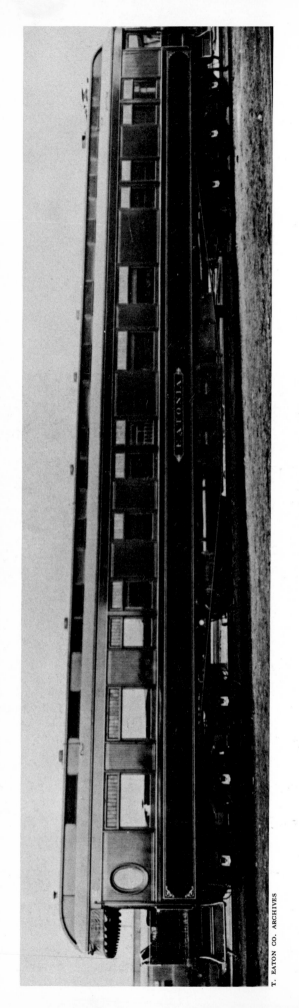

Two Eatonias were built for Sir John, the first (above) by Barney & Smith at Dayton in 1908, and the second, after the earlier car had been destroyed by fire, by Pullman in 1916.

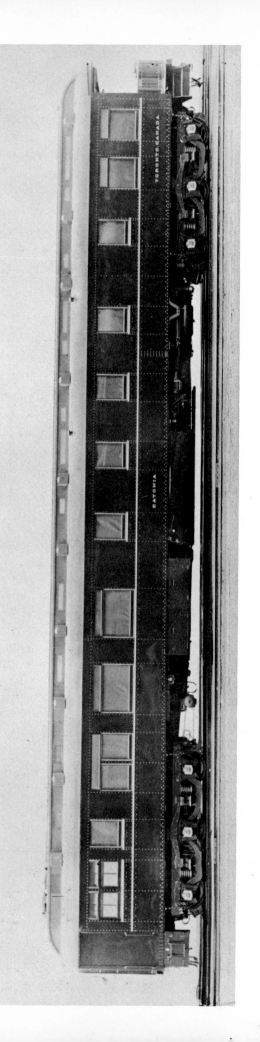

Like many members of the private car club, Sir John Eaton of Toronto owned successively two fine cars named for the family fortunes Eatonia. *Heir to the largest department store anywhere in the British Commonwealth, Sir John was a merchant prince of swaggering proportions and a director of Canadian Pacific. In the days before the 1914 war a happy group posed aboard first* Eatonia *as shown below; it included Colonel W. F. Eaton, George Beattie, Lady and Sir John Eaton. A notable patriot, Sir John saw to it that one of the first missions for* Eatonia II *after it was delivered from Pullman in 1916 was to be dispatched laden with doctors, nurses and medical supplies to Halifax after the great munitions explosion there in 1917. Second* Eatonia *later was taken over as a business car of the vast railroad enterprise of which its first owner had been an important director.*

T. EATON CO. ARCHIVES

"Eatonia *covered countless thousands of miles up and down and across Canada and the United States,*" *wrote Lady Eaton in her memoires of the family's first private car of that name.* "*I always felt it to be the most luxurious kind of travel, though I must say there was nothing for show, but everything for comfort and ease of service. . . . Two stewards, Kirk and Carter, were always on duty and knew their business perfectly.*" *The two interiors of first* Eatonia *on the opposite page are rare items of railroad lore in that they depict Barney & Smith decor and construction in private varnish at the turn of the century. On this page the master stateroom of second* Eatonia *represents convenience and esthetic satisfaction for a director of the Canadian Pacific Railway and a tycoon of commerce within the Commonwealth.*

TWO PHOTOS: T. EATON CO. ARCHIVES   PULLMAN STANDARD

One of the die-hard members of the private car club was Bruce Dodson, a Kansas City insurance magnate who enjoyed a nice train ride to his Palm Beach winter home aboard two successive cars named Helma. Here he is standing beside Helma II, which had originally been built by Pullman as Alicia for Boston moneybags A. C. Burrage. A perfectionist, Mr. Dodson insisted that his cars in their every mechanical aspect function like a fine Swiss watch, and the two Helmas were shopped each year at Pullman to maintain trucks and brake rigging in meticulous order.

HOLIDAY MAGAZINE

In the eighties when the private car Newport (left) was carried on Pullman's list of available per diem cars, French mirrors and Honduran mahogany were essential to stylish travel for the well-to-do, even if some of the party slept in open section berths. The Georgia Northern's second Moultrie (above) has greater privacy in its master apartments and was at one time the Chicago & Eastern Illinois' Mount Vernon. After Charles Pidcock, owner of the Georgia Northern, sold Lucius Beebe and Charles Clegg the car that became The Gold Coast, he soon replaced it with Mount Vernon. First Moultrie, also owned by the G.N., had been original varnish car of Henry M. Flagler, the Florida empire builder.

PULLMAN STANDARD   GEORGIA NORTHERN RAILROAD

A man who knew what he wanted and almost always got it eventually, Montana's Senator William A. Clark looked the part he played to the hilt of a rich, acquisitive frontiersman with an eye to the main chance. He aspired to millions and he acquired them. He aspired to the toga and got that too, after a contest that has become legendary in the political annals of the Old West. He wanted a fine private car, and Pullman was glad to oblige so discerning a customer. On these two pages are shown the Senator himself in his great days in Washington, the master bedroom and brass bed on No. 2001 and the observation salon, where he rode in substantial if somewhat gloomy grandeur, the archetypal, silk-hatted old moneybags of an age that saw nothing wrong either in acquiring money or spending it once it had been made.

PULLMAN STANDARD

The type and image of a senatorial aristocrat at the turn of the century, everything about Clark bespoke his contempt for mediocrity. An outstanding member of the private car club, he passed on his membership to his son Charlie, whose equally splendid if less upholstered car Errant is depicted on the pages immediately following.

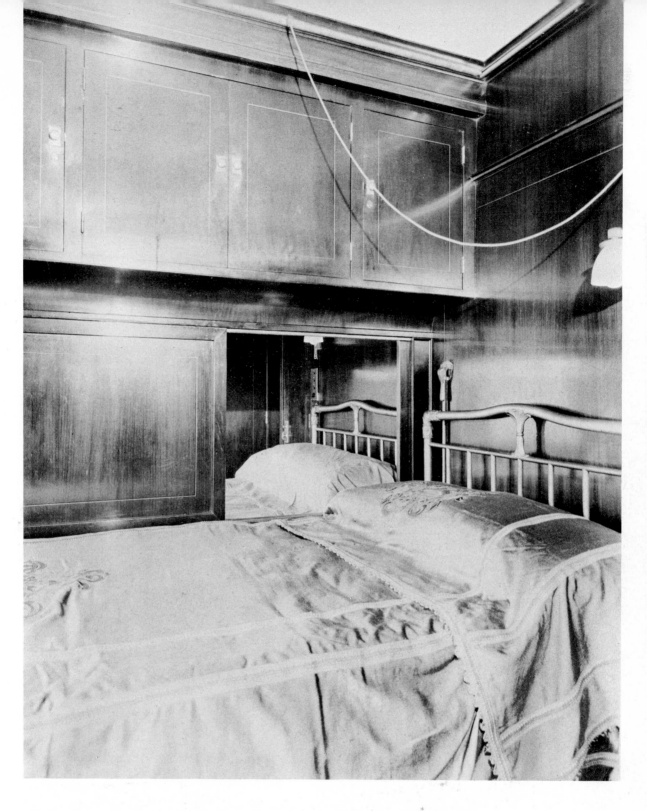

When, in the foreword to Mansions On Rails, *the author wrote, "In vain would*
one search (aboard private cars generally) for the convenience through whose
agency the pressure of a button from the owner's bunk dissolved a partition to
find it joined on roller bearings by the bed from the adjacent cabin," he couldn't
have been more wrong. Such an ingenious device was indeed incorporated into
the master suite of Errant *when it was built in 1926 by Pullman for Charlie Clark,*
son of Montana's legendary Senator William A. Clark, and it is depicted here. On
the page opposite, in a father-and-son grouping, are Errant *and Senator Clark's*
No. 2001, both Pullman-built to demonstrate that a nice taste in private varnish
may be inherited like a penchant for yachting or Madeira.

433

Whitehall *was built by Pullman in 1916 to the specifications of Mrs. Henry M. Flagler, widow and third wife of the Florida empire builder, hotel magnate and Standard Oil partner, and its decor, shown on the page opposite, and Pullman standard construction may be taken as typical of* Pullman's ultimate *expertise in the technique of carbuilding.* Whitehall *bore the name of the $15,000,000 mansion at Palm Beach that Flagler had built for his third wife and which subsequently became a hotel and one of the landmarks of the Florida Gold Coast.*

EVERETT DE GOLYER

FORD MOTOR CO.

FORD MOTOR CO.

Henry Ford's venture into railroading in the form of the Detroit, Toledo & Ironton Railroad running south from Detroit through the heart of the industrial Middle West was freighted with comedy from the beginning. Ford, known as an eccentric of the first order by this time, attempted to regulate the habits of his railroad employees as to whisky and tobacco without marked success. Until his rolling stock began pounding itself to pieces he relaid miles of track with cement ties, which he thought would be "durable." Irreverent executives wired details of monstrous catastrophes that sent wrecking crews on sleeveless errands, but the streak of rust proved one of the best investments in Ford's entire manufacturing empire.

Its line ran across and interchanged with a variety of carriers, the New York Central, Wabash, Baltimore & Ohio, Norfolk & Western, Erie, Ann Arbor, Pennsylvania and the Chesapeake & Ohio and broke a distributing bottleneck at Detroit which had long been a source of anguish. As an established railroader, Ford ordered his celebrated private car Fair Lane from Pullman, and he is shown here aboard it with a party of friends, including Edsel Ford and his wife, Ford himself and Thomas A. Edison in a D.T. & I. special. On the page opposite, Fair Lane is shown on delivery from the builder and later in the livery of the Cotton Belt, which acquired it after the arch-millionaire's death as its presidential car.

KAUFMANN & FABRY

The transition from general service to special equipment and the reverse are a commonplace in the record of Pullmans, but not always as available to the photographic record as in the car depicted on these two pages. Opposite is the drawing–observation salon of Golden Peak, built in the early years of the air-conditioned thirties for service between St. Paul–Minneapolis and the Northwest in the Great Northern's Oriental Limited. When this train was replaced on the G.N. timetable by the streamlined Empire Builder, Golden Peak was traded in and appeared on Pullman's used car lot south of Chicago. It was purchased by Lucius Beebe and Charles Clegg, extensively recompartmented and rebuilt by the

Western Pacific at Sacramento and decorated by Robert Hanley, Inc., of Hollywood as the private car The Virginia City, named for the Nevada community where Clegg and Beebe lived. Although the trade in private railroad cars has abated in recent years, a similar metamorphosis took place in the case of Chesapeake & Ohio's business car No. 28, assigned to Robert Young until the time of his death, when it passed into private ownership and emerged as the personal property of Mrs. Charles S. Payson of New York, a sister of John Hay Whitney and member of a family which for three generations has taken private cars for granted on an impressive scale.

439

MAYNARD PARKER

Posed aboard her private Pullman in the course of her 1911 tour of the United States, Sarah Bernhardt models a Persian lamb coat while on the adjacent banquette a chinchilla wrap is negligently thrown to suggest the dimensions of her wardrobe. It was an age when stars of the stage and opera regarded private cars as status symbols, and their provision was stipulated in their contracts. This extremely rare Bernhardt portrait is from the collection of Edward S. Tolan, a nephew of Edward J. Sullivan, Bernhardt's personal manager on the tour.

Above, a photographer of 1911 snaps Bernhardt on the platform of her private car with her manager, Edward J. Sullivan, while, below, the company poses for its portrait before departing from Grand Central Depot in New York.

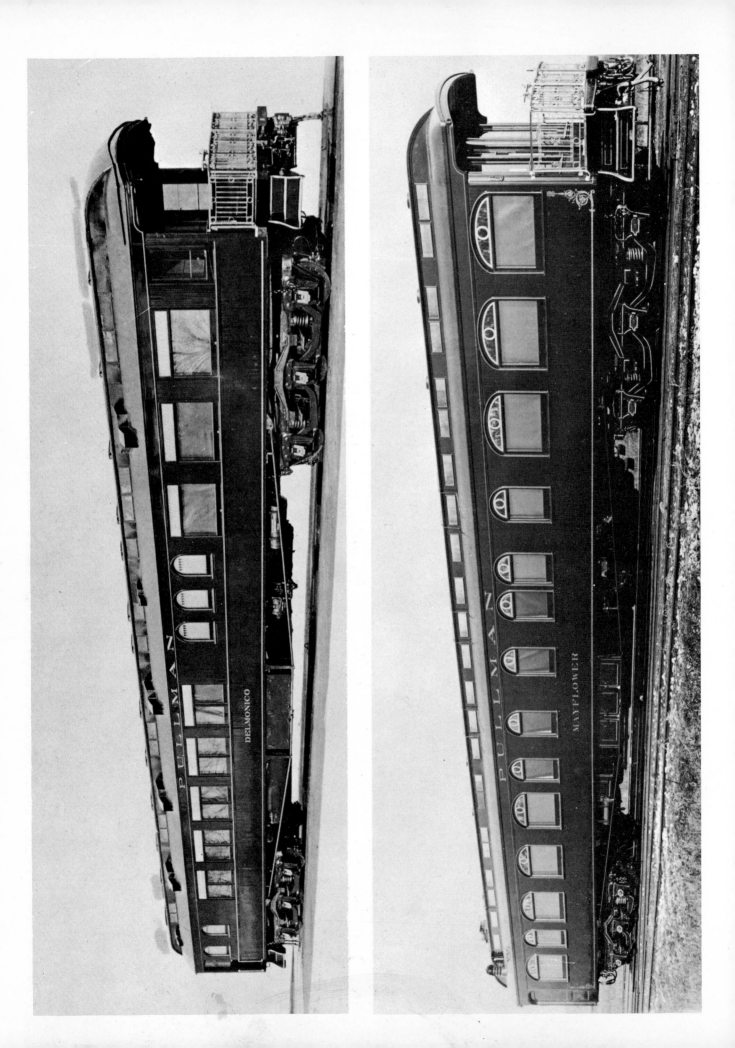

In 1901 anyone with a penchant for travel in the grand manner and approximately $100 a day to spend in addition to the eighteen full first-class fares required by the carriers themselves, could rent *Mayflower*, shown on this and the opposite page, from Pullman's pool of per diem hotel cars. For the price there came with the car a cook and waiter, and many men of wealth and importance found it more convenient and economical to rent a private car when the occasion demanded than to own one outright, with its not inconsiderable initial cost and carrying charges. *Mayflower's* beautiful lines represent the high-water mark of Pullman design before refinement of decor and rich ornamentation began to yield to mere utilitarianism. A decade later he might well have rented *Delmonico*, also shown on the opposite page. Outshopped in 1909 *Delmonico* was still an extremely handsome private car and a credit to the nabob who might roll up aboard her at Palm Beach for the Washington's Birthday Ball at the Royal Poinciana or at the Louisville & Nashville depot at Louisville for the Derby.

THREE PHOTOS: PULLMAN STANDARD

Most approved modern practice of enclosed solariums to replace traditional railed observation platforms is suggested by Harry S. Black's Esperanza *(right) and U.S. Steel's presidential varnish car* Laurel Ridge, *occupied, when this was taken, by Benjamin Fairless.*

RON CHRISTISON   PULLMAN STANDARD

Union Pacific's No. 100, built for its president in 1915, clung to brass-railed verandah of the great tradition.

PULLMAN STANDARD

The Santa Fe's presidential private car Santa Fe *illustrates a compromise between streamlined protection and open observation platform in the grand manner of other years.*

SANTA FE RAILWAY

By the late twenties and the year 1930, the Pullman-built private cars of the well-to-do represented on the page opposite by William F. Kenny's St. Nicholas, A. C. Burrage's Alicia and Paul Block's Friendship had surrendered the distinguishing individuality of brass-railed observation platforms, which had, in any event, been rendered obsolete by high-speed train cardings that made them untenable with comfort or safety.

Although the rolling stock represented here was valued in the aggregate at well over a million dollars, exterior hallmarks of character were supplanted by uniformity and conformity. The observation lounge of W. R. Reynolds's Winette, shown on this page, represented the era with comfort and urbanity of decor where, half a century previous, flamboyant opulence had been the rule.

FOUR PHOTOS: PULLMAN STANDARD

When in 1925 Pullman built St. Nicholas for
William F. Kenny of New York the glory years
of private varnish were already past and the carbuilder's expertise had reached its zenith, even as
twilight impended. Only a few more cars for private owners were to be listed as contemporaries
of St. Nicholas: Paul Block's Friendship, W. R.
Reynolds's Winette and Harry Payne Bingham's
Pawnee, but all were to be of a superb final vintage. On these two pages are the observation room
and dining salon, respectively, of St. Nicholas as
it came from the builder.

TWO PHOTOS: PULLMAN STANDARD

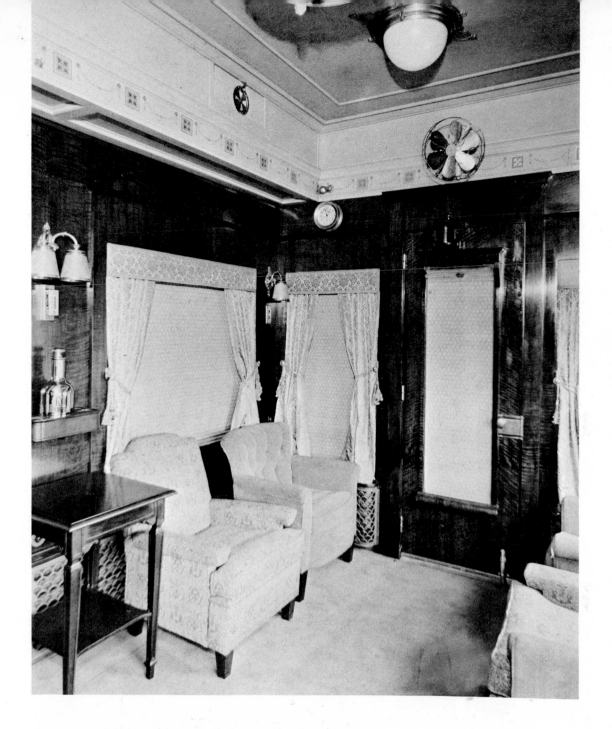

So private was Harry Payne Bingham's Pawnee that the legend of its privacy appeared twice on its rear door, as shown opposite. Its interior appointments suggest the restrained taste and simplicity of decor characteristic of the closing years of the age of private car transport. Pullman built Pawnee in 1930.

FOUR PHOTOS: PULLMAN STANDARD

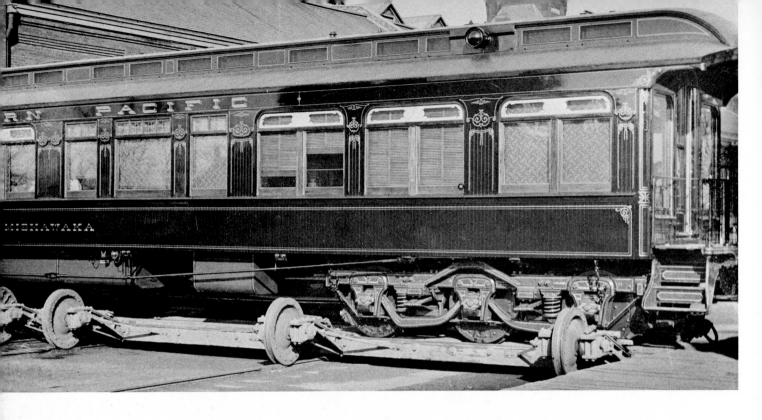

Representative of the styling of Pullman private cars in the early nineties are
Mishawaka and Ogontz, *built to the personal specifications of Charles Crocker,
powerful San Francisco nabob of Southern Pacific fame, and Robert Garrett, of
the Baltimore & Ohio. On the page opposite, the principal salon of* Mishawaka
*is visual evidence of the pride of craftsmanship taken in their handiwork by the
Black Forest cabinetmakers and woodworkers imported by Pullman to work in the
firm's celebrated* Marquetry Room *at Pullman, Illinois.*

THREE PHOTOS: PULLMAN STANDARD

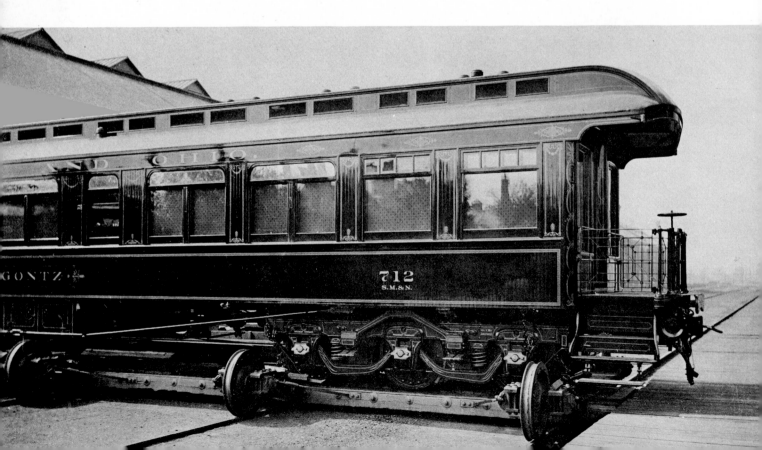

New York Central's No. 5, built in 1931 for occupancy by William K. Vanderbilt, represented the high tide of Vanderbilt participation in the carrier's affairs. It was already an economic liability in the light of the market debacle of 1929.

Built in 1902 to replace his earlier Wagner-built private car Pilgrim, William Collins Whitney's magnificent Pullman Wanderer was rebuilt in 1913 and remained in service in the Whitney family until the time of the 1941 war. Whitneys and Vanderbilts together formed the largest single family membership in the private car club over the years.

In 1931 two fine new conveyances were placed at the disposal of William K. Vanderbilt II, former president and senior director of the New York Central Lines. One was the yacht Alva, a 264-foot diesel-powered personal ocean liner built at Kiel by Krupp Germaniawerft at a cost of $2,500,000; the other, his railroad's official car No. 5 built by Pullman at an undisclosed but somewhat smaller cost. No. 5 was one of the handsomest and the very last private car to be built for a New York Central's executive of the Vanderbilt dynasty. Later that year Central,

which in 1929 had sold for 256½ on the New York Stock Exchange, touched 8¾ and the Vanderbilt private car years were over. In contrast to No. 5, whose interior is shown on this page and its handsome all-steel side elevation opposite, Genesta, a New York Central car built at the turn of the century, seemed comparatively modest, but there were undoubtedly stockholders in the railroad, some of them Vanderbilts, who would gladly have exchanged the era it represented for that symbolized by No. 5.

THREE PHOTOS: PULLMAN STANDARD

Noble examples of private varnish dating from the age of all-wooden construction and open platforms at both ends are shown on the page opposite in Pullman's No. 99 for the Nashville, Chattanooga & St. Louis in the years when that Deep South carrier enjoyed a distinguished individuality and autonomous management, and Michigan, of whose purchaser the Pullman records contain no trace and which must be ascribed to a railroad of the region suggested by its name. Shown above, snow-mantled as befits its years, is the ill-fated Ontario & Western's venerable office car Warwick. When at last the Old Woman closed its books to become the largest main line abandonment in the record, Warwick was purchased for an upstate museum by Charles R. Diebold. It is shown here before making its last run out of Buffalo in 1957.

TWO PHOTOS: PULLMAN STANDARD

CHARLES R. DIEBOLD

SOME NAME TRAINS

IN THE ECONOMY of every railroad of consequence in the United States its showcase and advertisement was its passenger service, and it must be remembered that until approximately 1930, passengers constituted a major source of railroad revenue. A carrier's reputation rose and fell on the quality of its dollar dinner and the splendor of its club cars. The name trains of the golden age of steam transport: the *Broadway Limited,* the *Twentieth Century Limited,* the *Black Diamond,* the *Overland Limited,* the *Bar Harbor Express,* the *Panama Limited,* the *Merchants Limited,* the *Florida Special,* the *Royal Blue,* the *Empire Builder* and the *Empire State Express* were household words. To have ridden them was a reflected glory and a mark of distinction. A man derived positive social and economic stature from patronizing the *Twentieth Century Limited* and bragged about the steaks on the *Sunset.*

And the ultimate in grandeur bore the name of the great over-all patron and genius of luxury travel. It was the all-Pullman train.

To list a flyer on a limited schedule, often with an extra fare attached, composed wholly of sleepers, room cars, parlor cars, diners, lounges and observation cars all manufactured and maintained by Pullman was to mark a railroad as having achieved the highest imaginable operational status. It represented the big time of republican snobbism. Coach trains with their chair cars, be they ever so comfortable or ornate, were for farmers and the peasantry and definitely second-class. Where trains were composed of both coaches and Pullmans the occupants of the former were strictly interdicted from intruding upon the diners and club cars of the preferred patrons.

To go Pullman was a way of American life. Even the socially elect hoboes and drifters bragged that they rode the brake gear and unguarded open platforms of nineteenth-century Pullman equipment, while more humble and less dexterous stiffs rode the slower freights, which they in turn designated side-door Pullmans.

The names of the great American passenger trains of only yesterday are the sonorous, the soaring syllables of majestic tradition, as resounding as the names of the knights who gathered at Arthur's Round Table or those of English victories at sea. They possessed a grandeur of character and regional romance that has never been associated with any other category of identification: the *Shenandoah*, the *Cascade*, the *Lake Shore Limited*, the *Golden Triangle*, the *Creole*, the *Congressional*, the *East Wind*, the *Navajo*, the *Banner Blue* and the *Corn King*. There were the less august names of less pretentious runs, characterized by suburban bounce and pride: the *Hustler*, the *Sooner*, the *Zipper*, the *Hoosier*, the *Tippecanoe*, the *Bluebonnet* and the *Planter*.

And rising above the French horns and oboes of the great symphony of movement was the soaring fiddle music of the lordly name trains that dominated the imaginations of men. They still sound splendidly in the ear: the *Broadway Limited*, the *Overland Limited*, the *Grand Canyon Limited*, the *Twentieth Century Limited*, the *Spirit of St. Louis*, the *Empire Builder*, the *Pony Express*, the *Yankee Clipper*, the *West Indian Mail*, the *Forty-niner*, the *Chief*, the *North Coast Limited*, the *Florida Special*.

The names of famous trains ran the gamut of variety from regional geography and identification of place to statesmen, railroaders, birds and Indians. Some, like the *Fast Flying Virginian*, the *Oil City Flyer*, the *Cannonball*, the *400* and *St. Louis Zipper* suggested the speed of their going. The *Forty-niner*, the *Twentieth Century Limited*, the *Exposition Flyer* and the *Panama Limited* suggested epochs, eras or events in the national legend. Most common of all designations were those of place: the *North Coast Limited*, the *Florida Special*, the *Golden Triangle*, the *State of Maine*, the *Lake Shore* and the *Denver Special*.

A few trains were named for birds: the *Flamingo*, the *Gull*, the *Night Hawk*, the *Mountain Bluebird*, the *Redwing*, the *Nightingale*, the *Owl*, the *Blue Bird*, the *Lark*, the *Humming Bird* and the *Flying Crow*. One was named for a woman, *Ann Rutledge*, and one for a racehorse, *Nancy Hanks*. Statesmen have been remembered in the *De Witt Clinton*, the *Jeffersonian*, the *Abraham Lincoln* and the *George Washington*, and less personally in the *Diplomat*, the *Legislator*, the *Judiciary*, the *Senator* and the *President*. Railroaders were memorialized in the *Empire Builder*, the *Commodore Vanderbilt*, the *Dixie Flagler* and the *Henry M. Flagler*. Indians achieved a measure of immortality in the *Chief* and the *Super Chief*, the *Navajo*, the *Seminole*, the *Hiawatha*, the *Ute*, the *Pocahontas*, the *Powhatan*, the *Chickasaw*, the *Black Hawk*, the *Iroquois* and the *Sioux*.

Flowers and trees rated in the *Portland Rose*, the *Bluebonnet*, the *Royal Palm*, the *Orange Blossom Special*, the *Maple Leaf*, the *Pine Tree Special* and the *Columbine*.

The longest train name the author has encountered was the Denver & Rio Grande Western's train No. 3, which the *Official Guide* in 1900 listed as *The Trans-Continental, San Francisco, Butte & Portland Express*. The shortest was the New Haven's *Owl*. The least felicitous were perhaps the Chicago & Eastern Illinois' *Spirit of Progress* and the Père Marquette's *Furniture City Special* between Chicago and Grand Rapids.

Just when the practice originated of giving trains distinguishing names in addition to the numbers that identified them on the company's time cards isn't altogether clear. That it was reasonably early in the record of railroad operations is apparent from the lithographic posters that advertised train travel in the mid-nineteenth century, and one of these soliciting patronage for the Lake Shore & Michigan Southern in 1862 lists four name trains maintained over "The American Route to the West": the *Day Express*, *Night Express*, the *Express Mail* and *Lightning Express*.

Not very imaginative samples of nomenclature, they at least served the useful purpose of identifying the passenger runs in the public imagination, which could hardly be expected to cope with official listing by number. They were also an improvement over such pedestrian designation as the Buffalo–Cleveland train or the Columbus–Indianapolis local. *Lightning* and *Cannonball* were universally popular and marked the dawning awareness on the part of the public that trains might have personalities of their own and, even on the same run, different characteristics of service and accommodations.

Antedating even these primeval name trains was the Illinois Central's *Lightning Express*, which in 1856 was carrying sleepers on the night run between Chicago and St. Louis.

With entire appropriateness, the first name train on an American railroad the author has been able to discover was a New England institution. It was also the longest lived of all name trains, for in 1937 when the *Fall River Boat Train* finally suspended because there were no longer boats for it to meet, it had been in continuous operation for ninety years.

The *Boat Train,* as it was generally abbreviated during those nine decades, ran between Boston and Fall River every evening over the rails of the Old Colony Railroad, and later the New York, New Haven & Hartford, to meet the down steamers of the Fall River Line to New York and to go up again the next morning.

The train and its connecting steamers came into being before through rail connections between New York and Boston were available and it is testimony to the affection in which this rail–water route was held by entire generations of American travelers that it continued in profitable operation long after the running time of crack direct connections over the New Haven's Shore Line had been reduced to five hours between the South Station and Grand Central.

Equipment for the *Boat Train,* because of its comparatively short haul, was simple: coaches and parlor cars. No diner was included for the ample reason that the cuisine on the steamers *Pilgrim, Puritan* and *Priscilla* were world-famous and, in the esteem of many Bostonians the peer of Parker's Hotel in School Street, while New Yorkers asserted it was every bit as good as Delmonico's and afforded a sea view to boot. The only spectacular innovation it ever inaugurated was in the form of two English-style compartmented parlor cars, which were entered from separate doors along the side while the conductor passed along an outside footboard to work his train. These daytime carriages, suggestive as they were of Colonel Mann's boudoir sleeping cars, were successful enough but finally were supplanted by parlor cars named *Pansy* and *Violet,* which in their own right became household words in the lexicon of Bostonians.

The conductor on the *Boat Train,* who was assisted in taking up his tickets by a clerk who roughly corresponded to the later train secretary on the *Broadway* and *Century,* was invariably the senior conductor of his time and a man of position and importance in the community. Alvin F. Harlow, official historian of New England railroading, records that only ten men occupied this exalted post in the ninety years of

the train's existence, most celebrated of them being Asa R. Porter, who rode back and forth continuously between the train's two terminals for thirty-two years.

Porter was a friend of presidents and on terms of grave and courteous friendship with all the important captains of industry who constituted an important part of the passenger list. A boutonniere invariably adorned his frock coat of office and he wore short chin whiskers and a clean upper lip which gave him the appearance of a stage Yankee, but so great was his dignity that even superior officials of the railroad addressed him as "Mr. Porter" and men of the great world liked to boast of his acquaintance.

The *Boat Train* was not without competition, stiffest of which was offered by the Merchants Steamship Line sailing in direct rivalry out of Providence. Passengers getting off the cars at the Merchants pier were served tea before going up the gangplank, and a band played encouraging airs on the pierhead. The general manager in top hat and tailcoat greeted his patrons warmly, shaking hands with each and every one of them, his hands encased in a pair of white kid gloves, fresh daily. The signal for hoisting the gangway and departing was the manager's taking off his gloves and, with a lordly gesture, tossing them into the harbor.

Still another elegance that was for many years a feature of the New Haven's service was the daily private-run, space aboard which was held by annual subscription and which amounted to an entire train of club cars every afternoon between Boston and Wood's Hole. It was widely known as the *Dude Train,* an extra-fare and socially exclusive consist which left Boston at three o'clock and ran the seventy-two miles to Buzzards Bay on a limited schedule so that residents in the favored resort might arrive in time for tea. The *Dude Train* was a casualty of the 1914 war.

Indisputably one of the great name trains of the railroading record and one whose character so established itself in the awareness of the community it served that it is fondly remembered almost seven decades after it finished its last run was the New York & New England Railroad's *New England Limited,* more generally known as the *White Train.* In its conduct, personnel, patronage, and most of all in its decor, the Yankee passion for individuality found expression to a degree that today seems almost riotous.

Imagine a train the coal in whose locomotive tender was sprayed white before every run in order to harmonize with the over-all color scheme! Or one whose regular engineer was equally esteemed as a commencement speaker and as a ballast scorcher! Or one aboard which the president of the railroad urged ostentatious disobedience to the general manager's specific orders in order to be on time for a club dinner in Boston!

The state of genial operative chaos of which these are only a sample endeared the *White Train* to New York and Boston patrons for only four years before the run was terminated and a more conventional flyer inaugurated in its place between Boston and New York by way of the Connecticut meadows, but they established it for all time in the folklore of down-East railroading as a property as well-remembered in the Boston legend as Deacon Shem Drown's grasshopper weather vane on Faneuil Hall.

The New York & New England Railroad operated over two routes between Boston and New York, each in conjunction with the New Haven. One was via Hartford and New Haven over which the *Fast Day Express* made the 226-mile run in six and a half hours. The other was over what was known as the Air Line, which was a cutoff that avoided Hartford and ran straight across country by way of Middletown and Williamantic. Both were, of course, in indirect competition with the New Haven's Shore Line through New London and Providence. The *New England Limited* dated back to the Centennial Year of 1876 and by 1889 had shortened its eight-hour schedule to six over the Air Line from Grand Central Depot to the company's Boston terminal at the foot of Summer Street where the South Station was later to stand.

Thus things stood with the N.Y. & N.E. until March 16, 1891, when the *Limited* inaugurated its service in an all-new dress and on a schedule that was shortly to be reduced to five hours and forty minutes.

The Pullman Palace Car Company had built for the upgraded *Limited* seven parlor cars, four coaches and four "Royal Buffet Smokers" which were divided between two trains, one of which was owned by the New England and the other by the New Haven over whose rails it ran between Grand Central and the

Elm City. The respective railroads each supplied a diner that was cut in for its end of the run out of Willimantic. Heating was by steam, illumination by Pintsch gas.

The parlor cars, where luxury ran riot, were furnished with velvet carpets, silk draperies and white silk curtains, chairs upholstered in old-gold plush and large plate-glass mirrors on the bulkheads which reflected the proper Bostonians in genteel attitudes as they perused the *Boston Evening Transcript* or the latest novel by William Dean Howells. Three of the parlor cars had twenty-six seats and a private stateroom; the other four seated thirty persons each.

"The Royal Buffet Smokers," chronicled the *Boston Herald* at the time, "will be run in addition to the ordinary smoking cars and are decorated in the same manner as the parlor cars. They contain twenty handsomely upholstered chairs for the accommodation of parlor car passengers. Two card tables with stationary seats and writing desks with all needed stationery for letters and telegrams are also provided. The regular passenger coaches seat sixty each and are comfortable and easy riding."

It is obvious from the *Herald*'s account that coach passengers, while they might ride easily, were not encouraged in the Royal Buffet Smokers.

The Pullman diners were distinguished for affording privacy at table for diffident patrons by means of draperies extending from floor to transom which could, in effect, make each table into a private booth or could be looped back against the wall if not wanted. The Boston diner was under the supervision of a Mr. Parker who knew the tastes of all Frothinghams and Higginsons and deferred to the wishes of Thayers and Saltonstalls in matters of scrod and other regional dishes. Tea was served at five o'clock to parlor car passengers, but not in the coaches. Everybody knew their place in those days.

But the transcending glory of the *White Train* was, of course, the color scheme from which its name derived. Royal Buffet Smokers, coaches, Pullman parlor cars, company diners one and all were painted from buffer to buffer in creamy white and delicately lettered and ornamented in gold. This startling innovation raised a number of eyebrows and had been subject to considerable discussion in railroad circles before its inauguration in actual service, but at the February meeting of the New England Railroad Club, a Mr. Adams who was identified as master carbuilder for the Boston & Albany Railroad had boldly advocated the scheme, saying that "their durability will be increased, the heat will affect them less and, properly taken care of, white will last longer than any other."

To match the cars with a white locomotive was not deemed prudent, but a step in that direction was taken daily when, before the locomotives coupled on at their respective terminals, the coal in their tenders was liberally sprayed with whitewash. Also Conductor M. W. Crowley and the brakemen and porters appeared in new white caps with gold bands, while Engineer E. C. Potter, a noted throttle artist of the old school, stroked his walrus mustaches while leaning from his cab window splendidly attired in a white driving coat, such as was affected by stylish horsemen, and white engineer's cap.

It may be remarked parenthetically there had already been a vogue of limited dimensions for painting the cars of fast mail trains in very light colors. It was inaugurated by William H. Vanderbilt, who painted the cars of the New York Central's *Fast Mail* between New York and Chicago in pale cream with beautifully engrossed Post Office emblems in red and gold. There were also white mail cars on the old Vandalia Line, later the Pennsylvania between St. Louis and Indianapolis, and on March 10, 1884, the Chicago, Burlington & Quincy had inaugurated a *Fast White Mail* between Chicago and Omaha. After the *New England Limited* had passed into history at the turn of the century the Great Northern was still running trains as part of what was called "The White Fleet" between Seattle and St. Paul.

The rehabilitated *New England Limited* was an immediate success. As a prestige symbol it almost at once assumed the same dimensions as were later to attach to riding the *Twentieth Century Limited* and the *Super Chief*. The railroad boasted that its crack flyer was never late and State Street bankers and Murray Hill brokers with affairs in Boston rode it in ostentatious display of the importance of their time. Maître d'Hôtel Parker's service of lobster Savannah and Mouton Rothschild from the cellars of S. P. Pierce & Company, the ordained grocers of Copley Square, was acknowledged to be perfect. Railroad men came from all over to study the *White Train's* operation and only a few shook their heads at the Maltese cross that constituted the company's insignia on the tender. The superstitious held it an emblem of bad omen.

The newspapers along the route gave the *Limited* a fine hand, and its progress through Putnam, Willimantic and even lesser metropolises was the daily occasion for small crowds to gather on depot platforms and at grade crossings. Inevitably somebody paid tribute to the *White Train* in verse:

> Without a jar or roll or antic,
> Without a stop at Willimantic,
> The *New England Limited* takes its way
> At three o'clock on every day.
> Maids and matrons, daintily dimited,
> Ride every day on the *New England Limited*
> Rain or snow ne'er stops its flight,
> It makes New York at nine each night.
> One half the glories have not been told
> Of that wonderful train of white and gold
> Which leaves each day for New York at three
> Over the N.Y. and N.E.

The meter may be a trifle uneven and the *Limited* did stop at Willimantic, but in a day innocent of the singing commercial this was promotion at its most lyric pitch.

Usually the *New England Limited* ran with six or seven cars behind a high-stepping American type 4–4–0 with a capped stack and the perhaps ill-omened Maltese cross on the tender. The cars were open platform units, vestibules not having come into common use then, with wide picture windows with an art glass transom above each of them. It is easy to imagine it running through the misty Connecticut meadows near Middletown under a full moon, the golden lights of its all-Pullman varnish cars gleaming through the twilight as Gene Potter wheeled them at eighty and better to meet his tight schedule. At one stage in the game the *White Train* was equipped with twin headlights, and photographs show them mounted high on the rim of the smokebox where they must have contributed materially to the impression of a ghost train speeding through the night between two distant terminals.

Its reputation for running on the advertised contributed materially to the *Limited* legend and Alvin F. Harlow, dean of New England railroad historians, told in his *Steelways of New England* of an occasion when Charles P. Clark, president of the road, was riding one of the Royal Buffet Smokers and heard another passenger who was unaware of his identity bitching about the train operation. It was thirty minutes off the card at Willimantic and the customer was sure it could never make up so much on the remainder of the run to Boston. While it paused for a service stop at Willimantic, Clark sent word forward by a brakeman to the peerless Potter that he would appreciate being in Boston on time. Potter ran her over the eighty-six miles at a speed that made up the half hour and a few seconds better, but next morning when Superintendent Allen heard of the exploit he issued a firm ruling that precluded any such running in the future.

Only a few nights later Clark was again on board, the train was again off schedule and he repeated his request to the engineer, explaining that he wanted to get in for a late dinner at the Algonquin Club in Commonwealth Avenue. Again Potter made up the time in direct violation of the Superintendent's order and next morning got a message to report to Allen's office. He was sure it was serious trouble.

Potter by fortunate chance encountered President Clark in the corridor just as he was about to wait on the Superintendent and explained his predicament. "Would you like me to see Mr. Allen in your place?" he asked the troubled man of valves and gauges. It was the last anyone ever heard of the matter.

Not only did the *White Train* achieve an enviable celebrity in the daily press of its age, it was immortalized in belles-lettres by no less a titan of literature than Rudyard Kipling. Kipling was vacationing in New England during the train's brief but exciting lifetime and was moved to write a short story, ".007," about an eight-wheeled American locomotive "worth $10,000 on the company's books." Just why the English author should be so stunned by the rather modest value set on Gene Potter's No. 167 is at this remove unexplained.

In 1895 the *White Train* was discontinued on the excuse that its light-colored cars required too much maintenance, but it passed into history as the most stylish train to serve New England until then and one of the pleasant memories of the pleasantly remembered nineties everywhere.

In the glorious noontide of Shore Line travel over the New Haven between New York and Boston a reciprocating fleet of name trains, awash with parlor cars, club cars and compartmented sleepers rolled around the clock to convey Saltonstalls and Higginsons on their occasions of profit or pleasure. The *Mayflower, Bay State, New Yorker* and *Puritan* filled the morning hours; the *Puritan, Shore Line Express* and *Gilt Edge* took care of afternoon traffic. At one and five o'clock came the big moments of the New Haven's day when from either terminal there sailed the flagships of the company's service, the *Yankee Clipper* and *Merchants Limited,* solid Pullman, extra fare, de luxe daylight trains with no coaches or baggage cars to mar the flawless symmetry of their solid green which ended in a brass-railed observation platform that

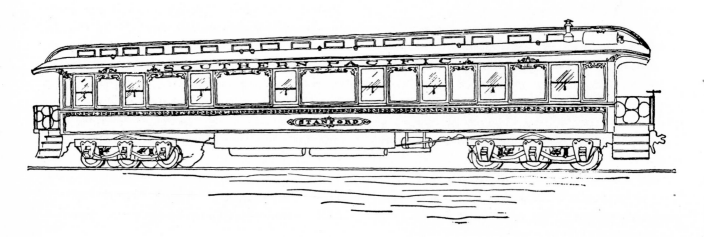

gleamed like an oriflamme from Providence to New Haven to Bridgeport. Afternoon tea was served on the *Clipper.* On the *Merchants,* which was largely populated with bankers and brokers traveling between State Street and downtown New York, stronger matters were in request. Popular rumor maintained that the New Haven cleared a handsome profit on the highballs and cocktails sold on the legendary five o'clock run and it may well have done so.

There were maids and porters in profusion. Dinner-jacketed maîtres d'hôtel knew many of their more distinguished regulars by name, and the chef knew that Mrs. Thorndike liked her scrod well-browned and Governor Fuller wanted his steak rare. Probably the New Haven's parlor cars were the last in service where gentlemen in morning coats exchanged derby hats for cloth traveling caps as they settled into their seats and where monocles and gloves were worn throughout the trip without attracting notice.

Many Bostonians whose affairs took them to New York weekly or more often maintained apartments in the Belmont Hotel directly across Forty-second Street from Grand Central, which was accessible through a private tunnel under the street, and the distinctive accents of Marlborough Street and The Fenway were clearly audible in the Belmont's ornate bar as the hour of five approached and passengers on the *Merchants* kept an eye on the clock.

The *Merchants* didn't run Sundays, but there was a sort of stand-in for its services called the *Cabana,* which ran in summer months at four in the afternoon. At midnight the solid Pullman sleeper *Owls* left in either direction with no coaches, and the timetable bore the legend "Receives passengers only to the extent of sleeping capacity."

In addition to the Shore Line name trains there were through trains connecting Boston with other points in the great world, the daylight *Senator* with parlor cars and lounges to Washington, the *Federal,* a full sleeper consist over the same route, the *Quaker* with sleepers for Philadelphia and the *Pittsburgh Express* with sleepers out of Boston and Springfield for the city of its name.

Travel on the New Haven was something of a New England family affair and partook of a cosy and personalized quality deriving from the regular use of its service by the same families for generations on end. Memory serves of an enormously tall, thin, colored man named Fred Wright, who was for many years club car attendant on the *Knickerbocker,* the original one o'clock afternoon train later supplanted by the *Yankee Clipper.* He knew and inquired after the members of the author's family whenever I rode with him, mentioned the last time they had ridden with him, and then, further afield, inquired after the health of my various uncles, Marcus, Decius and Frederick, who were Bostonians of consequence in their time. Fred's mind was a repository of social annals that could have served Charles Alexander, for several decades society editor of the *Boston Evening Transcript,* and without whose approval, it was said, no family alliance among the proper Bostonians could be contracted or even contemplated.

The writer's father, Junius Beebe of Boston, claimed to have been robbed of a Collins & Fairbanks overcoat in the New Haven's New London depot in 1875 and a recriminatory correspondence continued between him and every successive president of the road until his death in the thirties. The attenuated charges and denials of responsibility became a matter for jocular comment in the Algonquin Club in Commonwealth Avenue and at long last, sixty years after the original loss, a New Haven president, J. J. Pelley, finally ended the controversy by sending me an 1875 paddock coat he had discovered somewhere, complete with the velvet collar and cuffs of the period. The railroad, I think, was saddened to terminate a longstanding and highly enjoyable feud with one of its oldest families of patrons.

Wrecks on the New Haven at the turn of the century had been sufficiently drastic to merit mention in the stage conversation of *Life With Father,* but by the twenties these had long been a thing of the past, even characterized by a sort of affectionate recollection as having involved only the best people and occurred under the most distinguished auspices. Like San Francisco after the earthquake and fire, the debris were "the damndest finest ruins, nothing more and nothing less."

Although the average student of the railroading past doesn't associate the Illinois Central with the highly competitive Chicago–Twin Cities passenger business, the record shows that at one time it maintained two trains daily, the *Chicago, Minneapolis & St. Paul Limited* and the conventional *Fast Mail*, both overnight runs over the 503 miles of track by way of Waterloo and Albert Lea where it left its own right of way to achieve its northern terminal over the rails of the Minneapolis & St. Louis. It ran no mean trains—the *Limited* carrying a combination stateroom and open-section Pullman sleeper, a buffet–library–smoking car, a dining car serving supper from Chicago to Freeport, "the sleeping car electrically lighted throughout." The *Mail* ran a buffet–sleeping car about which no details are available, but it must have been the direct lineal descendant of Pullman's first hotel cars, furnishing shelter, food, sleeping accommodations and transport all under one hospitable, turtleback roof of the design known as Harriman.

The I.C.'s Chicago–Twin Cities service, like that of the vanished Wisconsin Central with its Tuscan red observation–cafe cars and fine Brooks engines, has long since vanished from the *Official Guide,* but it is pleasant to remember the electric lights throughout and its sleepers prowling gently through the night and shedding their glow briefly on depot platforms at Toeterville, Stacy, Mona, Lyle and London.

In the nineties the two I.C trains to St. Louis were operated via Pana, Illinois, and the Big Four Railroad, but by 1900 the I.C. had purchased the Peoria & Northern Railroad between Springfield and East St. Louis and its trains were now operated entirely over I.C. iron. During the St. Louis Fair of 1904 an entirely new *Daylight* was built with an eye-fetching decor of green, gold and brown and became locally known as "The Gold and Brown Train," in much the same way that a contemporary, far to the east and running on the New York & New England, was known as "The White Train."

The Illinois Central's service to the westernmost terminals of its system that was eventually to be maintained by the *Hawkeye Limited* overnight between Sioux City, Sioux Falls and Chicago began in December 1870 with an unnamed sleeper and coach train that required twenty-eight hours to cover the 510 miles involved. By the mid-twenties, however, the *Hawkeye Limited* was a complex of sleepers and complementary services requiring nine locomotives, two

baggage cars, two mail-storage cars, two Railway Post Office cars, seven coaches, four chair cars, one diner, three cafe coaches and twelve Pullman sleepers of various diagrams. Eastbound trains from Sioux City and Sioux Falls, respectively, were consolidated at Cherokee, Iowa, and this train consolidated with a string of varnish out of Omaha at Fort Dodge.

We have already remarked briefly on the establishment of through sleeping car service aboard the home-built, transom-roofed wooden sleeper *Amboy* and its companion cars by the Illinois Central on the Chicago–St. Louis run in 1856 and the probability that this is not only the first sleeping car of a Pre-Cambrian era of railroad geology, but that the *Lightning Express* in which it ran was among the first name trains.

Throughout the seventies and eighties the I.C.'s entry to St. Louis was over the Vandalia Railroad via Effingham and a nameless day train and equally anonymous sleeper haul connected to two cities. But in 1891 the I.C. blossomed with publicity for a new and splendid sleeper train on this run to be known as the *Diamond Special* as a salute to the carrier's diamond-shaped heraldic insigne, and two years later the *Daylight Special* was inaugurated, also in connection with the Vandalia. The principal feature of the *Diamond Special,* and one on which the advertising-copy writers of the time were pleased to dwell at length, was the fact that the train was gaslit throughout, this being a departure from the coal-oil lamps of an earlier era in favor of the Pintsch lights Pullman had been so assiduously promoting.

In the years before the 1914 war, cut-throat competition existed among the carriers serving Colorado for the rich seasonal traffic from the East to Rocky Mountain summer resorts whose entrepôts were Denver and Colorado Springs. The three major roads out of Chicago, the Burlington, Union Pacific and Rock Island vied in the splendor of equipment assigned to such trains as the Burlington's *Chicago–Denver Special,* the Rock Island's *Rocky Mountain Limited* and the Union Pacific's *Colorado Special.* Most trains of the period carried brass-bound observation cars in various combinations of lounges, cafes or sleepers. Many featured compartmented sleeping cars, library cars, buffets and handsomely paneled smoking apartments, luxury elements which carried over into the thirties aboard the Union Pacific's *Columbine,* which carried two parlor lounges upholstered in gold mohair with valet and barber service, and the Burlington's *Aristocrat,* which featured similar appointments. The U.P.'s blue and silver observation car *Colorado Club* had both tub and shower baths, and rivalry in the dining departments provided magnificent meals— dinners at $1.25—as late as 1939.

Probably the greatest prestige train the world has ever known until it was deliberately downgraded as an act of managerial sabotage was the *Twentieth Century Limited,* the peer in romantic implications of the *Blue Train* of Continental legend and the *Simplon–Orient Express* with its international couriers, plotters and traveling royalty in the days of the old bearded kings of the Balkans.

The *Century,* for a full fifty years of immaculate operation, was to rail travel what Rolls Royce has always been to the world of motors, an institution that smiled serenely on competition and defied imitation. It arrived and departed impervious to the seasons with the regularity of lunar tides, its progress at once majestic and tranquil, its sailing list the great names of a world in which greatness still obtained. Few things hindered its progress. Occasionally in the early years the elements delayed it, but contretemps in the conduct of its arrangements was almost unknown. The *Twentieth Century Limited* was a standard of excellence in a scheme of things in which the best of everything mattered to people who knew no other way of life.

The *Century* came into being in 1902, a by-product at once of the competition of the Pennsylvania, which had always been breathing down the neck of the New York Central on the New York–Chicago run, and the laying of new 100-pound rails, which made its operating speeds possible. When its twenty-hour schedule was announced there were those who took a dim view of such excessive speed. "The operators will soon find they are wasting fortunes keeping their property in condition," sneered one English journal of opinion, "and then, loving money better than notoriety, the project will be abandoned."

The train was a sensational success from the start. Its equipment was announced to be finer than that of the *Lake Shore Limited,* which until then had been the flagship of the Central: three Pullman sleepers, a buffet car and diner with barbershop, ladies' maids, valet and stenographer over and above the conventional train staff, and electric light in all cars generated from the axle, then the newest improvement in carbuilding *expertise.*

A passenger on the first hair-raising run was John W. (Bet a Million) Gates who was so enchanted with the ride one way that he stayed on the train and made it back again in the other. In Manhattan he diplomatically told the waiting newspaper reporters: "This train makes Chicago a suburb of New York." At the western terminal he told the reporters: "This train makes New York a suburb of Chicago."

The demand for space immediately made it necessary to add more cars until in the nineteen-thirties the *Century* sometimes ran in seven sections of sixteen cars each in one direction alone. Its profits to the road were astronomical.

Always the train was run in the grand manner. A crimson carpet was laid every afternoon before its departure from Grand Central and the flashes of news photographers, at first with magnesium flares and later with speed guns, flickered like summer heat lightning as names that made news followed their luggage down it to the appropriate car. Flowers for the dining cars of the *Century* alone ran up a florist's bill of $2,000 a month, and their table butter derived exclusively from the blooded Holsteins on the Vermont estate of Dr. William Seward Webb, a son-in-law of William H. Vanderbilt and for many years president of the Wagner Palace Car Company.

The grand manner was also reflected in the train's operational economy in the years when the J-3a Hudson locomotives were its conventional power. Lest any slightest defect in a road engine should be allowed to delay the *Century* for any least repair, stand-by J-3a's were maintained under full head of steam at every division point along the route and spotted near the end of the depot track where they could be cut in as replacement without the loss of a moment's time.

Primarily, during its golden years of prestige and pre-eminence, the *Century* was a train patronized by bankers, brokers and industrialists generally whose

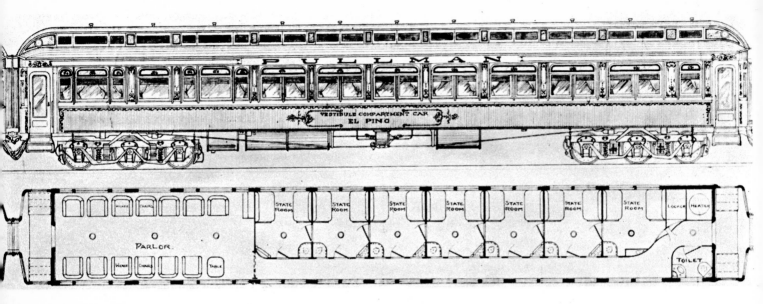

names had a cachet of the Chicago Loop and Gold Coast about them. Palmers, Wrigleys, Armours, Morrisons, Insulls, Blairs, Fields, Swifts and Harveys were represented on almost every run for five full decades, and the *Century* itself became a repository of their legends of thought and habit, dress, drinking, dining and manners generally.

The last regular passenger on the *Century* to arrive with a body servant whose duty it was to substitute her personal bed linen for Pullman sheets and pillow slips before she retired was a Mrs. Pickering from the perfumed precincts of North Astor Street. Colonel Robert McCormick of the *Chicago Tribune* traveled in a suite of two or three connecting rooms even though he was alone. Rufus Dawes, the Chicago banker, knew every old-timer on the train crew by his first name. Harry Sinclair, Herbert Hoover and Ethel Barrymore never came aboard with fewer than two personal servants, sometimes more. When Eddie Cantor went westward with a radio show he would take six or seven staterooms opening up as a single apartment and work all night with his gag men, script writers and music directors.

Once, as the eastbound section was approaching Harmon in the morning and J. Ogden Armour was having breakfast, the multi-millionaire packer sent for Harry Taggart, the dining car steward on duty.

"Is this my ham I'm eating?" he demanded.

Although there was a Swift at the other end of the car and a Cudahy across the aisle, Taggart knew his lines.

"Yes, sir. Of course it is!"

"All I wanted to tell you is that it's damned bad ham," roared Armour fit to be heard the length of the car.

The *Century* carried a train secretary who knew the identity of every person aboard from a checkup conducted at the train gate when the passenger surrendered his passage to the two conductors representing Pullman and the railroad. He could take dictation and in general served as a chief of communications and conveniences, posting urgent telegrams, apprising the diner stewards of special preferences in the matter of dinner and breakfast, gentling tycoons who were in wine and gratifying the unpredictable whims of opera and film stars. He could use his own discretion about informing passengers of the identity of fellow travelers but was strictly interdicted from making introductions between strangers, especially those of opposite sexes. The management never conceived of the flagship as a rolling love nest.

The departure from Grand Central and the La Salle Depot of the twin section of the *Century* came in time to take on overtones of the ceremonial. A 300-foot-long red carpet with the train's name woven in its fabric reached from the train gate past the rear cars, coming to an end only in the twilight of the train-shed where its absence wouldn't be missed. Redcaps with mounds of luggage on their trucks waited to make a concerted assault on the cars rather than trucking their loads in haphazard. Press photographers were almost invariably in attendance and women boarding the *Century* wore their smartest traveling outfits and most opulent corsages as a result.

Few passengers arrived in the final moment before train time; going on the *Century* was too important a ritual to permit the haste and confusion of last-minute boarding. By the time the conductor was ready to give his highball, the car doors were already shut, the carpet rolled up, the crowd dispersed and the train rolled into the night in subdued grandeur.

Conforming to the practice of even the most de luxe trains which made a point of being all-Pullman, the *Century* for many years slept its most exalted passengers in open sections. Drawing rooms in the early years were for invalids, newlyweds and royalty. J. P. Morgan might command privacy with an eye to a business conference en route, or Julia Marlowe as a tribute to her professional standing, but Diamond Jim Brady had not hesitation about folding his immense person into a lower, and De Wolfe Hopper and many another trouper in the top brackets of the theater slept soundly and well in the rocking uppers, as the cars raced silently along the Water Level Route so much publicized by the railroad.

In 1937 the management of the Central inaugurated a new *Twentieth Century Limited* which took the form of an all-room all-Pullman train, the first in service anywhere in the United States and a departure which put a dramatic period to the era of open sections for patrons who could afford privacy at a slight premium. The streamlined consist with its rubber draft gear, tight-lock couplings, air conditioning, Muzac and blue and silver decor was a sensation in the travel world and the Pennsylvania was shortly afterward to inaugurate similar innovations in its rival *Broadway Limited*. On both trains staterooms, drawing rooms, single bedrooms and the new and economical roomette held a complete monopoly of sleeping space, setting a new standard of de luxe appointments for other railroads in the land to envy and eventually approximate.

Of all the railroads in the golden age of luxury travel the Santa Fe approached the matter of de luxe runs in the most direct way imaginable and at various times had no fewer than two trains on its dispatcher's sheets called the *De Luxe*. The first of these seems to have been a daylight run between La Junta and Santa Fe, branching from the main line at Lamy. It was often hauled by the road's primeval locomotive *Uncle Dick,* named for Dick Wootton whose toll road the rails followed up the Raton Pass. Its plush attraction to justify the name was a parlor car purchased from the Intercolonial Railway of Canada with huge red velvet upholstered armchairs from which the tourists might view the Rocky Mountain scenery. The chairs were mobile, being mounted on casters, but after one trip the casters were removed and the seats fixed to the floor after the grade above Trinidad had caused the entire carfull of passengers to slide in one fell moment of supreme disorder to the rear end of the conveyance.

The second *De Luxe* more adequately justified its name and was operated on a sixty-three hour schedule between Chicago and Los Angeles with a $25 extra fare, no mean sum in the year 1911 and one which restricted its passenger list to the eminently well-heeled. It carried only seventy top-flight customers on its once a week departure each way with two all-drawing room sleepers, a compartment car, observation lounge, club car and diner. The diner had the first air cooling ever installed on a train and there were, in addition to the conventional quota of train-men, a lady's maid, a manicurist, hairdresser, and barber presiding over a tub bath and a shower, electric curling irons, a fiction library, telegraphic news bulletins and stock reports and stereoscopic views of the scenery in case the passenger didn't want to look out the window.

At Summit, California, atop the Cajon Pass, a uniformed boy in those halcyon days boarded both the *De Luxe* and the line's other luxury flyer, the *California Limited,* with free flowers for every passenger, boutonnieres for the gentlemen and bouquets of violets and roses for the women. There were also for a time, gift wallets of real alligator skin lettered with the name of the Santa Fe in gold and bearing a likeness of the train. For $25 the line believed in giving value received.

As late as 1935 when the old *Chief,* running with

Pullman Standard equipment and in steam, was still an extra-fare proposition, the author recalls an occasion when the surcharge was refunded as the train rolled into Los Angeles half a day off schedule because of snow in the Raton. The confusion was intense. Passenger representatives boarded the cars at San Bernardino and undertook the distribution of a cash refund to each passenger in the hour and a half remaining of the run. As the refund was on a prorata basis—so much to the through patrons from Chicago, less to one who had come aboard at Kansas City and so on—and a record was kept of each transaction, the corridors soon resembled nothing so much as Hallowe'en at the madhouse. The extra fare to be refunded because of tardiness shortly disappeared from the tariff schedule.

When the first run of the *De Luxe* left Chicago on December 12, 1911, an interested passenger was Bud Fisher, the cartoonist and creator of the immortal characters of Mutt and Jeff. A few days later a cartoon was syndicated in which Mutt asked Jeff why the Santa Fe ran through so many graveyards, and Jeff had to explain to his dim-witted companion that those weren't tombstones, just milestones along the right of way.

Like such glittering name–contemporaries as the *Century,* the *Broadway,* the *Overland* and the *Sunset Limited,* the Santa Fe's *Chief* had its origins in the era of Pullman Standard and survived the transition into streamlining and stainless steel with its reputation for fine appointments almost undimmed by time.

Before the advent of the *Super Chief,* the *Chief* in steam and standard cars had established a reputation as the conveyance of glamour names to and from Hollywood. Actually, of course, there are at any one time five fully equipped *Chiefs,* either en route between Chicago and Los Angeles or being serviced at either terminal, no problem to an organization that once dispatched twenty-two westbound and twenty-three eastbound sections of the *California Limited* in the same day without overstraining its car pool.

Superficially the *Chief*'s greatest bid for fame has been the sailing lists of screen players, famous directors, visiting celebrities and glamour generally that were first associated with it in a day before flying was a common property of exhibitionism; to railroaders and amateurs of rail travel its fame rested on the perfection of comfort it afforded patrons and the superlative cuisine of Fred Harvey's restaurant cars. Mention the name of the *Chief* to any old hand at California travel and he will at once recall to memory the fresh trout put aboard the diners at La Junta, the profusion of cut flowers that were replaced twice a trip in the public rooms and the celebrated Santa Fe library–buffet cars with their deep leather upholstery, superb barbershops and comforting shower baths that dispensed ice-cold Niagaras before air conditioning in the American Southwest.

Later on in the forties Frederic Wakeman's provocative novel, *The Hucksters,* portrayed an exotic night life aboard the sleepers of the *Chief* and *Super Chief* with cinema stars of legendary beauty engaging in perfumed interludes of romance in staterooms, drawing rooms and compartments with captains of industry, international bankers and gilded playboys as their amorous partners.

While a great transcontinental de luxe flyer may very well now and then have served as a ninety-mile-an-hour love barge speeding through the New Mexico night, this aspect of existence on the *Chief* was more fostered in the Sunday supplements than in reality, and it is difficult to imagine such notables as Douglas Fairbanks, Lon Chaney or Clark Gable, all of them regulars on the train, in compromising attitudes as the cars smoked their way down the far side of the Cajon.

The author of this chronicle once occupied a room adjacent to that of Laurence Olivier, later Sir Laurence, aboard the *Chief* on the occasion of that actor's first visit to Hollywood. Well-wishers, not all of them above pulling a celebrity's leg, had warned him against the wild ways of the American West in much the same manner that visiting Englishmen a century earlier had been warned by Cunard captains against the hostile Indians that abounded just west of Broadway. Olivier carried a Webley revolver and was prepared to sell his life dearly if the train was ambushed at Albuquerque. The first morning out, as we were double-heading up the Raton out of Trinidad, Olivier tentatively inched up the window blind in his bedroom, ready instantly to slam it shut if gunfire were attracted. By happy fortune the trail beside the right of way contained but a single occupant, a fat Mexican padre astride a mule who carried an enormous sunshade overhead to protect his devotional reading. Boldly Olivier dressed for breakfast, reassured by evidence indisputable that religion still obtained in a region widely advertised as godless.

Perhaps one of the most heartening legends of the Santa Fe Railroad and one that, understandably, nobody is at any great pains to deny, tells how in the early days of his eating houses along the ever-westering iron of the railroad through Kansas and Colorado, Fred Harvey, the founding father of the system, discharged a restaurant manager for not showing what seemed to him to be a big-enough monthly operating deficit. The restaurant pioneer was out to sell good food in a big way and it was indicative of his spaciousness of concept that he thought that, for the beginning, good will and a fair reputation were more important than immediate profits.

Any such extravagant notions of management had disappeared from the Fred Harvey organization long before the first run of the *Chief* in November 1926, but down to the very immediate present Santa Fe trains have been among the foremost in upholding the article of American faith which maintains that "real railroading," by which the general public means the best dining cars, doesn't begin until you get west of the Mississippi.

Dining car stewards on the *Chief* used to receive their menus one trip ahead, in plenty of time to make appropriate requisitions from the terminal commissary. The table d'hôte dinner is fairly standardized on all Santa Fe runs, but the customers can express their personalities on the à la carte bill of fare and many of them make a point of doing so. Basic stock for a run may include such items as sixty dozen eggs, ten pork tenderloins, ninety pounds of beef sirloin, forty of tenderloin, forty-five pounds of butter, twenty-five pounds of bacon, fifty pounds of coffee, seventy-five pounds of sugar, four tenderized hams, two Virginia smoked hams, four crates of strawberries and half a dozen of oranges, the *Chief* being celebrated for its promotion of California citrus products. Trout, melon and fresh vegetables are supplemented from commissaries at La Junta and Albuquerque. Fresh creamery butter is used for all cooking purposes except deep frying and nobody has ever known the *Chief* to run out of champagne.

It is only fair to report that, spurred by the fame of the competition on the Los Angeles–Chicago run, the Union Pacific has made an effort on its *City of Los Angeles* to rival the Santa Fe's cuisine and may well have done so.

The writer recalls once in the mid-thirties, when the *City of Los Angeles* was new and sported a dining car with portholes which gave it a curiously seagoing atmosphere, being a guest at dinner with Lady Suzanne Wilkins, wife of Sir Hubert Wilkins, the arctic explorer, when the management wanted to show a lady of title what it could do when *Burke's Peerage* was represented on the passenger list. I have the menu before me reading:

Caviar Frais de Beluga
Tortue Clair
Timballe d'Homard Grimaldi
Endive Braise
Coeur de Filet de Boeuf Coquelin
Cailles à la Turque
Le Panier de Bagatelles
Coup au Marrons
Café Filtre

With this trifling collation were served a Mersault Perrier 1926 and Bollinger champagne 1929 in magnums. Nobody went to bed hungry, but the *City of Los Angeles* is of the diesel age and hence not strictly embraced by this inquiry into the amenities of the golden age of railroads.

In the heyday of the cars there were many trains of local celebrity and importance in regional folklore that only infrequently emerged upon the national awareness. Some of these were homely runs of country landfarings among bread and cheese people, others such as the aforementioned *Dude Train* on the New Haven were integrated to more exalted destinies and passenger lists of importance.

In the latter category and with emphasis was the Southern Pacific's *Del Monte Express*, inaugurated early in the eighties as "the fastest train west of the Mississippi" between San Francisco and the railroad's newly opened and toweringly stylish resort hotel at Del Monte on the Monterey Peninsula. The *Express* covered the 125 miles between Third Street and its southern terminal on varying schedules in its eighty years of existence but always with a full complement of Crockers, Tevises, Haggins, Spreckelses and other consequential California names on board.

From the beginning it was a train with class and in its latter years was distinguished for the presence of a parlor car on which tea was served on the down trip and light breakfast on the up and which was named the *Oliver Merritt* in honor of a porter whose long years of service on the Monterey run had endeared him to two full generations of San Francisco commuters.

In the era of private cars the *Del Monte* frequently trailed clouds of additional glory deriving from the presence on its rear of the varnish cars of nabobs of both local and national dimensions bound for the polo fields and other exalted *plaisances* for which Monterey Peninsula was celebrated, among them Charles Crocker's *Mishawaka*, Lloyd Tevis's *San Emidio* and Governor Leland Stanford's somewhat redundantly named *Stanford*. Sometimes, too, there rolled grandly down of a Friday night the unnamed private car of old moneybags Darius Ogden Mills or the off-line varnish of a visiting Vanderbilt or Armour from the East. In the final years of service to Monterey the last private cars to be spotted within view of Monterey Bay were *The Gold Coast* and *The Virginia City*, the successive cars of Charles Clegg and Lucius Beebe.

The only train in the record to be named for a racehorse was the Central of Georgia's *Nancy Hanks,* which was briefly scheduled for eight months in 1893 on the run between Atlanta and Savannah. The train was on an eight-hour schedule, fast for the time, and its usual consist was a mail and baggage combine, a smoker, a first-class coach, a second-class coach divided for white and colored occupancy and a parlor car, and during its short lifetime it ran in two different liveries, the first of bright vermilion red and the second in equally eye-filling royal blue, with the name "Nancy Hanks" in full gold leaf on the side of each car.

Nancy Hanks, a diminutive bay mare which in turn had been named for Abraham Lincoln's mother, was very much in the news of the sporting world in the early nineties and in 1892 at St. Paul she clipped three

seconds from the standing world's record of 2.07 minutes over a measured mile. The Central's General Superintendent George Dole Wadley was an ardent follower of horse racing, and when a new fast train was proposed for the trip between Savannah and Atlanta the name *Nancy Hanks* seemed just the thing.

On the nameboards of each car the foreman of the Central's paint shops had painted a shield with the likeness of the celebrated horse, and a similar device was painted on the end bulkheads inside each car. On each car's sidewall appeared the flag of the Central of Georgia with "Nancy" on one side and "Hanks" on the other, beautifully done in gold. Still another likeness of the precipitous mare was blown in the frosted glass above each window of every car. The train was strictly a tailor-made job.

Although its career was short, the *Nancy Hanks* in its lifetime achieved a considerable measure of regional fame in the Deep South and became the subject of a folksong or ballad, still included in anthologies of such matters, whose first stanza ran as follows:

Some folk say the *Nancy* can't run,
But stop, let me tell you what the *Nancy* done done:
She left Atlanta at half past one
And got to Savannah by the setting of the sun.
The *Nancy Hanks,* she ran so fast
She burnt the wind and scorched the grass.

So well-remembered in Central of Georgia territory was this picturesque flyer that fifty-five years later when the railroad was casting about for a name for a new streamlined service on the same run it named it *Nancy Hanks II.*

Local or regional peculiarities were often reflected in the personnel and conduct of trains serving a particular countryside, none more than the New York Central's *Wolverine* and *Twilight Limited* in the twenties when they passed, en route via the Michigan Central, through the resort of Battle Creek, Michigan.

Stewards aboard Michigan Central dining cars en route to Chicago noted an appreciable rise in demand for tender steaks, rich desserts and strong coffee among passengers who got on at Battle Creek. The phenomenon became so pronounced that the management of the railroad began stocking specially succulent viands on this particular run and items not conventionally found on diner menus: *filet mignon* with Bernaise sauce, Eastern lobster which could be had Thermidor or Newburg, French vanilla ice cream and extra-proof drip coffee. The exacting customers, it was discovered, were refugees from the Battle Creek sanitarium maintained by the Kellogg brothers, fugitives from diet desserts, decaffeinated coffee and a nut butter and protose regime. Many of them were members of the Kellogg medical staff itself en route to learned conventions in Chicago at a time when, providentially, Irene Castle was dancing at the Blackstone and a tidal wave of the best bootleg champagne had been reported as inundating the College Inn. Michigan Central diner waiters, noting the pinched faces and undernourished appearance generally of passengers boarding the cars at Battle Creek, anticipated liberal tips after the steak and French fries, and greeted the afflicted: "Here comes the Porterhouse Brigade."

It was during this halcyon era, too, that Florida seasonal trains catered to a less miscellaneous clientele than later embarked for Miami and St. Petersburg. Bostonians of circumstance and conservative New Yorkers headed for winter vacation at the Royal Poinciana at Palm Beach rode with train crews, especially aboard the diners of the Seaboard and Florida East Coast who were not only familiar at first hand with their names and identities, but with their preferences in food and service. These diner crews and their captains and maîtres d'hôtel worked the resort circuit. In summer they were employed in the great resort hotels of New England, at Saratoga Springs, Bar Harbor and the White Mountains. During the then brief Florida season which began at Christmas and ended promptly with the great Palm Beach ball on Washington's Birthday, they turned up at the Breakers, the Poinciana, the Ponce de León and other recognized spas in the Palmetto State. Between times many of them worked the diners of the *Florida Special, Orange Blossom, Everglades* and *Havana Special.* The darky who had served your breakfast one summer morning at the Profile House at Franconia, New Hampshire, a month later would be presenting your entree in the mammoth dining room of the Poinciana.

Florida travel in those days was a family affair. A conductor on the run might serve the same conservative and mannered residents of Brookline or Murray Hill for decades and often enough a second generation of the same seasonal travelers. It was a well-ordered and reassuring way of life.

In the early twenties the writer was dining with his father aboard a Seaboard Air Line train en route to Florida and, as the waiter was serving the pompano *amandine,* the dining car steward, a benevolent autocrat with vast expanse of white linen waistcoat secured with a gold Albert watch chain, paused at our table to remark: "I'll wager, Mr. Beebe, that you don't remember where you were just forty years ago tonight."

Understandably, my father did not and asked for enlightenment.

"You were being married, sir, in the Vendome Hotel in Commonwealth Avenue," he was told by the man of menus, "and I was on the buffet serving the lobster aspic."

This sort of thing in those times was good for a gold double eagle at the end of the run.

One of the last all-Pullman trains to inaugurate service on a transcontinental run was the beautifully organized *Forty-niner* which the Southern Pacific and Union Pacific jointly operated over the Overland Route between Chicago and San Francisco in 1937. This streamlined, steam-powered, extra-fare flyer was placed in three-times-a-week service as a stylish panache to the *Overland Limited, San Francisco Challenger* and *City of San Francisco* with an eye to the de luxe traffic sure to be attracted by the San Francisco Exposition scheduled to open at Treasure Island in the following year.

The *Forty-niner* embodied a number of innovations in structure and operation that gave it character of its own, including a diner with round tables similar to those of conventional restaurant usage, the first split-level room sleepers to go into operation west of the Mississippi and a lounge—observation—buffet—sleeper unit occupying two cars at the rear of the train.

The duplex sleepers were not notably successful, although the train was often sold out, because the upper-level bedrooms lacked sufficient headroom for normal-sized passengers and contained almost no baggage space, a serious consideration with transcontinental travelers. But the *Forty-niner* as an operation was admired by everyone who encountered it and remains to this day a pleasant memory along with San

Francisco hospitality during the two years of the Exposition. In construction, it was entirely Pullman-built to the joint order of the two principal carriers involved. On the divisions west of Omaha, once it cleared the Chicago & Northwestern, it was powered on all but the final run through the Sierra by specially assigned steam locomotives painted to match the cars and maintained by the U.P. and Espee with the special touches of motive power on a highly regarded run.

The cars as they came from Pullman were painted a subdued bronze, presumably a reminder of gold-rush times of '49, an illusion of historic continuity heightened by the names of the units: *Donner Lake, Angel's Camp, Gold Run, James Marshall, John Sutter, Joaquin Miller, Bear Flag* and *California Republic*. As an anthology of the names of history, geography, personalities and belles-lettres, it is doubtful if any train has ever been more resplendent.

In keeping with the best practices of the time, the *Forty-niner* had a barbershop, and valet and ladies' maid services were taken for granted, but a feature that attracted uncommon attention was the two-car unit at the far end of the train. The first car, *California Republic*, was a room car containing sixteen rooms, two of which were conventional double staterooms, the other fourteen being staggered so as to alternate on the floor level and at three steps elevation from the deck. Beds in these upper and lower rooms were built transversely instead of lengthwise and each room had complete toilet facilities, a plumbing plan whose intricacy was reported to have been a major headache at Pullman. Six of the downstairs rooms could be opened *en suite* and four of the upper contained connecting doors forming a veritable rabbit warren of compartmented slumber nests.

The other car of the two-car unit, named *Bear Flag*, contained an observation lounge with twenty-six seats, lounges and sofas. Half the car was occupied by the lounge and beyond it was a buffet. The front end contained a compartment and three double bedrooms, two of which were available to occupancy *en suite*. The decor was *moderne* without being offensive to patrons with more conservative tastes in such matters, while the enclosed solarium at the extreme rear afforded a generous vista of the receding rails and came nearer than any such arrangement within the writer's

memory to suggesting the glories of the old-time open observation platform of revered memory.

Wonder and glory of the *Forty-niner* was its diner, a two-car unit whose restaurant proper, *Angel's Camp*, seated forty-two with a lounge for eight and was combined with the kitchen-dormitory car, *Donner Lake*. Writing a contemporary account of diners generally in *Collier's*, James Marshall mentioned it as follows:

The supercolossal diner of them all was one built by Pullman for Morales y Machado, President of Cuba. He ordered it shortly before he was tossed out on his ear, and the new administration, with an eye to the proletarian vote, cancelled the order. The car was full of plate glass and hand carved mahogany, with thousands of dollars worth of imported rugs, silk drapes and upholstery, and it had round tables at which as many as seven diners could be seated. This little number was the pride and joy of *The Forty-niner* operating between Chicago and Oakland. Gourmets used to wait to take passage on it, to eat in all this magnificence.

Nor did all the prestige associated with the *Forty-niner's* diner derive from its dimensions, décor and resources of gastronomy. In charge of its management was a steward fully as supercolossal as Mr. Marshall described the car itself to be. Wild Bill Kurthy was a legend along the Overland Route whose profanity, lavishness and exuberant personality were not soon forgotten by passengers privileged to eat under him, if the phrase may be pardoned.* Wild Bill was the boss man of everything in sight, crew, customers and all, no matter how exalted their status elsewhere in the world. They ate what Wild Bill suggested, which had nothing to do with diets or calories which hadn't been invented then anyway. Frilly little old ladies who would normally have asked for China tea and a watercress sandwich found themselves confronted with rare Porterhouse flanked by mountains of little thin hot cakes swimming in the best melted creamery butter.

* In the Middle West, Wild Bill Kurthy had an opposite number, albeit less outrageous and flamboyant, in the person of Dan Healy, the celebrated dining car steward aboard the Milwaukee's *Pioneer Limited* in the St. Paul–Chicago run. Healy, a friend of presidents and other traveling magnificoes, had served aboard the first dining car west out of Chicago in 1877 and came to the Chicago & North Western in 1893. In 1923, as dining car steward on the Milwaukee, he was dean of his profession and far and away the senior diner manager in the United States in point of service.

Elderly captains of finance and industry accustomed to a strict dietary regimen got onto the ferry at Oakland encouraged by three days of roast pheasant, eastern oysters, rare roast beef and the kind of desserts favored in truck stops. Specially regarded customers, already gorged to repletion when they retired to their staterooms, heard a knock on the door at bedtime and a grinning waiter would present, with Wild Bill's compliments, a huge tray of ham sandwiches, chicken sandwiches with mayonnaise and approximately a gallon of cold milk. "The Wild Man doesn't want you to be hungry in the night" was the accustomed explanation. If the passenger protested that he really was able to last till morning without more food, the darky would assume a look of abject terror. "The Wild Man'll kill me if you don't take them." The cold collation was almost invariably accepted.

On every run Kurthy summarily discharged each member of the dining car's staff, publicly, profanely and explicitly in front of the entire company assembled for lunch or dinner. For the least imagined fault of neglect or improper service the menial was fired in terms of bellowed outrage and told to take his worthless person and possessions ashore at Grand Island, Cheyenne or Ogden, wherever the train stopped next. He was always on duty when the next meal came round.

When the 1941 war came and the *Forty-niner* was only a fragrant memory, Wild Bill was assigned to the *City of San Francisco.* Informed travelers in that era of food shortages and associated inconveniences made a practice of having to travel to the coast on the section in which Kurthy's diner was part of the consist. War or no war and rationing to the contrary notwithstanding, there was always a profusion of steaks, butter, thick cream and other delicacies in supposedly short requisition. Rumor had it that other diners on the run fared far more leanly. Wild Bill had a way at the commissary.

Of all the geographic locales served by railroading in its classic dimension, Florida perhaps received the most opulent treatment in the field of travel promotion, because here the word artist assigned to detail the wonderments of travel over the Florida East Coast or the competing rails of the Plant System was not confined by the measurements which inhibited carbuild-ers; he was able to overflow into the landscape itself and invoke the classic legend of Ponce de León as an adjunct to operating schedules and seasonal tariffs.

During the winter season of 1905–6 the Southern Railway's *Palm Limited,* one of the pioneer luxury trains on the seasonal Florida run, connected New York and Jacksonville over the rails of only two carriers, the Pennsylvania to Washington and the Southern's own tracks from there, "1,057 miles in twenty-seven hours at an average speed of almost forty miles per hour including stops.

"The traveler has had his own exclusive bedroom and as good a luncheon, dinner and breakfast as well cooked and served as he could in any New York hotel," read a company brochure. "He has the latest magazines or novel from the train library and he has had several hours to catch up on his correspondence. He has enjoyed a quiet, restful journey, being translated at marvelous speed from the frigid atmosphere of the North to a land of perpetual sun and flowers. The train is limited in capacity, being composed of only seven cars so that it may make its rapid schedule. . . . The patrons of the *Palm Limited* are usually particular people and accustomed to the best that life affords."

As with many contemporaries, the Southern management wanted it known that it catered to a superior clientele and said flatly: "The appropriateness of the name and splendor of the train were promptly recognized by the largest number of the better class of well informed tourists last season. . . . Palms are indicative of victory and superiority and so it was deemed appropriate that this very superior train should bear their name."

The *Palm Limited*'s apartments were, of course, "richly furnished with desks supplied with exquisitely engraved stationery . . . lighted by electricity at night and served by electric fans when needed on the Southern portion of the route." It left New York at 12:40 P.M. and arrived at St. Augustine the following afternoon at 3:30.

Social standards aboard the Santa Fe's *Colorado Limited* in the same year the *Palm Limited* began its traffic in the *hochwohlgeboren* were somewhat more democratic as became its Western setting and clientele, but still firm in matters of finance. "These palatial cars may be occupied by any respectable citizen who is provided with the necessary ticket," read a company brochure. Probably the matter of social standing wouldn't have been brought up at all except that sleepers in the *Colorado Limited* were named *Windsor, Holyrood, Balmoral, Versailles* and *Kremlin,* palaces which in 1905 or only a few years earlier had boasted royal occupants.

The cars were finished in highly polished St. Jago mahogany, the drawing rooms in koko wood, smoking rooms in tigerwood, while "Parisian green moquette is used in the main compartments, blue moquette in drawing rooms. The color combinations are very effective."

"The trimmings throughout are 'Bower-Barff' whose unobtrusive black is in pleasing contrast to the usual glitter of polished brass and silver plate," said the Santa Fe with an oblique smirk in the direction of the competition. "The Pullmans are perfect in every detail."

Observation-sleepers were reminiscent of Bobby Burns and the Waverly novels, being named *Ben Wyvis, Ben More, Ben Doran,* and for other Scotch landmarks, to the probable confusion of drummers in hardware from Bridgeport who occupied their sections and drawing rooms. On the train "white appareled waiters bore viands from a hidden kitchen," thus conforming to the lexicon of the time which forbade anything as simple as mere food. Viands were invariably ample and tempting, sometimes rare and exotic, the latter usually on extra-fare trains.

The *Colorado Limited* left Chicago at six in the evening and arrived at what was customarily spoken of as the Queen City of the Plains at ten the second morning out. The fare was $25 round trip, exclusive of Pullman charges.

"It is a luxurious train," said the Santa Fe in a final and unexpected burst of simplicity.

At the turn of the century the electric light was the coming thing of the railroad world, widely advertised by numerous carriers such as the Pennsylvania and the Northern Pacific as one of the up and coming aspects of progressive operation and their finer trains. None placed their confidence with fewer reservations in the hands of Thomas A. Edison than the Chicago & North Western, whose various trains included the *Pacific Limited,* the *Denver Limited,* the *Overland Flyer,* the *Chicago Limited* and the *Vestibuled Limited,*

the last of which ran on an overnight schedule between Chicago and St. Paul–Minneapolis with supper served in a buffet–sleeper to passengers from Duluth. As a Vanderbilt affiliate, all luxury equipment on the North Western was, of course, Wagner in origin until after the year 1900.

So great was the pulling power of electricity—promotionally if not tractively speaking—that in 1900 a specially elaborate brochure illustrated with colored tintblocks was prepared to hymn the glories of illumination aboard the *North Western Limited,* which had been scheduled on the old run of the *Vestibuled Limited* of a few years earlier between the Twin Cities and Chicago:

Each compartment is brilliantly lighted by ELECTRICITY. . . . The standard sleeping cars are each ELECTRICALLY lighted. . . . Berth reading lamps conveniently arranged and chandeliers which supply both ELECTRIC and Pintsch light provide satisfactory illumination. . . . A special feature is the provision of ELECTRIC BERTH READING LAMPS operated by a simple device that can be lighted or extinguished at pleasure. . . . The dining cars are perfectly lighted by ELECTRICITY. . . . The free reclining chair cars on the North Western Limited are brilliantly lighted by ELECTRICITY. . . . ELECTRICITY lights the seats in the smoking compartments. . . . On the buffet–smoker and library cars ELECTRICITY in lamps of unique design is arranged with specific reference to reading. . . .

The forward-looking North Western saw to it that the customers and their every activity were brilliantly lighted on their way around the Great Lakes by the same radiance that lighted its Vanderbilt owners on their occasions in the serried brownstone mansions that were by now one of the landmarks of upper Fifth Avenue in far-off New York City.

Competing in the long names sweepstakes with the Rio Grande's *Trans-Continental, San Francisco, Butte & Portland Express* were two trains of the Rome–Watertown & Ogdensburg Railroad listed in the *Official Guide* for 1895 as *The Niagara Falls & Thousand Islands Club Train* and its overnight opposite number *The Celebrated St. Lawrence Steamboat Express.* An adjective-conscious management allowed that the first of these, on the Suspension Bridge, Niagara Falls and Clayton run, was "a superb day train comprising a Wagner vestibuled club car and Wagner vestibuled parlor car." The night train included in its consist "magnificent Wagner sixteen section vestibuled sleeping cars," and either or both must have been joy unmitigated to the leathern-lunged train announcers of the day to whose rolling periods even such orators as William Jennings Bryan listened with awe.

That the Deep South had its share of distinguished name trains and all-Pullman runs is suggested by the presence in the *Official Guide* of the late eighties of the *Richmond & Danville Limited* operated by the Richmond & Danville Railroad, now part of the Southern Railway System, between Washington, D.C., and New Orleans over its own rails and connecting lines. In later years the train was known as the *Washington & South Western Vestibuled Limited* and the Pullman photographic files for 1892 depict truly splendid club cars and sleepers custom-built for this luxury run and closely resembling in external decor the stunning cars built for the *Pennsylvania Limited* at approximately the same time.

The train left Washington at 11:00 P.M. and arrived at New Orleans at 7:45 the second morning out. It was, according to the *Guide,* "A magnificent train of Pullman Vestibuled Palaces, consisting of drawing room, dining, sleeping and buffet–smoking room and library cars of the latest and most magnificent and luxurious designs built expressly for this service and run daily. Only passengers holding Pullman tickets will be admitted to these trains between Washington and Atlanta. Minimum Pullman fare $2.00."

One of the buffet–library cars was the Pullman *Ulysses,* a circumstance that causes confusion among car collectors and historians because of the inclusion of an almost precisely similar car of identical name a few years later in the *Pennsylvania Limited.* The livery was, of course, different but does not show in the black and white photography of the time.

When the *Pennsylvania Limited* predecessor of the later classic *Broadway Limited* went into service on the through run between New York and Chicago, company literature was relatively subdued, evidently content to let the train speak for itself:

One composite car, one dining car and three sleeping cars constitute the train leaving Chicago. A vestibuled sleeping car from Cincinnati joins the train at Pittsburgh, and thence the run is made to Harrisburg, Philadelphia and New York. From Harrisburg a parlor car is run to Baltimore and Washington for the exclusive accommodation of 'Limited' passengers. The first of the Pullman vestibuled trains has been described in dozens of newspapers, and was inspected, when on its exhibition trip, by at least one hundred thousand people in the prominent cities of the country, from Boston and New York to Kansas City; from Cincinnati, St. Louis and Chicago to St. Paul and Minneapolis. As implied by their name, the prominent feature of the cars is the vestibule formed by enclosing the platform.

Its structure is primarily a broad, thick frame of steel extending from platform to roof, and supported by pressure derived from strong elastic springs. When two cars are connected these frames press tightly against each other, forcing back the steel springs. This gives close contact throughout the entire surface of the frames sustained by high pressure. In this way great steadiness of movement is imparted to the whole train. It will also be perceived that the steel frames act as spring buffers from top to bottom of each car, constituting a powerful barrier, if not absolute protection, against telescoping.

In the interior the vestibules are carpeted and furnished. Sheets of rubber, arranged in folds like those of an accordion, cover the points of contact, and by stretching while the train is rounding curves make the entrance of wind and dust impossible. Cut glass doors that are barred while the train is in motion open out on the steps. The vestibules, therefore, serve as hallways leading from one car to another, relieving the passenger from the annoyance of the whirlwind of the open platform, from dust in summer, from snow and intense cold in winter, and from storms in all seasons.

The sleeping cars are finished in a rare kind of mahogany and upholstered in pale blue plush. The staterooms are finished in satinwood and upholstered in rich terra cotta.

The roomy interior of the dining car is provided with tables accommodating about forty persons. The French oak finish, myrtle green plush, china and silver table service, with cut flowers and tastefully prepared menus, form a tempting sight. The composite car, finished in English oak, contains a baggage-room, card-rooms, a spacious smoking-room, fitted in olive brown, with easy cushioned rattan arm-chairs, library and well-equipped writing desk, in the drawers of which is fine linen paper with the engraved name of the train, free for the use of passengers. This car also contains a barber shop, with all appliances, and a bath tub. The uniform motion given the train by the vestibules renders safe and pleasing the practice of the barber's art while the train is at full speed.

The floors throughout are covered with Wilton carpets. Beautifully decorated ceilings support numerous richly finished lamps. The Baker heater, which has never in case of accident caused the destruction of a train by fire, supplies needed warmth. Toilet rooms, complete in their appointments, are in each car.

But if the management of the Standard Railroad of the World was content to abide by the maxim that *res ipsa loquitur* in its eulogy of the *Pennsylvania Limited,* such was not the case with the Milwaukee when, on May 5, 1898, it inaugurated its new *Pioneer Limited,* "twin trains as bright hued as the yellow butterflies that flutter over the golden dandelions in early spring," on the Chicago–Twin Cities run.

The literature evolved to herald this nonesuch among name trains pulled no punches in hymning "the $250,000 worth of gorgeousness for the thirteen hours journey between Chicago, St. Paul and Minneapolis lived for that length of time in such harmonious surroundings which unconsciously subordinate the mind to a corresponding state of concord and bring the traveler to his destination in a well balanced mental condition. Yet such 'comfy' quarters, despite their elegance are not a bit stiffish."

Aside from the train's practical features [read the Milwaukee's brochure describing the *Pioneer*] the interior decorations are a liberal education in themselves, if you care to study and observe well. The inlaid work, styled *marquetry,* has taken months of time and American enterprise to bring from distant parts of the world and prepare. Rare woods from all parts of the forests have been drawn upon for material, and are employed profusely, differing in each compartment and car. All are most beautiful, many very rare—such as the tulip, amaranth, primavera, saffron, olive and cocobolo. They have been combined in their natural colors to produce the most artistic results, and in quantity alone are almost worth a king's ransom, while quality and beauty tell an extravagant tale. Set in the highly polished surfaces of vermilion wood, the different mahoganies and Circassian walnut, are mosaics of other woods, contrasting in color, which compose the graceful wreaths, garlands, draperies, and torches that form the decorative scheme of the Empire style used. This is the style of ornamentation exclusively employed throughout the trains, with a suggestion of the classic Greek—a combination peculiarly adapted to producing rich effects.

So fine and minute is the detail of these mosaics of marquetry, so carefully shaded and marvelously wrought, that to the casual glance of the indifferent traveler a false impression of painting is conveyed, but the initiate eye gazes with pleasure and wonder at the intricacy and delicacy of this marquetry work, the color and beauty of the rare woods, and the rich carvings that supplement the inlay. And so wisely is this seemingly extravagant use of material and wealth directed, so true the art principle employed, that what might be rendered merely showy in the hands of ignorant riches, here becomes an embodiment of all that is truly artistic.

The whole combination of woodwork, tapestries, hangings and carpets, as well as the bronze and glass work, has been treated as a color scheme, under the supervision of a thorough artist. Taking the different wood of each compartment as the keynote to this color scheme, the colors have been carefully modulated from floor to ceiling. The main room of each car has its own separate color scheme, while each compartment opening from it varies according to its particular woodwork. With the deep, rich red of the padouk or vermilion wood, a delicate blue harmonizes; with the mahoganies, a soft, warm olive, while the Circassian walnut takes a happy combination of warm walnut brown, Venetian red, and delicate cream. Or again, as in the main room of the dining car, which is finished in mahogany, the color is kept in the cool sage greens, softening from the dark-green Wilton carpet toward the ceiling, where the high lights reach a delicate silvery tint. The tables will appeal to the true instinct of every good housewife, with their heavy Irish satin damask, of acanthus leaf and snowdrop pattern, set with Haviland china daintily decorated, and silverware made from an especial design, displaying the rare old English oval shapes, varied by the use of the fluted corners, and finished with a graceful rococo border.

In the parlor cars, which consist of a main drawing-room, with smoking apartments at either end, and the usual toilet rooms, richly carved San Domingo mahogany is used as a basis with contrasting colors against it, the ceiling is painted in warm apricot tints, lightening toward the center and decorated with a graceful pattern in gold, the furnishing in green shades—upholstery of a light tone and draperies of India silk damask in green and white. Most of the hangings are of heavy silk velours lined with satin, the upholsteries of moquette plush and the carpets of imported Wilton of a special weave and design all of equal richness.

In the main drawing room of the standard sleepers, a most imposing effect is produced by dividing the long perspective in the center with ornate Corinthian columns resting on richly inlaid pedestals. The arches supporting the ceilings spring from their entablatures, on which a slight departure from the Empire style permits the introduction of a Greek pattern. The bulkheads and berth panels consist of the choicest specimens of vermilion wood, highly polished and elaborately decorated with marquetry, the ceilings brighten into a delicate robin's egg blue, ornamented with a design in gold and bright color. This same effect of a division is repeated by Ionic columns between the cardroom and the main apartment of the buffet–smoking car, and in the arch which they support is set a handsome bronze grille.

And summing up—though I have not described the half—I said to myself, " 'Tis a veritable *edition de luxe* bound in covers of yellow and gold, in which one may read of history, science and art, and drift on fancy's wing to the uttermost ends of the earth, and the forests which have contributed to its making."

When the Chicago, Milwaukee & St. Paul Railroad was finished with the *Pioneer Limited,* there was little left in the lexicon of superlative wonderments of travel in which to enshrine any trains that might have remained in the pages of the *Official Guide,* and it would perhaps be as well to conclude a survey of random name trains in the record on this high, indeed almost ineffable note.

The Golden State Special *was inaugurated by the Union Pacific and its Central Pacific connection in 1887 between Chicago and California with de luxe equipment, which included the eye-popping vestibuled library–observation car* Sybaris *shown on these two pages. There were also a diner,* Casa Monica, *the sleepers* Khiva *and* Rahula *and the composite baggage–smoker* Golden Gate *with the first bathtub (right) to roll across the Great Plains in general service. The observation car* Aladdin, *whose platform is shown opposite, was the opposite number of* Sybaris.

THREE PHOTOS: PULLMAN STANDARD

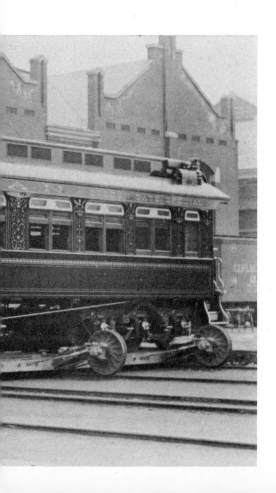

A wash drawing of the Golden Gate Special *pausing in the Nevada desert in the year 1889 is the endpaper for this book, executed by the distinguished railroad artist E. S. Hammack and depicting* Sybaris *in the noontide of its going and of the palace cars.*

Stunning examples of Pullman's most meticulous workmanship, the cars of the Florida & West Indian Limited also recall the proud tradition which built and assigned railroad equipment for specific runs and maintained it exclusively for service in the name train of its designation.

One of the oldest name trains on the through run between New York and Florida was the Florida & West Indian Limited, *which was known locally along the line, for brevity, as the* West Indian Mail. *It originated on the Pennsylvania and traversed the iron of the Richmond, Fredericksburg & Potomac, the Atlantic Coast Line and the various components of the Plant system through Georgia and Florida, including the Savannah, Florida & Western and the South Florida Railroad. In March of 1888 the* Limited *was running in two sections, the first of which—*Advance Mail *—comprised the regular day coaches and two private palace cars from the Lehigh Valley Railroad, occupied by A. M. Wilbur, son of the presi-dent of that carrier, and a party of vacationists Florida-bound. At Blackshear, Georgia, in the territory of the Savannah, Florida & Western, the first section was wrecked, as is shown below on this page. "The light train of four cars with its distinguished passengers dashed upon Hurricane Trestle," said a contemporary news account, "with unusual speed and the trestle promptly disintegrated killing twenty-five 'select passengers' and injuring a larger number." The second section with fourteen sleepers and other de luxe equipment was close behind but escaped injury. It was one of the few disasters involving private equipment to such a fatal extent.*

TWO PHOTOS: PULLMAN STANDARD

One of the celebrated name trains of the belle époque of railroad travel, the Lehigh Valley's Black Diamond, on the Jersey City–Buffalo run, was inaugurated in 1895 and posed on its first day in service behind the fine engine James Donnelly at Easton, Pennsylvania. On the page opposite the handsome coaches with the carrier's proud insigne on their nameboards assigned to the Black Diamond would suggest that on the Lehigh Valley, at any rate, coach travel was very little inferior in comfort to the palace cars that rode at the rear of the train.

TWO PHOTOS: PULLMAN STANDARD

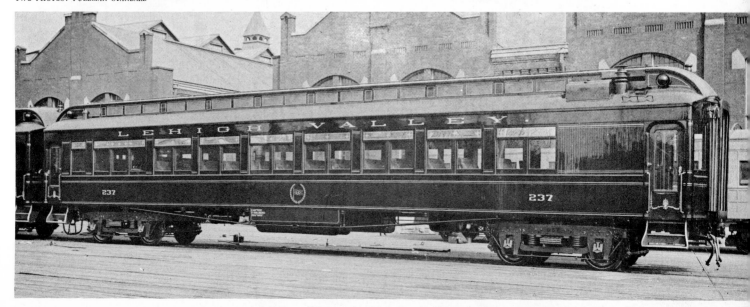

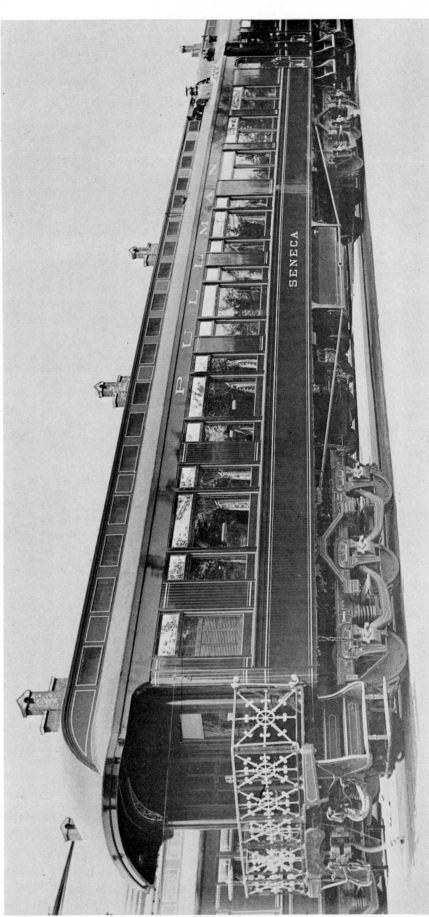

The ultimate in Pullman pride and craftsmanship went into the equipment for the Black Diamond, *so named for the coal that was the principal element in the Lehigh Valley economy. The cafe car No. 416 on the page opposite shows the head end on the first day's run, depicted on an earlier page. Seneca (opposite and above) was an observation–parlor car whose splendor of love seats, tufted upholstery and crystal chandeliers were the pride alike of the management and patrons of a swaggering and well-financed carrier.*

487

A companion car to Seneca, built by Pullman for service in the Lehigh Valley's Black Diamond when it was inaugurated in 1895, Veritas was outshopped two years later for the same run and represented a high-water mark in beauty of decor up to that time. The same elaborate furnishings obtained inside with love seats, inlaid ceiling and a profusion of the ornate devisings dear to the public imagination, still under the spell of the Chicago Fair of 1893.

Until the 1941 war, competition on the St. Louis–Chicago run bordered on the ruinous. Four main-line railroads, the Chicago & Alton, the Wabash, the Illinois Central and the Chicago & Eastern Illinois each maintained sleepers, diners, lounges and parlor observation cars and other first-class day and night equipment on trains on directly competing schedules leaving either terminal three times a day. Patrons had a choice of the Wabash Banner Blue, Bluebird *and* Midnight, *the C. & E. I.* Zipper *and* Midnight Special, *the Illinois Central's* Green Diamond, Night Diamond *and* Daylight *and the Alton's* Alton Limited, *shown here at East St. Louis in 1934,* Abraham Lincoln *and* Ann Rutledge. *Reminiscent travelers of the time recall the chicken stew with dumplings on the* Banner Blue *and its observation parlor car,* Helena Modjeska, *the elaborate buffet cars on the Alton run and the eighty-five-mile-an-hour spurts through the Illinois cornfields aboard the* Zipper. *Pioneer carrier on the St. Louis–Chicago run, the Illinois Central could trace its operations back to 1856 when its first name train, the* Lightning Express, *was running with compartmented sleepers known as "Gothic Cars."*

LUCIUS BEEBE

Where, three quarters of a century earlier, George M. Pullman's first primordial sleeping car (right) had seen service on the Chicago & Alton and Conductor J. L. Barnes had had to ask passengers please to remove their boots before retiring, the Alton Limited *(page opposite) rolled in the long afternoon of steam and the infancy of streamlining. Below is an Alton reclining-seat chair car in the year 1875 on the identical run between Chicago and Bloomington.*

PULLMAN STANDARD

New England Limited

alias

"The White Train"

"One half the glories have not been told

Of that wonderful train of white and gold. . . .

Pride and glory of the New York & New England Railroad in the Boston nineties, the New England Limited *poses for its portrait at the company depot at the foot of Summer Street where the South Station stands today.*

492

The White Train *parlor cars were peopled with proper Bostonians in an age when the silk top hat was still the accustomed attire of travel and a Gladstone valise contained all that was needful for a week end at New York's fashionable Waldorf-Astoria at Thirty-third Street and Fifth Avenue.*

On the page opposite, the New England Limited, *otherwise known as the* White Train, *rolls through the tranquil Connecticut countryside against a sunset backdrop near Middletown in a painting by Howard Fogg. On this page the interior of one of Pullman's royal buffet smokers reflects the subdued taste but solid comfort of Yankee preference. Here the captains of New England finance of the nineties conferred together over Lawrence's Medford rum and Overland cigars or read in the* Boston Evening Transcript *about the amazing empires of steel and railroads being built by Andrew Carnegie and J. P. Morgan, men whose achievements were faithfully followed and enduringly admired in Boston's State Street.*

HOWARD FOGG   PULLMAN STANDARD

The dining car of the New England Limited *shuttled back and forth daily between Boston and Willimantic in the charge of the knowing maître d'hôtel Mr. Parker, and its staff were familiar with the whims, habits and gastronomic preferences of all the proper Bostonians from Major Henry L. Higginson to Mrs. Jack Gardner of Fenway Court. A degree of privacy was available to diffident patrons by means of heavy curtains that could convert each table into a private dining room if desired. From its galley there issued a stream of dishes beloved to New Englanders, Maine lobster, Cotuit oysters and the best groceries in the world from the shelves of S. S. Pierce & Company of Copley Square.*

NEW HAVEN RAILROAD

With the peerless Gene Potter at the throttle, the N.Y. & N.E.'s Rogers-built 4-4-0 No. 183 backs into Summer Street depot at two fifty of an 1893 afternoon for an appointment to take the White Train *on the eighty-six-mile run to Willimantic. Below, the* New England Limited *pauses briefly at Middletown in deepest Connecticut; the crossover of the Hartford & Connecticut Valley Railroad is just beyond the depot.*

Less offensive to refined female sensibilities was the class of passengers who gave the Wagner cars of the New York Central a wide berth and patronized General Horace Porter's West Shore Railroad, which ran Pullmans. Built to blackmail the Vanderbilt lines, the West Shore was financially a calamity and a scandal, but for a time it maintained fine passenger service and Pullman parlor cars ran over its rails as late as 1930, when it had long since passed into the reluctant hands of the New York Central. Below is a Pullman compartmented parlor car in fullest flower in 1885.

In 1882 the late afternoon train between Albany and New York City was officially listed by the New York Central as the Buffalo Day Express, but because at Albany when the state assembly was in session it picked up so many politicians it became popularly known as "The Legislative Train." So boisterous was the conduct of the people's representatives and so profane their language that unaccompanied women hesitated to ride with them, and in its issue of March 11, 1882, Harper's ran this picture depicting two young ladies quivering with apprehension as the cars pass through Poughkeepsie.

The Wagner Palace Car Company still had two years of independent operations ahead of it before being absorbed by Pullman when the fine buffet car shown on the page opposite was built in 1897 for the Chicago & North Western, at the time a Vanderbilt road and hence a customer of Pullman's rival. It is shown below in service on the head end of a North Western express on the Chicago–Omaha run, where it supplemented the full diner service provided on the next to last car of this handsome train. Often the attendants on buffet cars of this sort, as shown above, turned out superlative food from their diminutive galleys, which were conducted with all the flourishes of the chef de cuisine at Delmonico's.

Whether expressed in terms of the carrier's beautiful two-platform business car No. 1902 [for a time the company numbered official cars for the year of their purchase; in the regime of the Moores, they became too numerous] or its handsome diner No. 717, evidencing the transition to all-platform-enclosed vestibule cars, the passenger equipment of the Rock Island in the years of its ascendant fortunes was the best that money could buy.

Either or both of the fine cars shown opposite might well have ridden across the Great Plains and through the heartland of America in the Rock Island's Denver–Chicago Express, *shown here in Denver Union Station in 1900. The run took a day and two nights at the time, and sleeping and dining cars were necessary for the trip. Posed beside the cap-stacked 4-4-0 No. 537 are the frock-coated conductor, the news butcher in knickerbockers, fireman, engineer and friend to represent forever a proud moment in Western legend and in the high noon of the Rock Island's affairs.*

Competing in service to the Northwest with the Hill lines and the Milwaukee, the Union Pacific has for six decades maintained service into Portland aboard a succession of name trains originating in Chicago. One of them was the Portland Rose, shown here in the glory days of steam near Hammett, Idaho, in an action shot taken on Medbury Hill by Henry R. Griffiths, Jr., with one of the U.P.'s famed 800 series 4-8-4's ahead of fifteen cars. Before the coming of the Rose, the crack train on the run was the Chicago–Portland Express aboard which, in all probability, Alfred Hertz encountered misfortune, as shown on the opposite page. Also shown is one of the fine Pullmans built expressly for this run in an age when luxury equipment carried the insigne of name trains to which it was assigned on its nameboards. In the diesel era the City of Portland took over the main line Chicago run and the Portland Rose was scheduled between the Northwest and Denver–Kansas City–St. Louis.

HENRY R. GRIFFITHS, JR.

Robbery aboard the cars was infrequent but sometimes it happened to the most distinguished people. In 1900 the Police Gazette was able to inform its no doubt enchanted readers that the great musical conductor Alfred Hertz had been robbed of his clothing en route to Portland aboard the Union Pacific and had been forced to make the informal entry to his hotel depicted here. Hertz played in bad luck on the road. Six years later he lost his wardrobe, this time in its entirety, when fire and earthquake destroyed the Palace Hotel in San Francisco where he and the Metropolitan Opera Company were staying.

At the time of Mr. Hertz's misfortune the Oregon Short Line was one of the complex of Harriman properties which included Union Pacific and Southern Pacific, and through service from Chicago to the North West was one of the highlights of the combined railroads. If Mr. Hertz lost his attire on a sleeper of the Chicago–Portland Special (below) it was at least from a name train that gloried in equipment specially assigned to its service and identified by nameboards.

PULLMAN STANDARD

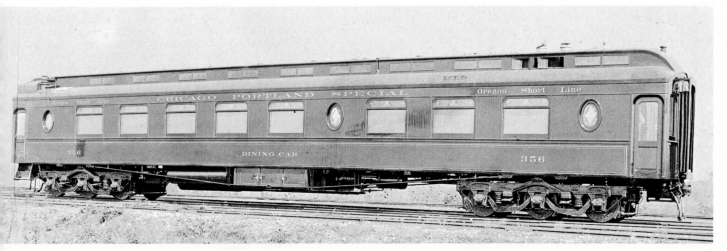

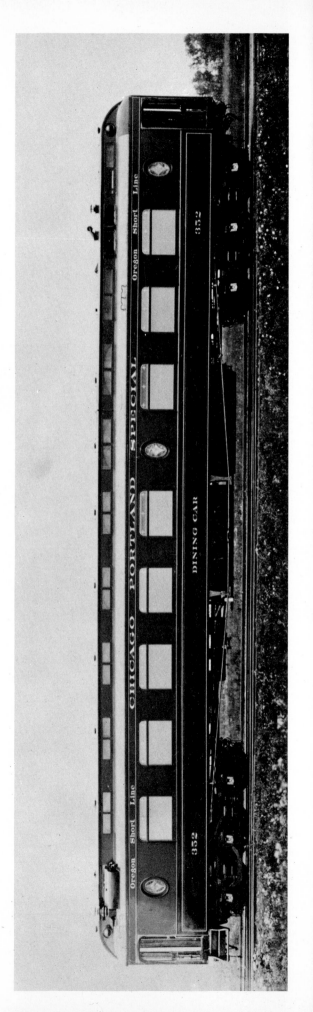

The glory days of the Union Pacific in the regime of E. H. Harriman saw specially designated equipment ordered from Pullman at a cost of millions, its luxury components engrossed on nameboards and sidewalls with the name of the train to which it was assigned.

Since the days when it had eased the stages of Wells Fargo off the main line of the Overland Trail to California, Union Pacific had been one of the proud proprietary names of the Old West, never more so than during its great reactivation in the Harriman administration. Its name trains, such as the Chicago Portland Special *over the* Oregon Short Line *and the* Overland Limited, *represented by special equipment on the opposite page, carried the U.P. insigne in smoking glory and on exacting luxury schedules. On this page is a wintry period piece by Fred Jukes showing the* Pacific Express *westbound out of Rawlins in 1907.*

When this fine diner was outshopped by Pullman for the Rio Grande's trains between Denver and Salt Lake, the carrier was already famed for breakfast menus that listed sixty items, including strawberries and cream, thirty cents, and sirloin steak for two, one dollar. At its western terminal, refreshed by a night's sleep in the high passes of the Shining Mountains, passengers could board the parlor–observation car of Senator William A. Clark's Salt Lake Line, soon to be absorbed by the Union Pacific.

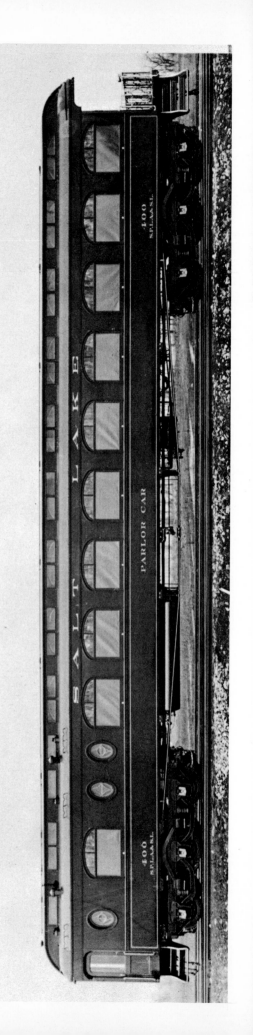

Successor to the Panoramic *on the Denver &
Rio Grande Western's Moffat Tunnel run between Denver and Salt Lake–Ogden in the thirties was the* Exposition Flyer, *named in honor*
*of the San Francisco fair at Treasure Island in
1939. The* Flyer *is shown here in the final years
of steam on the approach to tunnel No. 1 out of
Denver.*

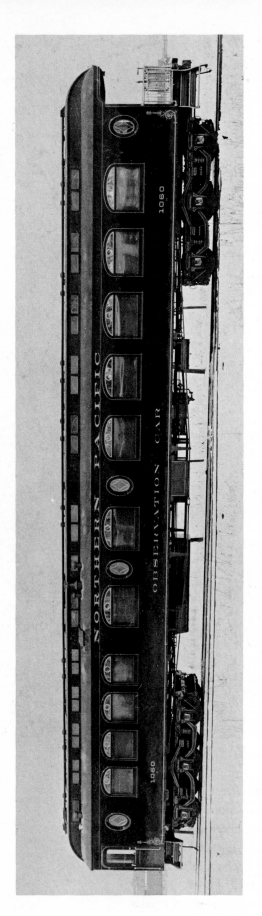

Pullman delivered these fine cars to the Northern Pacific shortly after the turn of the century for service in the North Coast Limited, already celebrated as the first train in the Northwest to be lit entirely by electricity.

In 1900 the Northern Pacific was not yet known as "Main Street of the North West," but in that year it established itself as a progressive railroad when, in April, it ran the first electrically lit train to go into service between Chicago and Portland. The North Coast Limited early in the game established itself as one of the great name trains of the continent for the food served in diners such as that on the page opposite, this despite James J. Hill's disapproval of passenger traffic generally. Here the new Edison dispensation is shown beaming from tulip-petal lampshades on leg-of-mutton sleeves and porkpie hats. That the Hill railroad's patrons could read is suggested by the well-stocked bookshelves in the charge of George, the Pullman porter.

511

Less formal than the dining arrangements elsewhere on the Northern Pacific's North Coast Limited on the opposite page are those in one of its sleepers in the year 1898 when the face of the world is turned toward Alaska and gold-seekers in thousands are headed for the sub-zero Yukon. The caption on this faded print identifies the beard in the middle distance as that of Soapy Smith, King of the Thimbleriggers, en route from Denver and Leadville to pastures new. He is shortly to die violently in Alaska. Lesser luminaries in the foreground are concerned with biscuits and cheese, but the circle of the elite dominated by Soapy and including Fred the porter, seem preoccupied with stronger and bottled matters. It is a moment to quicken the pulse in the Western epic, and the cry is "On, on to Nome!"

It seems impossible at this remove that things were as bad aboard the observation–club car of the Illinois Central's Florida-bound Seminole *in 1920 as is suggested by the faces in this picture. True, the market was soggy and prohibition was abroad in the land, but somewhere the sun was shining and Florida beaches beckoned. On the page opposite, Deep South travel in the age of steam is again represented, at the top by the Southern Railway's New Orleans–bound* Southerner *in streamlined dress under the catenaries at Washington, D.C., and below by the Southern's* Birmingham Special *in 1948, with three Pullman sleepers deadheading in front of the train's regularly assigned revenue cars.*

ILLINOIS CENTRAL RAILROAD   TWO PHOTOS: RAIL PHOTO SERVICE

Probably the longest train name in the Official Guide *for the year 1900 was that of the Denver & Rio Grande Western's No. 3, the* Trans-Continental San Francisco, Butte & Portland Express *shown here at Littleton, Colorado, a few miles out of Denver, with Pullman palace buffet sleepers in addition to conventional open section sleeping cars and coach and tourist accommodations. Although the Rio Grande's main lines had been standard-gauged in the early years of the previous decade, there still was a third rail for the accommodation of the carrier's narrow-gauge operations, which in 1900 provided access to remote mining communities in the Rockies impervious to the broad-gauge tracks.*

Builders' photographs from American Car & Foundry are rare items for car collectors because of the destruction of the company's back files at the order of an irresponsible executive in the fifties. This typical A.C. & F. diner interior was one of several beautifully designed restaurant cars delivered to the Denver & Rio Grande in the mid-nineties, and its square-topped chairs were a hallmark of the company's product. The photo is from the authoritative collection of Arthur D. Dubin of Chicago.

HOLIDAY MAGAZINE   ARTHUR D. DUBIN COLLECTION

*When, in 1895, the lordly Southern Pacific or-
dered four entire new trains for service between
Los Angeles and New Orleans in the* Sunset
Limited, *no expense was spared to make it one
of the handsomest trains on the continent and
one that reflected glory on both builder and
carrier. Typical of the interior appointments
were those of the sleeper* El Oro, *which reflected
the declining vogue of elaborate ornamentation
while still maintaining the richness of decor essential to a great name train and its owners.*

518

Nearly half a century after El Oro *was new the* Sunset Limited *was still rolling across the Southwest on its lawful occasions to be photographed in 1942 near Beaumont, in the California desert, by William Barham in a doubleheaded action shot of majestic dimensions.*

In 1934 the Missouri Pacific's train No. 1, the Sunshine Special, out of St. Louis daily at 6:30 P.M. with sleepers for Mexico City, Los Angeles, Houston–Galveston, Shreveport and Dallas–Fort Worth was one of the glamorous name trains of the final years of steam. On the West Texas leg of its landfaring over the rails of the Texas & Pacific it was powered by motive power of uncommon beauty, much of which carried the train name proudly on the smokebox.

TWO PHOTOS: LUCIUS BEEBE

In the deep Southwest where once the Sunshine Special had rolled over the Gould lines with a de luxe air-conditioned lounge–observation car with valet, shower, fountain and bar service, the early days of railroading out of St. Louis had been characterized by a certain element of hurrah, not the least of which derived from the presence of professional gamblers aboard the cars. A lady card-sharp named Poker Alice Ivers with irreproachable manners and an English accent played the Pullmans exclusively, claiming that the peasants in the coaches were beneath her notice, and a former Mississippi River con artist offered the Missouri–Kansas–Texas Railroad $25,000 a year not to be molested on its trains and promised to victimize only clergymen. Canada Bill Jones's offer was rejected, but his fame was nonetheless so great for skinning greenies on trains out of St. Louis that Leslie's ran this likeness of him in action with the caption: "Will You Take a Hand, Sir?"

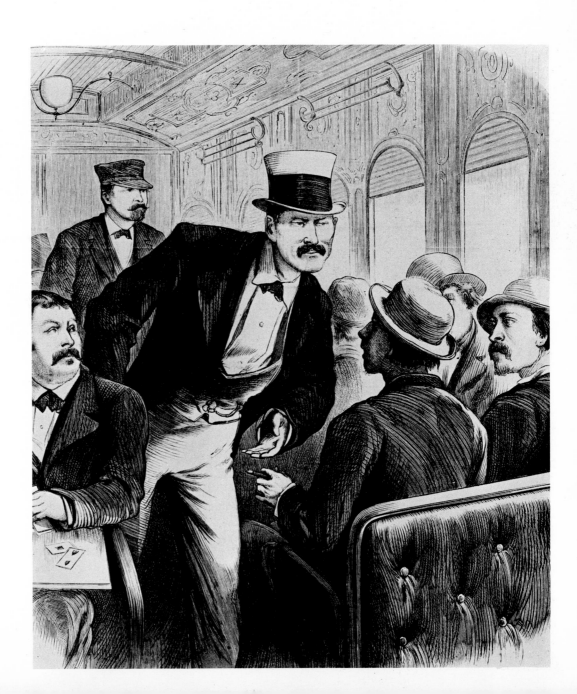

What was the first traveling salesman's story to be recounted in a railroad car and what primeval train was the setting for the event that was to cast its long shadow down the corridors of American folklore? Lacking scholarly investigation into the field, it can only be surmised that the event took place shortly after the dawn of rail travel and that the drummer's anecdote reached its finest flowering in the years after the Civil War when salesmen with every conceivable variety and brand of merchandise from the great manufactories and wholesalers of Boston and Chicago, St. Louis, Kansas City, Birmingham and Pittsburgh were abroad in the land, banded in a confraternity of continental commerce and occupying space on the cars from Bangor to San Diego on their professional occasions. Aboard the smoking cars of locals in Alabama and New Hampshire and in the compartments of open section sleepers past all counting on transcontinental name trains out of Omaha and Fort Worth, the drummers forgathered in relaxed moments over cigars and whisky and—in the lingua franca of their trade—the smoke-room story. Far away and long ago these derby-hatted travelers in the commerce of the nation posed aboard the Santa Fe's California Limited for a group photograph. "It seems there was a farmer had three daughters. . . ."

SANTA FE RAILWAY

Solid Pullman comfort characterized the Sante Fe's well-remembered Navajo, shown here in the Cajon Pass near Victorville, California, in a photograph by Herb Sullivan, a cameraman of the high iron who specialized in just such nostalgic railroad action as this.

HERB SULLIVAN

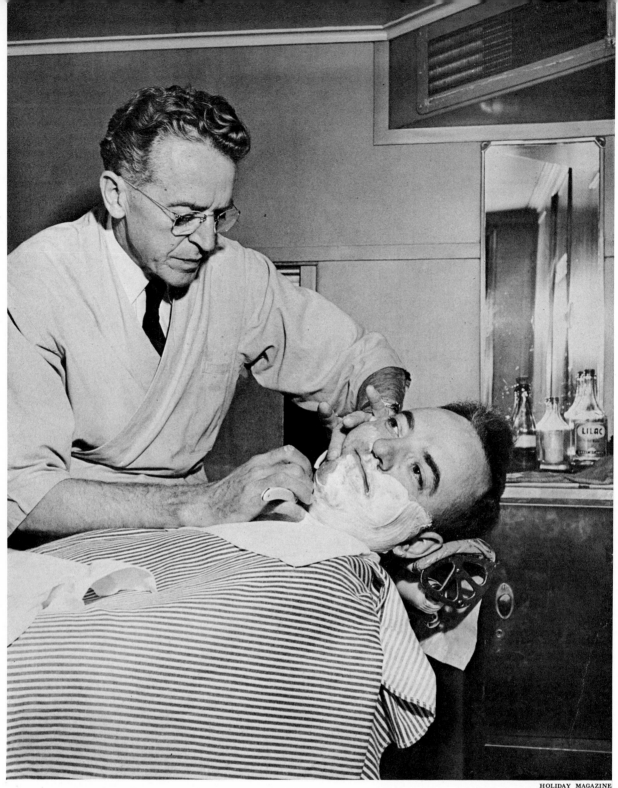

HOLIDAY MAGAZINE

Even in depression years when it sometimes ran with no more than seven cars, the Chief *maintained a resolute façade of elegance when it was pictured, on the opposite page, by Herb Sullivan in 1934 near Victorville in the Cajon. The posters suggest the grand manner of the De Luxe which had gone before.*

On the Chief *in the lean years there still were the traditional Santa Fe library cars, a brass-railed observation and, of course, a Fred Harvey diner, but the $25 extra fare of De Luxe and free corsages of orchids were gone forever. Here Train Barber Maurice Stansfield gives a customer the once-over crossing the Kansas plains.*

HERB SULLIVAN

TWO POSTERS: PULLMAN STANDARD

By the late eighties dining aboard the cars evoked many of the amenities of public dining in fine city restaurants in an age of ever-increasing gastronomic sophistication. Menus suggested that dining cars on the Baltimore & Ohio, Sante Fe and New Haven possessed resources of terrapin, antelope, quail, canvasback, Cape Cod oysters and Kansas City filets *that might compare favorably with Delmonico's, the universal standard of excellence of the time. Not everyone could have, as did J. P. Morgan, a steward in the person of Louis Sherry oversee his meals when he took the train, but on the diners of the Santa Fe an English perfectionist named Fred Harvey was serving food second to none off fine silver and the most expensive linen. Foreigners marveled at the food and service on American dining cars and went home to tell that every Yankee was a millionaire when he rode the cars. He was all of that when he had dinner aboard the Sante Fe's* Grand Canyon Limited, *whose second section is shown opposite at Victorville, California, in the Cajon Pass.*

ROBERT HALE

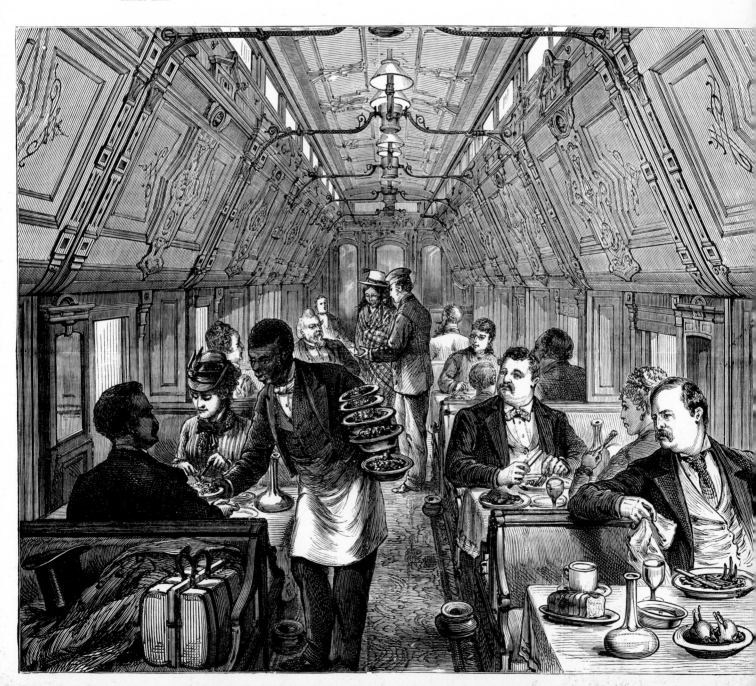

The seemingly limitless dimensions of the Shining Mountains and the grandeur of Western railroading are caught in this photograph by R. H. Kindig in the mid-thirties of the Denver & Rio Grande Western's doubleheaded Scenic Limited approaching Tennessee Pass on the Denver–Salt Lake run. On the right is the Arkansas River —setting for the great days of the fur trade before the railroads came. Behind the mountains lies Leadville, scene of one of the last and gaudiest of Colorado's bonanzas in precious metals.

R. H. KINDIG

A Rio Grande hogger and his conductor compare watches in a timeless gesture.

*Pastorals of the Colorado countryside un-
fold from the windows of the Rio Grande.*

*Servicing the cars at Pueblo is part of
train routine before starting up the hill.*

In the thirties the observation windows of the Scenic Limited
offered vistas of splendor as the train neared Tennessee Pass.

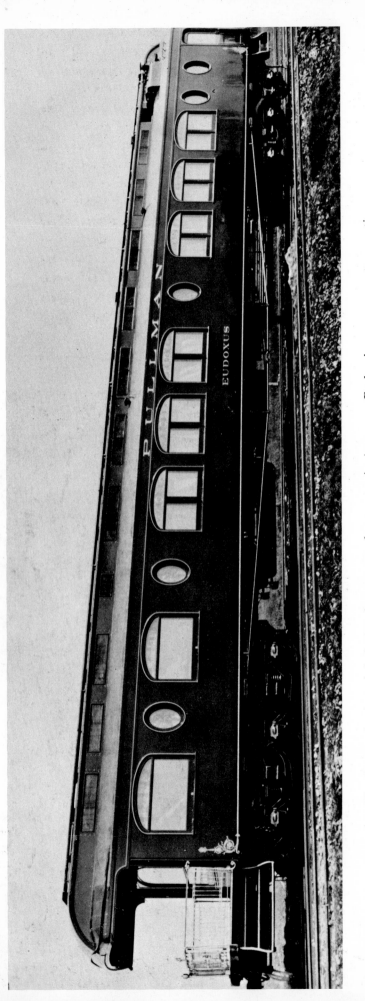

Flawless perfection of design and structure characterized the Pullmans Eudoxus and Endymion built for the first Twentieth Century Limited when the New York Central inaugurated the train in 1902. Endymion was an open section and stateroom sleeper; Eudoxus a compartment—observation lounge combine.

TWO PHOTOS: PULLMAN STANDARD

Eudoxus, *shown here, in addition to its private sleeping accommodations afforded such amenities of luxury travel as telephone connections at terminals, a reference library of business directories and manuals for the titans of finance who rode the* Century, *and a train secretary who was master of a primeval Remington typewriter as well as shorthand to cater to their least whim. Pierpont Morgan, Ogden Armour or Henry C. Frick could and did ride aboard* Eudoxus *with the assurance that it was part of a train whose every appointment was appropriate to the lords of creation. In the* Century *Pullman was commanded to spare no effort to build the handsomest train in the world—instructions precisely under which it had built the rival* Pennsylvania Limited *a few years earlier.*

NEW YORK CENTRAL SYSTEM

When the New York Central inaugurated the Twentieth Century Limited *as the world's finest and fastest long-haul passenger train there was a colored ladies' maid in attendance aboard the open section sleepers. Even in such stylish surroundings as those of the Central's showcase of elegance, the all-room sleeping car was still thirty-odd years in the future. Passengers were happy with lower berths, while invalids or groups reserved the staterooms at the end of each sleeper.*

Patrons aboard the first Twentieth Century Limited *found a barbershop, ladies' maid and train secretary in attendance, as well as conventional porters and waiters. The diner blossomed with ferns under glass, cut flowers, snowy napery and a palm-leaf fan in the light fixture above every place at table.*

Standard motive power assigned to the Twentieth Century Limited *in the days of steam and Pullman standard were the New York Central's classic J-3a Hudson locomotives which wheeled sixteen cars between New York and Chicago at better than an average mile a minute. Standby engines were maintained with steam up at every division point against the event of power failure to a train where delay was unthinkable.*

The red carpet departure from Grand Central of the Twentieth Century Limited
in the age of Pullman Standard provided a setting for the feminine fashions of
1925.

NEW YORK CENTRAL SYSTEM

The stage action of "Twentieth
Century," a Broadway smash
hit of the thirties starring Moffat
Johnson, took place in a stage-
wide re-creation of one of the
Century's observation–drawing
room cars faithful in every detail
of decor and atmosphere. Participants in the farce were a
stranded troupe of Oberam-
mergau Passion Players, including Christus seeking a producer
and defying the accustomed conduct and decorum of the world's
most celebrated extra-fare limited all-Pullman flyer.

RICHARD MANEY COLLECTION

In a happier day of railroading the Boston section of the Century *was an all-Pullman limited that rolled westward at five o'clock every afternoon through the Back Bay yards of the Boston & Albany with a smoking car such as this on the head end. A diner, open platform observation car from which to admire the Berkshire Hills and two sleepers on its regular schedule made it a glory of New England railroading to match the incomparable* Merchants Limited *on the equally haughty New Haven.*

LUCIUS BEEBE

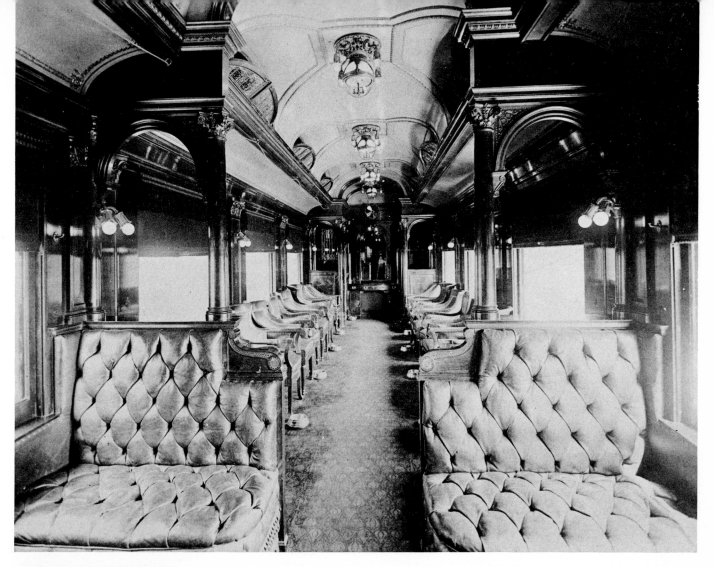

From the day of its first run, the Century *was a train of substantial comforts but subdued elegance of decor, as is suggested by the lounge depicted above. A fixed rule of the company prohibited the running of special equipment in the Central's flagship, and even the business car of august President Chauncey M. Depew (left) was carried in secondary trains. The photo of Depew on the platform of New York Central Business Car No. 1 was, in proper fact, taken toward the end of his life and long after he had retired from active participation in the road's affairs to become a living legend of after-dinner wit in New York's gas-lamp age.*

NEW YORK CENTRAL SYSTEM

Having its beginnings in the years that saw a retreat on the part of railroads and carbuilders from the luxurious decor of the nineties, the Twentieth Century Limited, *despite an abundance of services and operational superlatives, was never anything but an austere train to the eye. Decorative details in its public apartments were always at a minimum and fresh cut flowers the only adornment of its diners. While its direct rival on the New York–Chicago run, the* Pennsylvania's Broadway Limited, *was maintained in regal livery of Tuscan red and gold, the* Century *wore subdued tones of gray and blue. Ostentation, save in the matter of performance, had no part in the operation of the* Century. *Sleekly streamlined for its final years in steam, its club cars as depicted here were characterized by utilitarian austerity that cried aloud for the remembered splendors of Eudoxus.*

LUCIUS BEEBE

POMP & CIRCUMSTANCE

Even in an age of streamlining with the infamy of diesel just around the corner, the Century's sailing from Grand Central was still characterized by a crimson carpet and the pomp and circumstance of royalty. The dining cars of the 1938 train (page opposite) were designed—with a change from white to pastel-shaded linen and the turning up of a special pink lighting system and taped music—to become night clubs after the service of dinner was over. Placed in service just before the 1941 war, these opulent cars became the scenes of some notable skirmishes with the stuff that comes in bottles when the military took over most of the nation's travel resources for the duration.

541

TWO PHOTOS: NEW YORK CENTRAL SYSTEM

Passengers aboard the Santa Fe's luxury transcontinental flyer the Chief *in the days when it ran streamlined in steam (page opposite) were accustomed to the best of everything, including a barber and manicure, valet, stock reports and shower baths. Here a patron gets a trim at ninety miles an hour across the New Mexico uplands, while in the lower frame a chef to whom* caneton à l'orange *and mousse of foie gras are a commonplace prepares dinner in the stainless-steel galley for patrons of Fred Harvey.*

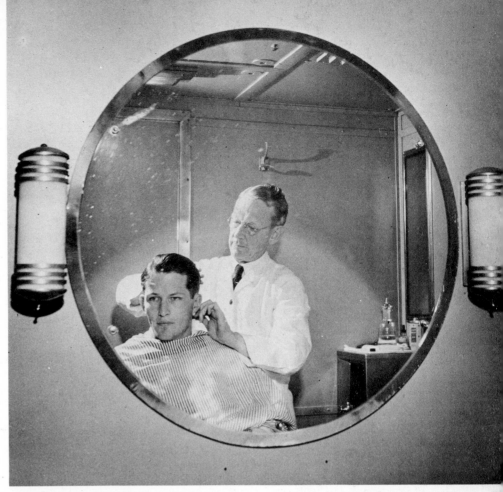

TWO PHOTOS: GRAPHIC HOUSE

Traversing some of the least spoiled and most scenic reaches of the West, the Union Pacific's Train No. 35, the Yellowstone Special *starts up the Continental Divide out of Big Springs, Idaho, with a baggage car and six Pullmans filled with summer vacationists and two Pacifics on the smoky end. In later years the Special succumbed to streamlining and diesel, but in 1949 when this picture was made steam still ruled much of the West and the durable Standard Pullman was the accustomed equipment.*

HENRY R. GRIFFITHS, JR.

A summertime-only run, from June to September, the Union Pacific's Yellowstone Special covers overnight the 328 miles between Salt Lake City and Ogden and West Yellowstone, entrance to the Yellowstone National Park. In its consist are coaches, Pullmans and a club lounge car for the use of sleeping car patrons. Here it is shown running three hours late in July 1951 near Ashton, Idaho, behind a trim U.P. 4-6-2 with eleven cars.

HENRY R. GRIFFITHS, JR.

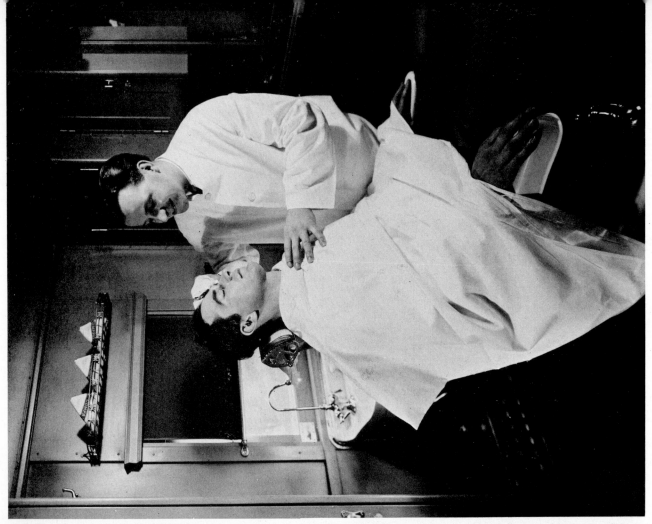

Inaugurated in 1937 with an eye to the impending San Francisco Exposition at Treasure Island the following year, the Southern Pacific–Union Pacific extra fare, all-Pullman streamliner, the Forty-niner, ran a round trip weekly with an eight-car train in steam from Lake Michigan to the Golden Gate. Shown at the left is the observation–buffet car California Republic. One of the handsomest of all Western trains (below) passes through the High Sierra near Gold Run on a June morning in 1938.

Gaily painted in brown, red and U.P. yellow, the Union Pacific's streamlined roller-bearing equipped 4-8-2 No. 7002 rolls down Sherman Hill at Borie in July 1937 with its consist of dark gray Pullmans. Specially assigned Southern Pacific motive power, as above, handled the crack flyer west of Ogden.

The diner of the Forty-niner, shown opposite, built for but not delivered to a Latin-American dictator, was presided over by Wild Bill Kurthy, a strong-willed steward who believed in letting the patrons have their own way so long as this involved eating the most and the best of everything, which Wild Bill provided in voluptuous abundance.

Typical of the competition in the thirties for passenger business between Chicago and St. Louis were the Wabash Banner Blue and the Chicago & Eastern Illinois Zipper shown top and below, respectively, on the page opposite. On almost identical schedules between the two terminals, these carriers were also in competition with the Illinois Central and the Alton with only slightly different intervening territory. All four roads prided themselves on maintaining top-notch service and fine dining cars with every amenity of comfort on both day and night runs. Shown here is the parlor–observation car Helena Modjeska that ran for many years in the Banner Blue, maintaining nominal continuity with Colonel William D'Alton Mann's penchant for naming his cars for the great in the worlds of opera and the stage.

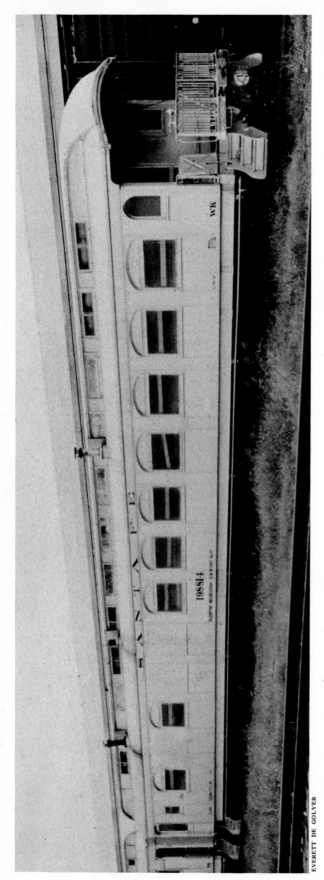

An exception to the usually austere design of even its most luxurious equipment was made by the Santa Fe in 1910 when it commissioned Pullman to build two observation–parlor cars such as that shown at the bottom of the page opposite for service in the Saint *and* Angel *running overnight between Los Angeles and San Francisco via Bakersfield. The exteriors were creamy white with mission bells in leaded glass in the Gothic window and brass observation railing. Above it is shown an end to grandeur: the same car as a sleeping and recreation unit in a work train at Dallas in 1960, a saddening commentary on the mutations of time.*

On the Bakersfield–San Francisco run in 1938 the Santa Fe's Golden State *ran with Pullman standard coaches, parlor cars, smokers and diners painted in distinctive livery as competition to the Southern Pacific's* Daylight *on the more advantageous Coast Route. It is shown here northbound at Fresno.*

The original Bar Harbor Express *and its successor the* Bar Harbor *was one of the great all-Pullman name trains that survived from the age of steam into the later days of streamlining and diesel. It operated week ends only during the summer between Washington, Philadelphia and New York and the Maine resort points at Brunswick, Augusta, Newport Junction and Bangor, originating on the Pennsylvania and being handled over the New Haven, Boston & Maine and Maine Central on its journey down-East. Originally a six-days-a-week train from June until October, it later ran three times weekly and finally only on week ends, with sleepers, a diner and club car. Its single bedrooms (above) have rested such Bar Harbor great as Mary Roberts Rinehart, Walter Lippmann, Walter Damrosch, Barrett Wendell, Dr. S. Weir Mitchell, E. T. Stotesbury and A. Atwater Kent. On the page opposite it is shown in 1946 running in steam behind a Maine Central 4-6-4 at Waterville in a photograph by Everett De Golyer, and below, leaving Ellsworth, whence it runs in reverse as far as Bangor.*

TWO PHOTOS: EVERETT DE GOLYER

Here the Union Pacific's well-remembered Los Angeles Limited *takes aboard a passenger in 1910, the suggestion implicit in the picture being that she has space in the rear car which combines sleeping space with a public salon. But whether its car rode in splendid isolation at the end of the train with markers to show its passing in the night or in the midst of a long consist of sleek green vestibuled cars, the Pullman open section of classic tradition with its soft pillows, immaculate linen and green baize curtains between the occupant and the strange jungle night life that flourished in the aisle will be a part of the American consciousness forever. It represented millions of hours of snug security and comfort in repose, a way of life for a restless people, and, of all the sorts and conditions of beds occupied by Americans for a full century, more slept in Pullman berths than in any other.*

PULLMAN STANDARD   UNION PACIFIC RAILROAD

The two
parlor lounges
of Colorado Club
were furnished
in ebony and up-
holstered in gold
mohair, and radio
fans could listen
to "Amos 'n' Andy"
on an eight-tube
receiving set.
The car was
built throughout
by U.P. artisans
in the company
shops at Omaha.

558

Just to prove that the great days of carbuilding were not dead, the Union Pacific in 1930 placed in service between Chicago–Omaha–Denver this stunning lounge-observation car, Colorado Club, on the then crack train on the Rocky Mountain run, the Columbine. The exterior (opposite) was painted royal blue and silver with the State of Colorado crest on the sidewalls. There was a barbershop, valet service and tub and shower baths; costly stuffs upholstered deep fauteuils. Colorado Club was one of the last great gestures of ornate decor and luxury before the ice age of moderne reduced all passenger equipment to faceless anonymity.

559

Bridging the transitional gap between the age of Pullman Standard and steam and the era of diesel and streamlining were such lightweight name trains still operating in steam motive power as the Southern Pacific's Daylight, *the* Forty-niner *on the Overland run and the* Dixie Flagler *on the Florida run out of Chicago over rails of the Florida East Coast and the Atlantic Coast Line, among others. On the page opposite, the New York's legendary* Empire State Express *rolled splendidly for a season beside the Hudson in steam and stainless steel. On this page the Santa Fe's prestige-laden flyer* The Chief *between Chicago and Los Angeles, over Santa Fe iron all the way, gets a highball out of Lamy, New Mexico, in the days when the superb 3700 series engines powered the head end in smoke and glory.*

560

The end of the road was almost at hand in 1937 for the open section Standard Pullman sleeper with one or more staterooms represented by Alabama College on the page opposite. Six years earlier the firm had already been experimenting with change in such forms as the duplex sleeper Wanderer, the third car of that name to come from Pullman's shops since 1902. Both previous Wanderers had been private cars. The age of lightweight, streamlined equipment was already inaugurated by the end of the thirties, and its expression in such trains as the Dixie Flagler (below) lasted into the final years of steam operations. Here the Flagler—one of the few trains ever to be named for a railroader and having its origins in Chicago over the rails of the Chicago & Eastern Illinois—is shown in a pastoral setting of rare beauty south of Atlanta, powered by an Atlantic Coast Line 4-8-2.

TWO PHOTOS: PULLMAN STANDARD   RAIL PHOTO SERVICE

Few of the most ornate products of Wagner or Pullman for carriers in the United States could hold the proverbial candle to Satsuma, a sleeper built for Canadian Pacific in the eighties by Barney & Smith. The theme of Satsuma was Spanish Renaissance executed in primavera woodwork and sage green plush upholstery, and it accommodated forty-four passengers in eight sections and two equally elegant staterooms. Among its appointments were separate retiring rooms for men and women and a bathtub, presumably available to either sex by prearrangement with the car attendant. The Canadian Pacific didn't need to tip its hat to anything south of the international boundary.

The gleaming buffet car with narrow vestibules shown here was built by Barney & Smith for the Milwaukee's original Pioneer Limited on the Chicago–Twin Cities run the year Dewey took Manila, and it is pleasant to contemplate the quantities of Kentucky sourmash, assisted on its way by the brew that made Milwaukee famous, that may have passed across its service bar. In 1934, when the below photograph was taken, the Milwaukee Road's Southwest Limited ran overnight between Milwaukee and Chicago and Kansas City, the two sections being amalgamated at Savanna, 138 miles west of Chicago. The observation car, which originated at Milwaukee, had all the latest facilities: air conditioning and radio.

In the noontide of the New Haven's fortunes, equipment such as this was assigned to the all-Pullman, extra-fare luxury runs Merchants Limited and Knickerbocker Limited. There were all-bedroom cars on the overnight between Boston and New York, and equally as fine parlor cars, diners and lounges rode the Gilt Edge, the Shore Line Express and the Colonial.

The New Haven's first steel Pullmans of 1913 had exteriors painted to suggest wood construction to reassure timid patrons afraid of electrocution in the event of mischance on the electrified tracks west of New Haven.

A threadbare witticism aimed at New England's puritanical morality once maintained that the best thing about Boston was the New Haven's five o'clock train to New York, but for many years the New York, New Haven & Hartford's Merchants Limited *was a fine thing in its own right, not only as an escape from the Hub of the Universe but as one of the radiant names in the lexicon of railroading. The* Merchants, *like its one o'clock opposite number, the* Knickerbocker, *was all-Pullman, extra-fare and a luxury train with implications of the great worlds of State Street and Murray Hill. Its "sailing lists" were perfumed with the names of Choates, Lowells and Thorndikes and, at the turn of the century, its club car stocked J. P. Morgan's special brand of cigars against the possible appearance of Jupiter himself en route to a Harvard overseers meeting. In the thirties the* Merchants *conductor, the venerable George Hall, was the last to wear a blue frock coat of office with a boutonniere fresh daily, and when Fred Wright, ranking steward on the train's club cars, retired it was a Sunday feature. The* Merchants *was the quintessence of upper-case Beacon Hill and Commonwealth Avenue, and at one time a train mouse lived aboard one of its observation cars. When the management threatened its extermination, passenger protest permitted it to ride back and forth over the Shore Line unmolested; it was a durable conversation piece at the Somerset Club. The* Merchants *is shown below at the South Station in Boston in 1913 as a prophetic afternoon sun was setting on the fortunes of a princely carrier.*

The Denver & Rio Grande's
Exposition Flyer (*left*) *shown
passing through Tolland, Colorado, in 1939, was a train of
classic dimensions with coaches,
Pullman sleepers, diners, and
lounge cars on the Denver–Salt
Lake run. Maintained in Chicago–San Francisco service over
the connecting rails of the Burlington and Western Pacific, it
was the predecessor of the post-
war California Zephyr.*

Long an institution in steam on the Chicago–
Los Angeles run over the Santa Fe, the Chief in
the year it was dieselized carried at its rear on
one section a belated tribute to the great carbuilder in the form of an enclosed observation-
lounge car George M. Pullman, *shown at the
bottom of the page opposite. Above: a Pullman
sleeping car interior from a brochure of the
much loved but long since vanished Colorado
Midland Railroad of 1890 depicting the joys of
luxury travel over its rails between Denver and
Salt Lake in competition to the well-established
Denver & Rio Grande.*

569

The two Pullmans shown on this page, Arthur Dubin believes to be among the most exotically beautiful examples of the golden age of car-building. Both photographs are from his collection. Progress and its companion Advance were built in 1906 as twelve section–drawing room–observation cars, the only ones ever built to this plan, for Toledo–St. Louis service in the almost forgotten Toledo, St. Louis & Western Railway's Commercial Traveler. Lorna was outshopped two years earlier for the Chicago & Alton. Painted dark red, it was assigned to the Kansas City–St. Louis run in the Missouri State Vestibuled Express.

In the year 1926 when the Chicago, Burlington & Quincy's Chicago–Denver Limited *carried at its end the solarium–parlor car* Burlington–Bridge, *the days of the open-end observation platform were already numbered. The wind and particles of roadbed picked up at high speeds as well as air conditioning indicated an enclosed sun parlor where once the glory of brass rail and folding stool had reigned.*

A name in railroading whose romance has endured long after its final run was made was the Great Northern Railway's Oriental Limited *between the Northwest and St. Paul–Minneapolis. It is shown at the top of the page opposite in 1907, two years after it began operations, along Puget Sound near its western terminal, and below, about 1921, when all-steel Pullman equipment had replaced the wooden sidewalls of an earlier period. Above is one of the diners assigned to the* Limited *in the twenties, scene of untold consumption of the Idaho baked potatoes, Wenatchee apples, and other on-line produce that the Hill carrier delighted to serve its patrons as well as carry in vast quantities aboard its merchandise consists.*

Long after the last Standard Pullman sleeper rolled from the shops, thousands of open section cars were still in service in the United States, snug, dependable and repositories alike of folklore and tangible comforts. A warm lower was still a good place to be when the above scene was photographed at the Chicago & North Western depot at Milwaukee in the fifties during a Wisconsin blizzard of epic proportions. On the page opposite, twilight on the high iron finds a long string of Pullmans of the Missouri–Kansas–Texas train No. 7, the southbound Blue-bonnet, slamming across the rails of the Texas & New Orleans main line two miles out of San Antonio. A prophetic mood of sunset melancholy and impending dark as the cars near their terminal suggests the night into which, at the end of day, all things must go.

574

CHICAGO & NORTH WESTERN RAILWAY   PHILIP R. HASTINGS